Mass Media,
an Aging Population,
and the Baby Boomers

LEA's Communication Series
Jennings Bryant/Dolf Zillmann, General Editors

Selected titles in Mass Communication (Alan Rubin, Advisory Editor) include:

Bryant/Bryant • Television and the American Family, Second Edition

Gunter • Media Sex: What Are the Issues?

Harris • A Cognitive Psychology of Mass Communication, Fourth Edition

Kundanis • Children, Teens, Families, and Mass Media: The Millennial Generation

Lang • Measuring Psychological Responses to Media Messages

Palmer/Young • The Faces of Televisual Media: Teaching, Violence, Selling to Children

Perse • Media Effects and Society

Wicks • Understanding Audiences: Learning to Use the Media Constructively

Van Evra • Television and Child Development, Third Edition

Zillmann/Vorderer • Media Entertainment: The Psychology of Its Appeal

For a complete list of titles in LEA's Communication Series, please contact Lawrence Erlbaum Associates, Publishers, at www.erlbaum.com.

Mass Media,
an Aging Population,
and the Baby Boomers

Michael L. Hilt
Jeremy H. Lipschultz
University of Nebraska at Omaha

LEA LAWRENCE ERLBAUM ASSOCIATES, PUBLISHERS
2005 Mahwah, New Jersey   London

Lawrence Erlbaum Associates, Inc., Publishers
10 Industrial Avenue
Mahwah, New Jersey 07430
www.erlbaum.com

Cover design by Kathryn Houghtaling Lacey

Library of Congress Cataloging-in-Publication Data

Hilt, Michael L., 1959–
   Mass media, an aging population, and the baby boomers / by Michael L. Hilt and
Jeremy H. Lipschultz
      p.   cm.
   Includes bibliographical references and index.
   ISBN 0-8058-4865-7 (cloth : alk. paper)
   1. Mass media and the aged—United States.   I. Lipschultz, Jeremy Harris, 1958–
II. Title.

P94.5.A382U647   2005
302.23'0846—dc22   2005045497
                                                                          CIP

Books published by Lawrence Erlbaum Associates are printed on acid-free paper,
and their bindings are chosen for strength and durability.

Printed in the United States of America
10 9 8 7 6 5 4 3 2 1

Contents

About the Authors

Michael L. Hilt is Professor and Graduate Chair (PhD, University of Nebraska, 1994) and **Jeremy H. Lipschultz** is Reilly Professor and Director, School of Communication (PhD, Southern Illinois University, 1990) at the University of Nebraska at Omaha. They are coauthors of *Crime and Local Television News: Dramatic, Breaking, and Live From the Scene* (Mahwah, NJ: Lawrence Erlbaum Associates, 2002). Hilt is the author of *Television News and the Elderly: Broadcast Managers' Attitudes Toward Older Adults* (New York: Garland, 1997). Lipschultz is the author of *Broadcast Indecency: F.C.C. Regulation and the First Amendment* (Boston: Focal Press, 1997) and *Free Expression in the Age of the Internet: Social and Legal Boundaries* (Boulder, CO: Westview Press, 2000).

Hilt and Lipschultz have written numerous scholarly articles in refereed publications such as *Journalism Quarterly, Journalism & Mass Communication Educator, Journal of Broadcasting & Electronic Media, Educational Gerontology, Journal of Social Behavior and Personality, Journal of Radio Studies, Simile,* and *Communications and the Law.*

CONTRIBUTORS

David Corbin (PhD, University of Pittsburgh, 1981) is Professor of Health Education and Courtesy Professor of Gerontology at the University of Nebraska at Omaha. He teaches and researches in the areas of health and aging, stress management, and human sexuality education.

He is author of *Reach for It: A Handbook of Health, Fitness and Dance Activities for Older Adults.*

John Dillon (PhD, Southern Illinois University, 1991) is Professor of Journalism and Mass Communications at Murray State University in Kentucky. He teaches in the areas of news, communications theory, and new technology and his research includes studies of attitude and Internet usage.

Hugh Reilly (MA, University of Nebraska at Omaha, 1997) is Assistant Professor of Communication at the University of Nebraska at Omaha. He teaches public relations and advertising.

James Thorson (EdD, University of Georgia, 1975) is Jacob Isaacson Distinguished Professor and Chair, Department of Gerontology at University of Nebraska at Omaha. He is the author of numerous books and articles including *Aging in a Changing Society* (2nd ed., 2000).

Foreword

This is a wide-ranging book of interest to a diverse audience because it deals with three different topics (mass media, aging, and the baby boomers) as well as with the intersection of these topics. There are numerous books on each of these topics separately, but this is the first to deal with their intersection and overlap. As a result, this book will be useful to:

- Students and faculty in gerontology courses and research
- Media students and professionals
- Advertisers and business executives (especially chapter 6)
- Politicians and policymakers (especially chapter 9)
- Healthcare providers (especially chapter 8)
- Other professionals such as clergy, lawyers, and social workers
- Baby boomers

It will also be of special interest to everyone concerned about the insidious social disease called "ageism." Indeed, there is so much information about ageism in this book that ageism could well have been included in the title as a fourth topic.

Hilt and Lipschultz are well qualified to deal with these topics because they have both done extensive research and published several books in these areas. The four contributors, who supplement the main text, are also experts in their fields.

The book is made attractive and easy to use with relevant photographs, case studies, figures, tables, and boxes. Each chapter also has a summary and review questions to help reinforce the information presented in the main text. The indexes are useful in looking up specific information.

In writing such a monograph, it is tempting to overgeneralize about a particular cohort, such as the baby boomers, or older or younger people. This would be another form of ageism—that of using stereotypes to represent an entire cohort or age group. This book is careful to avoid that temptation and often points out the diversity within cohorts such as the baby boomers.

The authors also manage to make sophisticated distinctions between various aspects of ageism, such as negative vs. positive ageism, stereotypes vs. attitudes, prejudice vs. discrimination, and personal vs. institutional discrimination. Too many unsophisticated persons simply equate all ageism with prejudice. While this is a major part of ageism, other aspects, such as discrimination, do more actual damage.

Much of the text deals with such controversial questions as how different are the baby boomers from the older (World War II generation) and the younger ("silent generation") cohorts? Will the baby boomers make a qualitative difference to our aging population or will they simply continue the trends of the last several generations? What are the positive aspects and opportunities of the baby boomers as well as their problems as they age?

This is a quite up-to-date book that provides the latest information on such things as television shows and their treatment of older persons, psychographics of various cohorts, research on uses of the Internet by older persons, and political issues related to aging.

There is a balance between "good news" and "bad news" throughout the book. For example, there is the bad news that broadcasters and print journalists emphasize a narrow range of themes in stories about older people, and most of them are negative (the dangers of older drivers, the fear of crime, and the vulnerability of older people to scams). On the other hand, there is the good news that "The mature customer is healthier, wealthier, and wiser, especially about money matters, than any other group of this age in our history" (p. 121).

In summary, this is a well-written book that will be useful to many different kinds of people—and especially to baby boomers, the face of future aging.

—*Erdman B. Palmore, PhD*

Preface

The United States is entering a time of dramatic change. The baby boom-er generation, born between 1946 and 1964, is heading toward their re-tirement years. Uses of mass media, as well as the images portrayed, are already being influenced by the demographic shift. For example, when Federal Reserve Board Chairman Alan Greenspan warned in 2004 that, in about a decade, Social Security and Medicare funding shortfalls would be driven by baby boomer retirements, the story was extensively reported in the press. Mass media coverage of aging issues is expected to expand, and scholars from a variety of fields have become interested. Gerontologists and speech communication researchers were some of the first to recog-nize the importance of this area of study, but there remains a need to of-fer a comprehensive examination of mass communication issues.

Traditionally, mass media and the elderly has been an important area of study because older people have been portrayed via negative stereotyp-ical images. Despite criticism, these portrayals persist. Mass media have tended to focus on youth culture and younger demographic age groups. These images help sell products and programming. In advertising, for ex-ample, sex is used to sell products. This represents a natural bias against the elderly. Even marketing in the area of prescription drugs for erectile dysfunction has shifted away from older people and toward baby boom-ers and younger people. Although age has always been an important variable in media use and health communication studies, there has been limited focus on the older age segment.

This book comprehensively examines the linkage between media and aging issues. Interpersonal communication has been the focus of previous research, however, the purpose here is to comprehensively address mass media theory and practice as it relates to older people. Aging baby boomers are an interesting group because of their lifelong experiences with mass media, including television. They were born at the dawn of the television age. Additionally, they have come to embrace the Internet in large numbers. Beyond this, the older World Wide Web users have, in some cases, enthusiastically adopted the Internet as a source of information and a means to maintain interpersonal communication with family, friends, and interest groups.

The introductory chapter explains why aging baby boomers are an important area of mass media study. The 77 million boomers in the United States are a segment of the population with political, social, and economic power. Chapter 2 reviews theory and research on communication and gerontology. Media images of older people may construct social realities for the public and have effects on individuals. Over long periods of time, stereotypical images may cultivate negative representations of aging. At the same time, the elderly sometimes suffer from disengagement because of declining health. Chapter 3 examines television as one replacement for interpersonal interaction. This chapter reviews the relation between broadcast news and the elderly. Chapter 4 focuses on print media. Older readers remain the most important audience for print media. However, poor eyesight among older people is one reason why they may forsake reading. Chapter 5 turns to the topic of entertainment. Because older people generally have more available free time, they use media for entertainment. Baby boomers are a distinct cultural group, which emphasizes leisure time. Media usage competes with other entertainment activities. In chapter 6, the impact of aging on advertising and public relations is explored. Products and ideas targeted at older people, particularly baby boomers, are marketed with specialized campaigns that emphasize entertainment and leisure. Chapter 7 extends baby boomer media use to the Internet and new media. Older adults' use of the Internet reflects their interest in news, information, hobbies, and family. Chapter 8 draws from the studies about health and sexuality to understand views of aging. A positive view of aging may be related to life span. In chapter 9, older people are viewed as important players in the political process because of the size of the demographic group. Chapter 10 addresses trends and predictions related to baby boomers and mass media. The influence of mass media on society, the dynamics of social change, and the aging of America combine to create new opportunities and challenges.

This book may be used in undergraduate and graduate courses in communication, gerontology, sociology, and political science. The text is appropriate for upper level undergraduate and graduate students. It may be used as a primary or supplementary reading, depending on the course. It could be used with a more general theory book. Increasingly, interdisciplinary studies are crucial to understanding complex social issues and trends.

ACKNOLWEDGMENTS

The authors appreciate the ongoing support and encouragement from communications editor Linda Bathgate of Lawrence Erlbaum Associates. Editorial assistant Paul Overmyer was instrumental during the production process. Also, we would like to thank James D. Robinson for an insightful review of the manuscript.

The School of Communication and College of Arts and Sciences at the University of Nebraska at Omaha have been very supportive of our research. We wish to thank our colleagues for their interest in this project.

The authors would like to thank their spouses and children. Mike's wife, Debbie, offered useful suggestions. She and the children, Adam and Eric, were very supportive throughout the process. Jeremy's wife, Sandy, offered many useful sources and ideas. Jeff and Elizabeth, Jeremy's children, continue to bring great joy and encouragement to the work. Sandy's mom, Faye, provided new insight into how older people use the Internet in their lives. We love you all!

—*Michael L. Hilt*
—*Jeremy H. Lipschultz*
Omaha, Nebraska
September 2004

Chapter 1

Introduction to Mass Media, Aging Americans, and Baby Boomers

The country is growing older. The baby boomer generation—the post–World War II bubble born between 1946 and 1964—is rapidly heading toward the retirement years. The youngest in this group are 40-plus, and face middle age with an eye toward their senior years. The oldest boomers should be planning retirement. All 77 million baby boomers are sure to influence politics, the economy, health care, leisure, and mass media (Alch, 2000). This is particularly true because Americans are living longer, with life expectancy beyond age 77. Other trends also point toward some obvious changes in America and the world:

- The Bureau of Labor Statistics reported that, by 2008, aging baby boomers would inflate the proportion of workers age 45 and older to 40%. This would be a 12% increase in a decade.
- Claritas Research predicted that, by 2007, the number of households headed by 55- to 74-year-olds would grow about 15%, to nearly 31 million. The number of older households with an annual income of $100,000 or more may double by the 2010 Census, to over 8 million.
- Beyond income, the Federal Reserve Board projected that family net worth for wealthy older people may average between $500,000 and $1.5 million over the next several years.
- The Bureau of Labor Statistics in 2000 found that older people spend about $72 billion on health care.
- The 2000 Census reported that almost one in four boomers belonged to a racial or ethnic minority—10 million Black, 8 million Hispanic,

1

3 million Asian, and nearly 6 million multiracial or other U.S. baby boomers.

- Bruskin/Audits and Surveys Worldwide found in 2000 that adults between age 35 and 64 spend an average of 248 minutes a day watching TV, which is 22 minutes more a day, on average, than adults age 18 to 34.
- The median age for the world increased from 23.6 years in 1950 to 26.4 years in 2000. The United Nations Population Division predicted that, by 2050, the world median age would reach 36.8.

Dychtwald (2003a) highlighted the impact of baby boomer wealth, in light of expansive pension earnings and soaring property values, on the future of Medicare and Social Security:

> America's mature men and women have experienced a phenomenal reversal of financial fortune. Society's poorest segment a few decades ago, they have become its richest. Today's 50+ men and women earn $2+ trillion in annual income, own 77 percent of all financial assets, represent 66 percent of all stockholders, own 80 percent of all money in savings and loans, purchase nearly half of all new cars, purchase 80 percent of all luxury travel, and account for the purchase of 74 percent of all prescription drugs. (p. 1)

These statistics reflect historic shifts for the country. In the United States, the average age of the population, after decreasing for several decades, has returned to a long-term trend of slowly increasing.

From 1820 to 1950, the U.S. population median age had been growing older. In 1820, when reliable data were first collected, the median age was 16.7, and it rose to 30 as the effects of the baby boom were about to take hold (Gerber, Wolff, Klores, & Brown, 1989). For the next two decades, baby boomers reversed the trend. As Gerber et al. pointed out, "Had it not been for the baby boom, Americans might have turned their attention to their elders sooner than they have" (p. 3).

This is significant because, in the latter half of the 20th century, American media promoted a youth culture, advanced a consumer market, and influenced people around the globe. Perhaps this is about to change: "The new needs of older consumers will ultimately fuel a continuation of the dynamic growth of consumption that has been a vital part of the American economy since World War II" (Gerber et al., 1989, p. 207). Humphreys (2003) argued that "the aging of the population will dramatically alter the typical basket of goods and services . . . purchased by the average American, which will expand markets for some products. In turn, the aging of the population will affect the prospects for many occupations, boosting demand for workers in healthcare, household services, and leisure travel" (p. 1).

By the time the first boomers reached middle age in the 1990s, the free spirit exhibited by a generation of individuals was leading to a "turmoil" between wants and needs: "On the one hand, they insist on the primacy of the individual—the right to do what they want when they want. On the other hand, the demands made on them by the communities in which they live—their families, their careers, their localities—are growing" (Russell, 1993, p. 10). Increasingly, older boomers will be dealing with issues such as retirement, health care costs, disability, and care giving (AARP, 1998). AARP identified the five segments of the baby boomer generation (Fig. 1.1, Table 1.1): the Strugglers (9%), the Anxious (23%), the Enthusiasts (13%), the Self Reliants (30%), and Today's Traditionalists (25%).

American mass media seem to be turning their attention to the influential baby boomer generation and their concerns. Passel (2003) noted that, by 2025, the nation will be halfway through the retirement of the baby boomer generation: "This is likely to create a number of problems for the federal government unless some of today's current leaders are able to come to grips with a problem 10 to 20 years in the future" (p. 1). Demographers

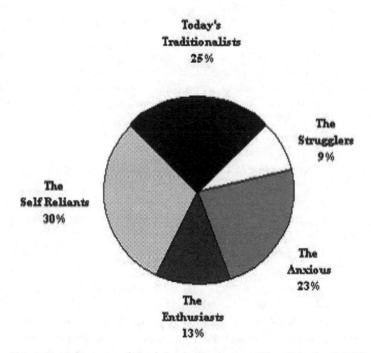

FIG. 1.1. Subgroups of the baby boomer generation. Data from 1998 AARP/Roper Baby Boomer Study ($N = 2,001$).

TABLE 1.1
AARP Segments of Baby Boomers

The Strugglers Lowest income group Disproportionately female	• No money in savings • Not satisfied with retirement savings amount • Current needs outweigh desire to save for retirement
The Anxious Apprehensive about future Limited income Striving to save Expect to keep working	• Pessimistic about retirement • Not satisfied with savings for retirement • Concerned about health care coverage
The Enthusiasts Plenty of money Eager to retire	• Do not plan to work *at all* during retirement • Optimistic about retirement years • Cannot wait to retire
The Self Reliants Highest income Highest educational levels Aggressively investing	• Currently investing in range of savings approaches • Confident about retirement income • Satisfied with amount currently putting away for retirement • Plan to work part-time mainly for interest or enjoyment sake
Today's Traditionalists Strong sense of confidence Trust in social programs	• Confident Social Security will be available • Confident Medicare will be available • Plan to work during retirement

also point out that increasing longevity and delayed retirement are factors that will place economic and political pressures on society.

Since the 1992 presidential campaign, for example, it has been argued that politicians and media have been strongly influenced by the baby boomers (Russell, 1993). In general, baby boomers, or at least their portrayal in media, seemed to be defined as a group that was not like their parents' generation (Mills, 1987).

Howe and Strauss (2003) predicted a "boomerizing of old age" as the generation moves through its 60s and 70s:

- They will retire later in life, due to economic necessity, forcing businesses to make room for older workers;
- Most will age in place, often turning their large houses into legacy homes for their grown children;
- Those who leave for active adult communities will show an aversion to planned living, and will spread out in places their parents seldom went, such as small towns, college communities, wilderness areas;
- They will continue to assert themselves in the culture, as consumers of products and lifestyles laden with cultural and religious meaning; and

- After initially resisting the idea of growing old, boomers will eventually embrace it, reinvent it, and try to perfect it—less as "senior citizens" than as elder stewards of a great civilization. (p. 1)

These predictions and others, such as whether or not the senior lobby will be influential, raise important social questions. As issues surface, the public, politicians, and media may engage in discussion about the growing impact of an older population. The purpose of this book is to examine how media and aging interact in the United States. How aging in the United States is communicated interpersonally and through media has both theoretical and practical value.

BRIDGING COMMUNICATION AND GERONTOLOGY

A strong interest has developed in the connection between communication and gerontology (Dillon, 2003; Hilt, 1997a; Nussbaum & Coupland, 1995; Nussbaum, Pecchioni, Robinson, & Thompson, 2000; Riggs, 1998; Williams & Nussbaum, 2001). Williams and Ylanne-McEwen (2000) argued, however, that "communication and aging, as well as life-span communication research, remain minority interests within the communication discipline" (p. 4). They studied elderly lifestyles in the new century. Williams and Ylanne-McEwen (2000) contended that "researching communication and aging should not be seen as tantamount to researching decrement, ill health, and disengagement from mainstream life" (p. 7).

There are concerns about how the generations communicate across age boundaries, and media studies also have begun to examine the portrayal of older people and their issues. However, there remains a need to offer a comprehensive examination of mass communication processes, content, and effects. Further, the Internet has created a dramatic need for updating the literature now available. For example, the development of computer-mediated communication as a field of study offers a basis for understanding how older people interact and build online relationships (Barnes, 2003; Jones, 1997). According to Barnes (2003), "Using the Internet to maintain or establish human relationships is a primary motivation for Internet use" (p. 137). In addition, older people seek information via the Internet on issues such as health, leisure, and travel. There is evidence that older people are motivated to use computers to obtain additional information, advice, and input on their decisions. As the baby boomers age, they should be even more likely to use the technology learned in the workplace as a tool to address new life challenges.

There is a need to broadly consider the relation between the fields of communication and gerontology, to focus on mass media, and to conceptualize a structure for interdisciplinary studies. As a starting point, previous research has identified media as one source for negative perceptions about growing older.

AGEISM, STEREOTYPES, AND CULTURE

The study of how media present ageist stereotypes is becoming increasingly important in the communication and gerontology fields. Ageism research began with Butler's use of the term in 1969 (Butler, 1969, 1995; Palmore, 1999). *Ageism* has been defined as "a process of systematic stereotyping and discrimination against people because they are old" (Palmore, 1999, p. 4, quoting Butler, 1995, p. 35). Ageism, like racism and sexism, is related to communication because of the social tendency of some to utilize particular frames in discussion of people and issues (Estes, 2001). Age may be treated as a positive or negative concept.

Ageism may be studied from a cultural perspective because "our culture is so permeated with ageism, and we are so conditioned by it, that we are often unaware of it" (Palmore, 1999, p. 86). In media studies, culture has come to be seen as a way of understanding how people live at any given time (Campbell, 2000). Media and culture have been seen as going hand-in-hand in defining our environment: "Societies, like species, need to reproduce to survive, and culture cultivates attitudes and behavior that predispose people to consent to establish ways of thought and conduct, thus integrating individuals into a specific socioeconomic system" (Kellner & Durham, 2001, p. 1).

Holladay (2002) examined memorable media messages about aging. Media are seen as being responsible for cultivating some views of aging:

> Through exposure to elderly television and movie characters we may develop conceptions of what later life might hold for aging individuals and ourselves. News reports highlight issues pertaining to members of the older population. Television commercials and print ads heighten our awareness of problems of aging, ranging from cognitive difficulties to impotence to financial insecurity. (p. 681)

However, advertisements may also show older adults being active in promoting the sale of products and services such as "supplements and antiaging creams or the use of security systems and medical devices that promote health, activity, and security" (p. 682). Media, then, serve to reinforce negative and positive stereotypes.

Television, for example, provides cues for the structure of society. Stevenson (1995), drawing from Williams' earlier work, contended that media transmit culture, as "known meanings and directions" and "common meanings" (Stevenson, 1995, pp. 11–12). For Carey (1992), culture implied "ritual," "mythology," and "the creation, representation, and celebration of shared even if illusory beliefs" (p. 43).

Perry (1999) explored "animated gerontophobia" looking for ageism and sexism in children's films. The research contended that American "society continues to revere youth and deplore aging" (p. 201). The study examined Disney films for evidence of promotion of negative stereotype portrayals. "I identified quite a few aging female villainesses who exhibited many of the negative stereotypes of aging" (p. 202). Six Disney animated films were viewed as important cultural icons. Perry emphasized, "The stereotype of the 'mean old lady' needs to be recognized for what it is—a stereotype—and we need to become aware of the insidious influence of stereotypical portrayals in the movies. By continually depicting aging as negative, the media creates a society that denies and mistrusts all persons who are past their youth" (p. 209). The author called for future research on older male characters, as well as the need to recognize social importance of entertainment media. Perry explained, "When a small child experiences the curious lack of positive mature female role models in Disney movies, he or she is inevitably influenced by it. We have an obligation to our children to present them with an affirmative view of the aging process and the aged, particularly since we are an aging society and our ranks of aged grow with each passing day" (p. 211).

In the case of shared beliefs about aging, it is possible that media provide a cultural explanation for our understanding of growing older—one that may offer easy negative stereotypes rather than complex description. Social definitions of aging, as presented by media, are influenced by the commercial realities of the media industry in a free society.

THE IMPORTANCE OF MASS MEDIA IN SOCIETY

Media consumption for the baby boomer generation is difficult to predict. Paul (2003) noted some generalizations, including that television may remain an effective mass medium for reaching this group. At the same time, boomers have been willing to embrace the Internet. One factor is the historically high level of formal education among boomers, and this leads them to be heavy readers, as well as having been raised on television. Analysts note that when mass media attract only 10% of boomers, this still accounts for nearly eight million readers, listeners, or viewers (Paul, 2003). Television viewing, for example, continues to increase among baby boomers. In 2001, older boomers favored three network shows: "CSI," "The West Wing," and "ER." Younger baby boomers, on the other hand, tended to watch "ER," "Friends," and "Survivor."

The Media Audit in 2003 surveyed the 85 largest television markets and found that the number of viewers age 50 and older grew from 41 to 47 million in just 5 years. This represented more than one third of the adult population. However, advertisers remained apprehensive because the age group is so diverse in terms of socioeconomic class. This is intriguing because, even though income drops dramatically at retirement age, more than one fourth of people over age 65 have assets over $100,000. For boomers age 55 to 64, 30.3% had this level of savings: "Their incomes put them below the 85-market average, but their liquid assets put them significantly above the same average" (Jordan, 2003, p. 2). This will translate into increased available money for the aging baby boomers. "If their home is paid for and their kids are gone, they will have significant buying power even though their incomes are less than those of younger adults" (p. 1).

Dychtwald (2003a), commenting on the aging baby boomers, predicted an impact on consumer behavior during the next quarter century. He contended that boomers favor experiences over material goods. According to Dychtwald (2003a), "A shift from the desire for products to services will lead to an explosion in educational programs that stir the imagination, travel that broadens one's perspectives, entertainment that stimulates the mind, art that enraptures the spirit, religion that inspires the soul—and even new botanical or pharmaceutical substances that alter one's perception of reality" (p. 1).

BOX 1.1. A Gerontologist Reflects on Media Coverage of Older People
By James A. Thorson

Of the 2.3 million people who will die this year, fewer than 20,000 (about eight-tenths of 1%) will be murdered. Our media will devote an inordinate proportion of its time to these people. Most, in fact, will not have been shot in dramatic circumstances or die in police chases. (What our media won't tell us about them is that they will, most likely, be male, young, of a racial minority, and dying in circumstances where drugs or alcohol, or both, are involved.) Despite this, or maybe because of it, we find people's demise to be vastly entertaining. It makes for the lead story on the six o'clock news, and I can't surf through my dozens of cable channels in the evening without finding the majority of the movies featuring somebody being blown away.

BOX 1.1. *(Continued)*

Hardly any time will be spent on how most people die: old and chronically ill. Being old and chronically ill, of course, isn't very sexy, and thus isn't very entertaining.

Forgive me, as a nonmedia professional, if these few observations blend the news media and the entertainment media. I think they've blended themselves for quite a few years, so it's kind of hard to pinpoint where one gives off and the other begins. The point of both is to be entertaining, of course. Isn't that why they get rid of female news anchors when they reach a certain age?

But, back to the point: Being old in our society is so uninteresting that we don't even mention it when someone old dies. Okay, the death of a movie star or other celebrity gets in the news now and then, but that's the function of celebrity. Neither you nor I will raise much media dust when we kick off. If our relatives want to announce our passing to the world, they'll be forced to actually purchase obituary space in the local paper, much as one would place a want ad.

I'm not suggesting that the six o'clock news should have a recitation of who died on any particular day, just that we get less interesting as we age, and those whose business it is to entertain us know this.

This is reflected nowhere so well as in prime-time television.

A vision of "old" on a TV show usually connotes humorously cranky, like Granny on "The Beverly Hillbillies." These kinds of images of the elderly as cantankerous have become so politically incorrect in recent years that they have disappeared almost entirely. We only see Redd Foxx in "Sanford and Son" or a character from "The Golden Girls" in reruns. In fact, if you think about it, about the only people we do see in prime-time anymore are themselves in their prime, between age 15 and 35.

Maybe we're too sensitive: Years ago, Johnny Carson had a character called "Aunt Blabby." Carson would don a long dress and wig and have a humorous dialog with Ed McMahon. The gag always was that the old girl was pretty well gone in an alcoholic haze, and she'd occasionally take a belt from a flask hidden in her cane. Well, the Gray Panthers had a fit about that, and for his last decade or so on the air, Carson didn't use Aunt Blabby. Similarly, "Sesame Street" once featured a Muppet named Professor Arid, who was so dull that when he lectured he put himself to sleep. That puppet disappeared when senior groups protested.

In fact, in an entertainment industry where everyone is attractive and no one wears glasses, I'm sure that producers are hard-pressed to put any old people at all on our screens, unless it's an avuncular Wilfred Brimley being kindly and wise or someone selling laxatives. Even the people in the ads in *Modern Maturity* look to be about 45.

One of our graduate students recently did a content analysis for her thesis, and she found that images of aging, at least on television, are no longer positive or negative: They aren't there at all. That is, because we can't make fun of foibles like forgetfulness, it's simply easier to displace older people

---

BOX 1.1. *(Continued)*

entirely—like they don't exist. There literally are fewer characters representing older individuals on TV currently that there were 20 years ago.

In news programs, of course, we still have the occasional formula story about old people. It seems that elderly individuals, despite the fact that they've survived quite well for 70 or 80 years, are now so uniquely stupid that they will fall for almost any con man or scheme to bilk them of their last few dollars. These stories invariably speak about scoundrels who "prey" on the elderly.

I'm not arguing that old people need to necessarily be represented proportionately on our screens, being blown apart by mad bombers or rent asunder by cyborgs gone wrong. I'm just pointing out the irony that there is an agnosia in our media—news as well as entertainment—which features death on a daily basis for entertainment purposes but ignores those who are in fact closest to it. In our youth-worshiping society, old people symbolize death and thus must be avoided—even if death makes for good entertainment.

Dr. Thorson is Jacob Isaacson Distinguished Professor and Chair of the Department of Gerontology, University of Nebraska at Omaha.

The Internet has become central to current definitions of mass media, which also include radio, television, newspapers, newsmagazines, public relations, and special interest information and entertainment. In updating the study of mass media and older people, key issues emerge concerning how the baby boomer generation will impact society worldwide as they influence the discussion of aging. U. Karsch and C. Karsch (1999), for example, found that in 1996, the Brazilian press publicized the death of 98 elders in a Rio de Janeiro long-term care institution: "The media has played an important role in raising the awareness of issues related to elders" (p. 153). The coverage led to new laws aimed at protecting the elderly population.

For older people, including the baby boomers, mass media offer the opportunity to access information and support in maintaining a quality of life over time. Older people face specific problems, such as how to remain healthy and active in a society that has not traditionally promoted their vitality. Further, American society presents a political struggle over Social Security and Medicare programs. The aging boomers head toward their extended retirement years with typical financial worries. Media coverage of issues and portrayal of culture represent perhaps *the* most important aspect of how we will come to define a future society where a significant portion of its living members are older.

CHAPTER SUMMARY

The 77 million baby boomers in the generation born between 1946 and 1964 are the focus of future discussion about aging. Statistics indicate that this group, particularly in the United States, will be important for setting social policy. Boomers will influence politics, the economy, health care, leisure, and mass media. Americans are living longer. With life expectancy averaging beyond 77 years, the study of aging must reflect the changing face of society. Culture and mass media are instrumental in understanding social change.

REVIEW QUESTIONS

1. Define the baby boomer generation. Why do you think it is important to study this group in the United States?
2. Historically, how has American culture presented older people? What role has the media played in the portrayal of aging?
3. How has the Internet become an important source of information for older people?
4. What is ageism and why is it important?
5. Why should the study of media and aging be important to you?

Chapter 2

Theory and Research on Communication and Gerontology

Although intergenerational speech communication concerns (Williams & Nussbaum, 2001) have received some attention, there has been less focus on mass media issues (Dillon, 2003; Hilt & Lipschultz, 1999; Riggs, 1998). Media are influential in framing or defining social beliefs about aging, yet the relation between media and ageism has been given limited attention in communication and gerontology. Concerns about communication difficulties and activation of fears dominate some areas of study. Likewise, in gerontology, the discussion of ageist stereotypes is not explicit in its consideration of media influence. At the same time, the aging baby boomers offer new reasons to study older people.

A conceptual framework would be useful for understanding aspects of media issues relating to older people. Media research and gerontology provide a theoretical basis for studying older people and the importance of communication in their lives. The lack of focus in recent years on older people and their use of communication is unfortunate because earlier communication scholars such as Gerbner, Gross, Signorielli, and Morgan (1980), as well as Schramm (1969), considered the general issue. However, until recently, the field did not systematically follow their lead.

As mentioned in the previous chapter, the older population in the United States is increasing dramatically as healthy Americans have longer lives (Barrow, 1996). Census projections show that, by 2040, the nation could have more people over age 65 than under age 21, and more than one in four Americans will be age 65 or older (Howe & Strauss, 2000, 2003; Usdansky, 1992). This chapter explores previous research on media and older people, and establishes a foundation for interpreting observations about media portrayals, uses, processes, content, effects, and culture as it pertains to people age 50 and older.

INTERGENERATIONAL COMMUNICATION, IDENTITY, AND FAMILIES

Research has focused on how people in different generations communicate with one another. There has been a particular interest in how intergenerational communication functions within families. Harwood (2000), for example, studied the degree to which communication between grandparents and grandchildren happened face-to-face, over the telephone, and through written media. Media richness, the theory that certain forms of communication elicit more information, offers one explanation for the nature of intergenerational interaction. Kahai and Cooper (2003), for example, found that richer media forms facilitated positive social perceptions and emotions. Leaner media, such as e-mail, offered more clarity but less in terms of social value. Williams and Nussbaum (2001) summarized that "a rich understanding of intergenerational communication is only made possible by first realizing that all communication takes place within a relational context" (p. 167).

Human communication studies on the elderly provide an important foundation for the focus on mass media:

> The environment of cities, neighborhoods, mass transit, crime, political agendas, governmental policies, and the media portrayal and reporting of all of these factors can create a communication climate difficult for younger and older individuals to master. Prior to any communication shared by the generations, each individual must first battle the real or perceived barriers to a successful communicative encounter. (Williams & Nussbaum, 2001, pp. 260–261)

Barriers to intergenerational communication may be raised by the emphasis in television of targeting specific age groups. When, for example, CBS News targeted an older audience, this may have magnified differences in available information used in conversations across age groups (Graber, 2001). In news and entertainment television, as well as other media, generational stereotyping may also influence the quality of interpersonal interaction.

PORTRAYAL AND EFFECTS

Estes (2001) offered a critical perspective on social policy and aging. She listed popular theories: disengagement theory, activity theory, productivity theory, social construction theories, age stratification, and conflict theories. Specifically related to media, Estes contended that media interpret aging for society, and media construct social reality: "Advocacy groups on the nightly news were dominated by the small pro-privatization 'Gen-X' organizations that appeared more than twice as often (five to two) as the American Association of Retired Persons (AARP), the nation's largest organization of aging (36 million members), or any other group" (p. 109). Research in the portrayal of elderly people includes such diverse subjects as Saturday morning cartoons (Bishop & Krause, 1984; Levinson, 1973; Powers, 1992), game shows (Danowski, 1975), television commercials (Francher, 1973; Hiemstra, Goodman, Middlemiss, Vosco, & Ziegler, 1983; Schreiber & Boyd, 1980; Swayne & Greco, 1987), fictional television (Greenberg, Korzenny, & Atkin, 1979), prime-time television (Cassata & Irwin, 1989; Dail, 1988; Petersen, 1973), and soap operas (Barton, 1977; Cassata, Anderson, & Skill, 1980, 1983; Downing, 1974; Elliott, 1984; Ramsdell, 1973). Elderly people tend to appear on television infrequently, and they are unlikely to have prominent parts in shows (Robinson & Skill, 1995). Additionally, talk radio may offer a form of communication that produces ageist stereotypes because of the narrow range of callers (Rubin & Step, 2000).

Harwood and Anderson (2002) found that older adult characters continue to be underrepresented in major network television programs. Older adult characters, when they are part of a story, tend to be portrayed more negatively than younger adult characters. However, the results failed to support Robinson and Skill's (1995) finding that older adults appear in peripheral roles. Harwood and Anderson (2002) found that older characters are treated similarly to minority and other marginalized groups.

Beyond entertainment television research, local and national television news coverage also has been important in understanding stereotypes about the elderly (Lipschultz & Hilt, 2002). However, researchers have not addressed how television news may frame older people within stereotypical portrayals. It may be speculated that if such images can be found within television news content, there is a possibility that these would contribute to societal norms about the elderly. For example, coverage of scams against the elderly may portray older people as frail, easily deceived, vulnerable, and confused. Older people also may be the subject of "good news" stories, where they overcome the perceived barrier of age by being physically or mentally active.

Limited research has been conducted into the content of magazines. Vasil and Wass (1993) examined nine studies investigating the portrayal of the elderly in various print media—magazine cartoons, magazine advertisements, newspapers, and birthday cards. Their evaluation of the quality of the portrayals produced mixed results. But few studies have looked at the *content* of magazine articles. One study investigated the content of articles in magazines, examining age stereotyping in *Time* (Kent & Shaw, 1980). A content analysis of named individuals appearing in 1978 issues found little age stereotyping. Hilt (2000) studied how *Time, Newsweek,* and *U.S. News & World Report* covered John Glenn's return to space in 1998. He found "few comments that could be considered ageist or demeaning to older adults" (p. 167). On the whole, however, little attention has been paid to how older adults are portrayed in magazine articles.

Pollack (1989) argued that mass media have done an incomplete job of educating themselves about social policy questions that affect the elderly, and too many editors see the problems of elderly people as too boring or depressing for regular coverage. Whitmore (1995) concluded that not enough is known about the portrayals of older people in all news media, including newspapers.

Paddon (1995) found that newspapers targeted older readers by publishing special features or sections. For example, the *St. Louis Post-Dispatch* published a "Fifty Plus" series in the early 1990s. Paddon was concerned about the ability of newspapers to sell an older audience to advertisers. However, she predicted the importance of older readers and warned newspapers about taking older readers for granted. Whereas seniors have begun to be seen as a target market, Paddon suggested that newspapers may use national feature stories rather than local content: "As local news staffs shrink and locally generated copy decreases, much more of the editorial content of interest to older readers will likely come from syndicated services" (p. 61).

Earlier, Stone (1987) summarized newspaper audience research and concluded that although reading patterns remain stable for adults through the working years, "reading frequency drops slightly after age 65, due possibly to health, eyesight, or finances" (p. 109). In one study of Alabama residences, there was a drop in newspaper credibility for those people over age 50 (Ibelema & Powell, 2001). Thus, newspaper credibility was lower than broadcast and cable credibility for this age group. The data did not fit a broader national historical trend: "In general, the elderly tend to find the media most credible" (p. 49). The oldest and youngest readers have been found to be least critical in their perception of newspaper image (Burgoon, Burgoon, & Buller, 1986). In response to the changing nature of newspaper readership, *USA Today* ushered in a new era in which newspaper design and style mimicked the video images seen by baby boomers raised on television. Hartman (1987) discussed how "McPaper" emphasized style over depth (p. 1). The baby boomers appeared to be most satisfied when information was coupled with entertainment. Thus, newspapers were faced with motivating younger readers through meeting psychological needs.

PSYCHOLOGICAL AND SOCIOLOGICAL IMPACT OF PORTRAYALS

Many Americans fear growing old. Friedan (1993) placed much of the blame for this fear of aging with media. Studies of television's portrayal of elderly people rarely conclude that the portrayals are positive, and research needs to be conducted on psychological impact. More is known about media content in this area than processes and effects.

The study of older people as crime victims has matured into one of the major areas of research in gerontology (Lipschultz & Hilt, 2002). The elderly and their fear of becoming victims of crime dominate the area. Rosenfeld (1981) found that the elderly perceive more threat from crime and feel more threatened than younger people; change their activities in response to increases in crime more often than younger people; and are far less likely to be victims of personal and property crimes, with the exception of larceny, than are younger people. Levine (1986) found that major market local television newscasts include very substantial doses of helplessness. Members of the general public are most often presented as helpless, and by implication, so are most viewers. Helplessness is one common feeling experienced by victims of crime (Wallace, 1998).

Of all media, television offers the most frequent view of older people (Tebbel, 1975). Consequently, television should be in a better position to eliminate misunderstandings, but this has not been the case. In a 1993 Cable News Network special focusing attention on people age 50 and older, gerontologist Ken Dychtwald noted that mass media should be leading the charge in creating a more contemporary image of aging. Whereas media may not be leading social change in this area, there is some evidence that news coverage is reacting to the changing face of its audience.

BOX 2.1. Congress Offered a "Boomer Wake-Up Call"
Excerpted from remarks by Ken Dychtwald

. . . When the leading edge of the baby boom first arrived, America and its institutions were entirely unprepared. Waiting lists developed at hospitals across the country; facilities and staff were inadequate; and in some hospitals, hallways were used as labor rooms. Similarly, apartments and homes didn't have enough bedrooms for rapidly expanding families; there was a shortage of baby food and diapers; and department stores couldn't keep enough toys in stock to meet the multiplying demand. When the boomers

BOX 2.1. *(Continued)*

took their first steps, the shoe, photo, and Band-Aid industries skyrocketed. Similarly, sales of tricycles, Slinkies, and Hula Hoops exploded as the marketplace was flooded with products for kids.

The boomers were born into a radically different world than that of their parents and grandparents, whose lives had been traumatized by World War I, the Depression, and then World War II. Struggling through decades of social and political uncertainty, often shadowed by the threat of poverty, the older generation was often forced to make peace with modest means and delayed gratification.

In response, these new parents hoped to give their own children a new level of stability and comfort—even luxury. "Gone, for the first time in history," announced *Time Magazine* in 1955, "is the worry over whether a society can produce enough goods to take care of its people." Notwithstanding their attempt to teach their children their own values of restraint and discipline, they also dreamed of showering them with abundance.

For example, while many parents of boomers were raised in the crowded confines of tenements or row houses, they envisioned a different environment for their children. In response, by the early 1950s, hundreds of thousands of new homes were built, in some cases resulting in the creation of new communities, such as Long Island's Levittown—America's first "suburb." By the late 1950s, more than 45 million Americans would call suburbia home. . . .

. . . Just like the hospitals a few years before, the public school system was also unprepared for the boomers' arrival. There weren't enough school buildings, classrooms, playgrounds, or teachers to meet the onrushing demand. By the 1960s, class size ballooned and many schools were forced to go into multiple sessions.

While public institutions' timing was belated, businesses once again pounced on the boomers' changing needs. During the 1960s, American adolescents drank 55 percent of all soft drinks and consumed vast quantities of fast food, contributing to year after year of 20 percent annual growth for franchise chains like McDonald's, Jack in the Box, and Kentucky Fried Chicken. . . .

. . . In their teens, marketers and political leaders began to notice that the boomers were not migrating through life's stages in exactly the same way as the smaller and more traditional generations before them. Much more self-reliant *and* indulgent, boomers were more inclined to question the status quo and challenge authority than previous generations. They believed themselves to be young, free, and in charge.

This youthful exuberance was tempered and twisted somewhat by the assassinations of John and Robert Kennedy and Martin Luther King. And as the media exposed the boomers to the injustices of racial prejudice and the existentially confusing war in Vietnam, many blamed their parents' generation for prevailing social problems; hence a "generation gap" emerged as the sociopolitical values of the young and the old diverged. . . .

BOX 2.1. *(Continued)*

. . . By the 1980s, the "tune in, turn on, drop out" philosophies of earlier years had subsided. As is common in the third decade of life, many boomers ratcheted up the economic ladder, and began to pursue increasingly materialistic goals. Just as the image of the "hippie" had come to stand for much of what made the '60s unique, the "yuppie," yet another version of the continually evolving, maturing boomer, came to stand for the '80s.

During the past decade, millions of boomers have been migrating into life's middle years, simultaneously juggling the responsibilities of increasingly powerful roles at work, child-rearing and providing long-term care to their parents. Perhaps the single biggest change compared with earlier generations is the complexity and multiplicity of roles that boomer women have courageously assumed. As careerists, moms, wives and "sandwiched" daughters, boomer women are truly a new breed of social pioneer. . . .

. . . On January 1, 1996, the first baby boomer turned 50. Now that members of this youth-oriented generation are within shouting distance of their maturity, they have begun to turn their attention toward the aging process itself. Most boomers would prefer to take their youth with them into old age. And, given impending breakthroughs in a wide range of scientific fields, this desire might actually be realized.

Currently, more than 100,000 anti-aging related research projects are underway in numerous disciplines in all corners of the world: *more resources have been deployed in the battle against aging in the past ten years than in the previous ten centuries.* . . .

. . . Just as society's institutions have been grossly unprepared for the baby boom, the teen boom, and the yuppie boom, we have—as yet—done far too little to prepare for the coming *elder boom*. Millions of new nursing-home beds will not appear overnight. Teacher shortages were patched over in the 1950s by occasionally pressing bright high school graduates into service, but it takes far longer to produce a neurosurgeon or oncologist. And, of course, so many boomers making demands on retirement benefits will place enormous strain on the Social Security and Medicare Trust Funds in the early decades of the 21st century. As a result of the unprecedented demographic, medical and lifestyle changes described above, a variety of aging-related societal crises could shake the foundation of our nation and rattle all aspects of our lives. . . .

. . . Although medical science has focused on how to prolong life, political and community leaders have not yet created a compelling vision for what tens of millions of long-lived men and women might *do* with those additional years. Currently, 40 million retirees spend an average of 43 hours a week watching television and the elderly have the lowest volunteerism rate of all age groups. Unfortunately, mature-oriented affinity and advocacy organizations have become more concerned about what their constituency might *get* from society than what they might *give*. Unless we envision and mobilize a new, productive role and useful purpose to life's later years, an *elder wasteland* could emerge in which more than 70 million couch-potato

> **BOX 2.1.** *(Continued)*
>
> retirees drift through their mature years watching TV, surfing the Internet, wandering through malls, and playing various games while siphoning off society's resources. . . .
>
> *Dr. Dychtwald is a psychologist, gerontologist and author of ten books on aging-related issues. He became known as the nation's leading proponent of "healthy aging," he became the founding President and CEO of Age Wave, an "idea lab" created to help corporations and associations prepare to meet the needs of an aging consumer marketplace, and he has served as a fellow of the World Economic Forum.*
>
> Source: Prepared by Ken Dychtwald in support of testimony given to the Senate Committee on Aging on November 8, 1999. Retrieved from http://aging.senate.gov/oas/hr42kd.htm

USES AND GRATIFICATIONS

Surveys consistently have found that television news is the public's most important source of information (Bower, 1985; Coulson & Macdonald, 1992; Iyengar & Kinder, 1987). Roper (1989) indicated 66% of those surveyed rely on television more than any other medium as their primary source of news. Elderly people spend more time with television than any other medium (Louis Harris, 1975; Moss & Lawton, 1982; Nussbaum, Thompson, & Robinson, 1989) and watch more TV than younger people (Bower, 1973). Older adults spend far more time watching television than reading newspapers, and watch more television than any other age group (Atkins, Jenkins, & Perkins, 1990–1991; Moss & Lawton, 1982).

While watching television, the older viewer prefers news, documentaries, and public affairs (Bower, 1973; Davis, 1971; Davis, Edwards, Bartel, & Martin, 1976; Davis & Westbrook, 1985; Goodman, 1990; Korzenny & Neuendorf, 1980; Rubin & Rubin, 1982a, 1982b; Scales, 1996; Steiner, 1963; Wenner, 1976). Older viewers are major consumers of television news, preferring it to other media (Doolittle, 1979). They view it as a way to become aware of current events rather than as a diversion (Davis & Davis, 1985).

Frequency of television use and total viewing time increases with age up to about 69 years, before showing a slight decline (Louis Harris, 1975). People age 55 and over watch an average of 7 more hours of television per week than younger adults (Nielsen, 1974). Nielsen found elderly people watch between 30 and 35 hours of TV per week. Bower's (1973) study confirmed Steiner's (1963) research that older people, more than any other age group, watch news. Bower reported that the 55-year-and-over group had the highest rate of any age group for viewing news, information, and public affairs.

Doolittle (1979) separated an older cohort into three subgroups: younger seniors (age 48–66), old seniors (age 67–74), and older seniors (age 75–93). Of the three subgroups, television news usage was the highest for old seniors (age 67–74). Overall, these respondents rated television as most credible. More than 20 years later, television, as a news source, remained more credible than print media (Ibelema & Powell, 2001). However, older people remain an important base for newspapers: "Consumers over 50 remain the strongest readers of newspapers" (Somerville, 2001, p. 27). For readers over 50 years old, the most important newspaper content appears to include the following:

- Community, obituaries, ordinary people;
- Home, health, food, fashion;
- Natural disasters, accidents;
- Government, war, politics, international;
- Movies, TV, weather;
- Advertising. (Somerville, 2001, p. 27)

If newspapers, magazines, and other print media reflect society's concerns (Wass, Almerico, Campbell, & Tatum, 1984), then they should be important arenas for discussing elderly issues. Among top-rated general circulation magazines, *Reader's Digest*, *TV Guide*, *National Geographic*, and *Time* are popular among older readers (Robinson & Skill, 1995). One study found that almost 20% of older adults read general interest magazines (Durand, Klemmack, Roff, & Taylor, 1980). The affluent elderly read many more magazines than their less affluent counterparts (Burnett, 1991). Burnett found that affluent elderly male readers were more likely to read *Newsweek*, *Time*, and *U.S. News & World Report* for news and information. News magazines also target content toward affluent elderly females, which is an audience that falls under the "well-off, well-educated stratum of the population that the promotion departments of newspapers and magazines like to describe as the 'opinion-makers' " (Grossman & Kumar, 1981, p. 62).

Williams and Nussbaum (2001), generalizing from their research on television and older people, found three important factors in media usage: an increase in leisure time available, an interest in news and public affairs, and the impact of age, gender, and income. These factors do not explain radio listening. Meantime, reading printed media is considered a special case: "The reading of books and magazines remains a popular activity throughout life, with a sharp decline starting around 65 years of age if eyesight begins to fail. The reading habits of older adults are also different from the reading habits of younger adults" (p. 257). Media use by older people may be, in part, explained by psychological and social factors, and physical decline also cannot be ignored.

During the past 30 years, one of the central issues of media studies has been what people do with news content. Uses and gratifications research works from a basic set of assumptions about the audience: They have psychological and social needs, they have expectations about consuming news, they make decisions based on their expectations, and they make decisions based on how well their needs were gratified (Palmgreen, Wenner, & Rosengren, 1985). The uses and gratifications perspective "suggested simply that we 'ask not what media do to people, but ask what people do with media' " (p. 11). In the case of older people, including the aging baby boomers, this implies that media use behavior will align with their specific needs. For example, older people may actively seek information about their health care concerns.

In the uses and gratifications model, audience members are active in making decisions about what to read, watch, listen, and use. McQuail (1985) contended that uses and gratifications research meets the needs of media scholars, practitioners, and audience members wishing to understand the lure of mass media. McQuail pointed out, "Viewed this way, the business of trying to find out what people are getting from their media experience and what their motives are seems a straightforward matter, requiring no more theoretical justification, attack, or defense than does the counting of audience members and the description of audience composition" (p. 150). However, there has been a lot of debate about the nature of this sort of research. Uses and gratifications research is a descriptive model that falls short of helping us to understand the varied motivations of viewers. Although audience members may actively make choices about, for example, which magazine to read, their stage in life may only partially explain the selection. Interest in a travel magazine may be driven by income and education, as well as by age and retirement status.

Still, it is fair to say that age is an important variable in understanding media use. In a study conducted by Kent and Rush (1976), 99% of the elderly persons surveyed said they watched television news. This heavy use of television news remained 14 years later, when Goodman (1990) found that older men and women favored television for their national news and information, but preferred newspapers for local news. Research conducted for the ABC Television Network found that viewers age 50 and older were significantly more interested in news than younger generations (Wurtzel, 1992). This is particularly important because Americans age 50 and older control half of this country's discretionary income and 77% of its assets (Grey Advertising, 1988), and the age 65 to 74 cohort has the highest percentage of discretionary income of any 10-year cohort (Wolfe, 1987). This age group also has particular interest in learning more about how to maintain their health and live longer lives.

Thanks to health care improvements, people in their 60s and older are living longer, and have more disposable income than ever before (Lieberman & McCray, 1994). Older people may be the targets for public health communication campaigns, and these are related to the motivation to seek new information. If older people are diagnosed with a medical condition, then they may become more attentive to news stories and television advertisements about prescription drugs that could impact their health. The diffusion of new ideas and products spreads among older people through mass and interpersonal communication channels (Rogers, 2003). Media messages are processed as cognitive information, which may trigger emotions and even behavioral change under some circumstances. Public health communication campaigns exist within a complex personal and social context. The diffusion of new ideas about health may be initiated by persuasive communication messages. Information and entertainment are sometimes difficult to separate when it comes to mediated communication, including television. Older people have an important asset in this regard: free time.

Although many older persons spend substantial time with TV and like to watch it, such viewers have not been a significant factor in commercial television programming decisions (Carmichael, 1976; Carmichael, Botan, & Hawkins, 1988). Programming decisions are often based on the number of people watching a particular show, in other words, the ratings. If the ratings are low, or if the advertisers do not buy commercial time because they do not want to market their product to the type of people who watch that program, then the show soon will be off the air. The ABC Television Network, along with the other major television networks (CBS, NBC, and FOX), considered its core viewers to be adults in the 18- to 49-year-old age group, teenagers, and children from age 2 to 11 (Wurtzel, 1992). The aging population remains an often-overlooked group by media executives and researchers.

Lieberman and McCray (1994) maintained that news and information needs to be relevant to all groups, if media want to keep their audiences. They found that 90% of people at retirement age or over said keeping up with the news is extremely important.

Numerous studies show that use of media increases during middle age through the retirement years (Dimmick, McCain, & Bolton, 1979). For example, Glick and Levy (1962) referred to the elderly as "embracers" of television. Their strong identification with TV may lead to passive and heavy viewing—a state of acceptance toward content that lacks critical consumption.

Several explanations have been given for age-related trends in media use. Comstock, Chaffee, Katzman, McCombs, and Roberts (1978) grouped the elderly along with the poor and ethnic minorities into the category of "disadvantaged." They said this group depends on television more than any other news medium for knowledge and information. The elderly audience's use of the broadcast medium may be related to the ease with which it can be received. Television, beyond the cost of the set, costs less than newspapers and magazines. In addition, failing eyesight can make reading difficult or impossible (Chaffee & Wilson, 1975).

A number of studies have focused on gratifications sought and obtained from television news (Davis & Edwards, 1975; Rubin & Rubin, 1981; Wenner, 1984). These studies indicate that, for some, the content of newscasts provides information of value in personal and social situations. For others, the process of viewing news may be an end in itself, because of its entertainment values and its ability to reduce feelings of social isolation. The television is readily accessible, provides a link to the outside world, allows the elderly to structure time periods of their day, and provides companionship.

Five gratifications have been identified (Palmgreen et al., 1980), which may provide insight into the television news viewing behaviors of the elderly. The five gratifications are general information seeking, decisional utility, entertainment, interpersonal unity, and parasocial interaction. Local television news allows older people to seek highly useful community-based information. Disengaged from the mainstream of social life, many older people find the local news to be a source of amusement, human contact, and a substitute for "real-life" communication. In this environment, disengaged members of a society may acquire a warped sense of, for example, the danger from violence.

SOCIAL GERONTOLOGY AND DISENGAGEMENT

The disengagement theory (Cumming & Henry, 1961; Passuth & Bengtson, 1988; Young, 1979) argues that society and the elderly are mutually obliged to withdraw from each other. Cumming and Henry maintained that the process is functional to both society and the individual; it enables society to make room for more efficient young people while allowing the elderly time to prepare for their eventual withdrawal from social life—death. They argued that the disengagement theory should actually be considered an interpersonal communication theory because mass communication researchers say television serves as a substitute for interpersonal contacts among elderly people. As Horton and Wohl (1986) indicated, "In television, especially, the image which is presented makes available nuances of appearance and gesture to which ordinary social perception is attentive and to which interaction is cued" (p. 185).

The theory of disengagement has generated much criticism. Barrow (1996) contended that one might just as well speak of society excluding the elderly as disengaging them; perhaps the withdrawal of older people is a reaction to a society that excludes them. It may be that older adults are being pushed out of society, and television contributes to the disengagement by not showing or speaking about elderly people in its programs. Thorson (1995) wrote that the disengagement theory, like many studies of the aged, tended to lump all older adults into one group and not allow for individual differences.

Brown (1996) analyzed social processes of aging. Brown contended that a new image of aging is emerging from three sources: personal observations of retired people involved in tourism or recreation, politics, and the mass media. The perception of older people is said to have moved from that of social disengagement toward active elderly entitled to more than their share of societal resources. "The growing discussion among politicians and journalists today about how 'entitlements' are an unfair financial drain on the society is a powerfully effective expression of that image" (p. 6). In fact, the elderly have been found to contribute to the economy and social life of their communities and the nation.

Another reason given for increased use of the media by elderly people is that television and newspapers have become substitutes for interpersonal contacts (Davis, 1971; Graney, 1975; Graney & Graney, 1974; Rubin & Rubin, 1982b). Because of loneliness and disengagement, older adults turn to mass media for their information about the outside world (Atkin, 1976; Hess, 1974; Powell & Williamson, 1985; Schramm, 1969). In fact, older viewers may participate in parasocial interaction, which is a process in which a viewer comes to see a television personality as an important person in their life (Horton & Wohl, 1986).

As discussed earlier, the disengagement theory of aging suggests that as people grow older they are likely to show less interest in society's problems (Cassata, 1985). Cassata found that television news allowed them to feel connected to the world, and the news also supplied them with the information required to adapt to social change and function in society. This finding has been offered as evidence to challenge the disengagement hypothesis. People disengaged from society would not seem likely to be interested in television news, but elderly people showed high interest. Atkin (1976) suggested that the preference for news and information in television viewing is a direct attempt to compensate for the stable and unexciting world of older adults. Schramm (1969) interpreted this as their way of keeping up with society rather than a means of disengagement. He wrote that older people use television to keep in touch, combat progressive disengagement, and maintain a sense of belonging to society. Lowenthal and Boler (1965) found that older adults who voluntarily disengaged from their social activities also decreased their media use. However, older adults who were forced to involuntarily disengage from society tended to increase media use as a substitute for lost activities.

Kubey (1981) suggested that television may be a substitute for the interpersonal information network that existed when the individual went out into the community to work. The increased leisure time that accompanies retirement may account for some of the higher consumption rates of television news by elderly people. The substitution theory has been offered as an alternative to the disengagement theory. The substitution theory of aging holds that older persons will tend to substitute mass media communication for interpersonal communication when the latter is unavailable, or extremely difficult to accomplish (Bliese, 1986).

Ryff, Marshall, and Clarke (1999) maintained that the disengagement theory has strong microlevel conceptualizations of social structure. Social construction of reality may also enter into a process because the "individual and society" are engaged in an ongoing relationship (p. 18). More will be said about this later, but reality may feed back on the individual, embodied in written and other institutional forms. Social construction of reality should first be examined through how older Americans use media content.

SOCIAL CONSTRUCTION OF REALITY AND FRAMING

Social construction of reality is a philosophical view about "symbolic universes" and "legitimations" by people, and it deals with subjective interpretation as creating reality (Berger & Luckmann, 1967, p. 128). Lang and Lang (1984) generalized that media constructions often seem "authentic" to people, and that visual content helps define events (p. 26). In general, "the act of making news is the act of constructing reality itself rather than a picture of reality" (Tuchman, 1978, p. 12). The "analytical technique" of framing has been used more recently in the study of "defining and refining issues for the public" (Endres, 2004, p. 8). Framing media stories about older people involves the entire news process.

For example, the construction of reality in news begins with the newsroom decision to cover a particular story. In the case of the elderly, stories about seniors might seem too boring to cover if there is no dramatic action. Social construction continues when, having decided to cover a story, the reporter and photographer arrive at the scene to gather raw material. The social construction of crime news is symbolic, and it is a form of newsgathering useful in the production of social reality. As Barak (1994) pointed out, "Media images or characterizations of crime and crime control in the United States are constituted within the core of the social, political, and psychological makeup of American society. Mass news representations in the 'information age' have become the most significant communication by which the average person comes to know the world outside his or her immediate experience" (p. 3). There are several reasons that news may be the basis for social construction of reality perceptions by the elderly, beyond the fact that it is a part of regular daily activities. News is dramatic. The elderly may pay attention to it for entertainment reasons (Bogart, 1980; Dominick, Wurtzel, & Lometti, 1975; Rubin, Perse, & Powell, 1985), and news is perceived as realistic by much of its audience (Rubin et al., 1985). For the elderly, reading, listening, or watching news may create a perception of a lack of personal safety (Perse, 1990). Also, news may influence an older viewer's thinking toward an issue of direct importance to them, for example, Social Security (Iyengar & Kinder, 1987). In short, social construction of news, based on news values of producers, may distort the world for those less engaged in social life.

CULTIVATION

Research in the fields of psychology, sociology, and communication are particularly helpful in making generalizations about how media content is processed. Lang (1994) explained, "The psychologists asked how communication affected individuals or small groups. The sociologists asked how communication affected organizations and societies. The result was that communication became what Paisley (1984) referred to as a 'variable field,' one in which the level of analysis varies" (p. vii). As applied to media and the elderly, this means that we need to draw from a variety of fields. For example, psychologists study individual differences in the ways that viewers look at the television screen, and this may help explain why viewers retain different information (Anderson & Burns, 1991). It is necessary to examine the importance of active audience members in defining the realities.

Gerbner and his associates treat media content, specifically television, as having direct impact on the audience. "In its simplest form, cultivation analysis tries to ascertain if those who spend more time watching television are more likely to perceive the real world in ways that reflect the most common and repetitive messages and lessons of the television world, compared with people who watch less television but are otherwise comparable in important demographic characteristics" (Morgan & Signorielli, 1990, p. 16):

> That means that television's independent contribution to such patterns is most likely to be in the direction of homogeneity within otherwise different and diverse social groups, eroding traditional social and other distinctions. . . . It means that large and otherwise comparable groups of regular television viewers from different walks of life share a stable commonality of meanings compared to the lighter viewers in the same groups, and the commonality reflects their exposure to the television mainstream, eroding other traditional group differences. (Gerbner, 1990, pp. 260–261)

In cultivation research, the amount of television viewing impacts a person's "conception" of social reality. As Morgan and Signorielli (1990) put it, "The basic hypothesis is that heavy viewers will be more likely to perceive the real world in ways that reflect the most stable and recurrent patterns of portrayals in the television world" (pp. 9–10). Heavy viewers of dramatic television content are hypothesized in cultivation research to be linked with their exaggerated estimates of victimization (Ogles & Sparks, 1989).

Considerable research has been conducted in two theoretical fields relative to the portrayal of elderly people in media. Cultivation theory holds that people watching television acquire a view of the real world shaped by the televised content they view. The following are among the findings:

- Gerbner (1969) noted that if elderly people are portrayed on television as incompetent, then viewers might begin to think that is true.
- Signorielli and Gerbner's (1978) prime-time television analysis of more than 9,000 TV characters found that elderly people were not often represented.
- When elderly TV characters were portrayed, they often had problems and were reliant on younger people for help (Northcott, 1975).
- Elderly TV characters were more likely to be villains than heroes (Aronoff, 1974); or, they simply were portrayed in a negative light (Davis & Kubey, 1982).
- Bell (1992) found that negative stereotypes of elderly people in prime-time television have been replaced by more positive stereotypes.

- Gerbner (1993) pointed out, in a study of women and minorities on television, that older people are greatly underrepresented, and seem to be declining instead of increasing as in real life.

Cultivation theorists would say that heavy television viewers might think that few people are elderly and elderly persons were of less consequence because they were rarely seen on television.

BIAS, STEREOTYPING, AND MYTH

Palmore (1999) studied negative and positive ageism. He defined ageism as "any prejudice or discrimination against or in favor of an age group" (p. 4). Prejudice may be divided into negative stereotypes and negative attitudes. For Palmore, stereotypes are "mistaken or exaggerated beliefs about a group, in this case the elderly," and attitudes are "negative feelings about a group" (p. 19). Palmore posited a systems model in which stereotypes produce attitudes, and attitudes support stereotypes. In extending the Palmore typology, it is important to consider the separate influences of mass media portrayals and interpersonal characterizations.

Mass media and interpersonal communication may reflect both positive and negative stereotypes and attitudes at both personal and institutional levels. This may be seen through behaviors of individuals and or-

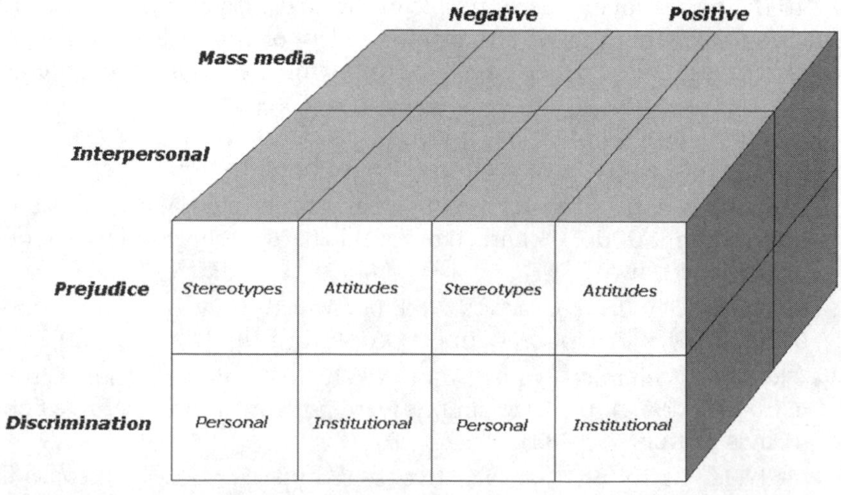

FIG. 2.1. Ageism and communication typology. Adapted from "Typology on Types of Ageism," in *Ageism, Negative and Positive* (p. 19) by E. B. Palmore, 1999, New York: Springer. Adapted with permission.

ganizations, as well as the content of their communication. In the case of mass media, prejudicial stereotypes and attitudes help explain why content about older people often fits conventional patterns and themes. This is contrasted with discriminatory behavior of individuals and organizations, which may contribute, for example, to hiring and firing in employment practices. Media portrayals may reinforce existing beliefs and attitudes of audience members. Additionally, interpersonal experience with the real lives of older people would be expected to mediate the influences of media messages. For example, if a person draws from a set of positive personal experiences about aging, media content that is also positive would be more likely accepted as factual. Likewise, negative personal beliefs about aging may be supported by stereotypical media content or the absence of attention given to the elderly.

Fisher (1977) purported that society's concerns do not include elderly people or the issue of aging. Information about elderly people and issues of importance to them has been inadequate (Hess, 1974). Hess wrote that mass media have missed "a truly big story" (p. 84). Media, according to a variety of studies, have been charged with failing to capture the reality of being old in America, and with creating and reinforcing negative stereotypes about old people (Bramlett Soloman & Wilson, 1989; Gantz, Gartenberg, & Rainbow, 1980; Markson, Pratt, & Taylor, 1989; Schramm, 1969). Although it is more than 30 years old, Schramm's research (1969) still rings true: Media have overlooked the emergence of elderly people as a major segment of the population.

Perhaps media have failed to provide adequate coverage of elderly issues and people because of news values. Gans (1979) identified news values as "ethnocentrism, altruistic democracy, responsible capitalism, small-town pastoralism, individualism, moderatism, social order, and national leadership" (p. 42). Brief definitions are as follows:

- *Ethnocentrism* relates to values that emphasize American culture. Media emphasize youth and action as central to the commercial culture.
- *Altruistic democracy* emphasizes public interest and service. The elderly may be seen as pulling back from their role in active participation in the community.
- *Responsible capitalism* trusts the business community. Elderly are often viewed as being on fixed incomes with little connection to business affairs. Additionally, they may be seen as "set in their ways" in terms of purchasing behavior.
- *Small-town pastoralism* yearns for the simplicity of rural life. When media do portray small-town America, they may focus on elderly

retirees with little to do. The town café may be the meeting place for finding opinions. This may be portrayed as the exception and representative of yesteryear.

- The preservation of *individualism* is viewed as promoting freedom. In the case of older people, some forms of individualism are treated by media as eccentric. However, as a group, the elderly may be portrayed as conservative and cautious.
- Media values of *moderation* discourage extremism. Older people may be viewed as having the benefit of experience, but news may focus on the unusual people with extreme points of view.
- *Social order* is displayed through routine coverage of day-to-day politics. Issues such as reform of Social Security or threats to its long-term viability are framed as elderly stories.
- The need for *national leadership* is portrayed as a means to maintain social order. Media coverage sometimes points out the age of certain leaders and, in some extreme cases, questions their abilities.

Media interpret news through words, sounds, and pictures. The imagery of news helps illustrate points (Gitlin, 1980). Media influence the way people think by focusing viewers' attention on specific issues (Nussbaum et al., 1989). They set the agenda for the audience by emphasizing certain topics and by slighting other issues through omission. Agenda setting could enter news coverage through event bias. News stories focus on events such as fires and accidents rather than issues such as the plight of elderly people. For example, television may reinforce stereotypical attitudes about elderly people (Gerbner et al., 1980). Additionally, elderly viewers may be more interested and affected. Lonely elderly viewers in one study showed greater interest in viewing negative rather than positive portrayals, whereas nonlonely subjects exhibited the opposite preference (Mares & Cantor, 1992).

Thornton (2002) studied myths of aging and ageist stereotypes. The author suggested three strategies to dispel current aging myths:

1. Patently false myths may be discredited as not scientific. "They should be challenged at all levels of public dialog (sic), in the media, in economic and social planning, in marketing, and in academe" (p. 310).
2. More research needs to be done related to the findings cognitive psychology. "Considering the aging population issues that need to be addressed in the next four decades, developmental and longitudinal studies of individuals and cohorts after middle age are extremely sparse and a priority" (p. 311).

3. Current myths of aging marginalize people, tend to be inaccurate, and may reinforce insensitivity: "They are demeaning and ageist statements, based upon false images, tired stereotypes, and untruths" (p. 311).

Results of a national survey published in *Parade* magazine (Clements, 1993) showed that more than one half of the respondents feel the elderly are portrayed favorably in television (62%), movies (59%), and advertising (55%). One respondent who disagreed said that the average person who does not have close contact with the elderly and only sees them through media would get an incorrect perspective. "This may be one reason why many people treat the elderly as children, as if someone else would be better at deciding what's best for them" (Clements, 1993, p. 5).

CULTURAL STUDIES AND MEANING MAKING

From a broader perspective, there are two communication models: transmission and cultural. The *transmission* model is the traditional linear view of communication that focuses on how media messages are sent to the audience. In contrast, the *cultural* model emphasizes shared meanings and spaces: "Without this common reality, communication would be impossible, and in fact, the vast majority of our communication merely serves to ritualistically reproduce that system of shared meanings within which we live" (Grossberg, Wartella, & Whitney, 1998, p. 20). In this view, we take for granted the role that culture plays in helping us make sense of what we see in mass media. A community must be able to share the meanings. Older people may come to rely heavily on news and entertainment media to identify and interpret community life. Media relate to them consistent ideology and culture (Lull & Hinerman, 1997). For those older people who have become disengaged from everyday social life, media create a sense of engagement. In producing meanings that are shared by nearly everyone in the culture, the images and stories enables viewers, readers, and listeners to stay connected. For example, the phrase "9–11" came to be interpreted through the images of terrorism as shown on television. For those disengaged from the daily workplace, there may have been a sense of community via the media coverage.

CHAPTER SUMMARY

This chapter has explored previous research on media and older people. A foundation has been set forth for interpreting observations about media uses, processes, content, effects, and culture as it pertains to people age

50 and older. It has been argued that communication and gerontology provide a useful intersection for addressing theoretical concerns about media and aging.

REVIEW QUESTIONS

1. Define the disengagement theory. How can we use it to study media and the elderly?
2. How might aging affect use of media? What impact would life circumstances (e.g., poor health) have on an older person's use of media?
3. Do you believe that portrayals of the elderly in media conform to stereotypes? Why or why not? Is there any reason to believe that this is changing or will change in the future?
4. How does culture serve as a basis for interpreting meanings about older people in our society?
5. Explain how and why an older person may be interested in sports television as a way to stay connected with others. Do you believe watching such programming can be a substitute for attending events?

Chapter 3

Radio–Television News and the Elderly

Older people are an important segment of the audience for radio and television news broadcasts. Traditionally, older people have more of an interest in radio news, talk radio, local television news, and network newscasts.

In the case of radio and radio news, aging baby boomers appear to search for substance:

> Baby Boomers listen to the radio an average of 21 hours per week, about two hours more per week than most other adults. Program preferences differ slightly between older and younger Boomers. According to Arbitron, news/talk is No. 1 for older Boomers and rock is No. 5, while rock is No. 2 with younger Boomers and adult contemporary is No. 1. And just as Baby Boomer viewing supported the rise of cable news networks, their avid ears have led to the enormous popularity of talk radio. (Paul, 2003, p. 25)

Paul (2003) concluded that as boomers age, they try new media but keep older media habits. Boomers do not multitask as much as younger people, but their large amounts of increasingly available free time allow them to sample media. Boomers readily adopt new technologies, such as cable television and the Internet, but aging does not diminish their traditional interest in information and entertainment.

THE AUDIENCE FOR NETWORK TELEVISION NEWS

The overall audience for American network television news has declined because younger people are less likely to watch than their predecessors. At the same time, the aging audience has become a prime segment to target. The median age for network television viewers has risen: CBS, 61; ABC, 59; and NBC, 56 (Johnson, 2002, p. 3D). However, as the boomers grow older, analysts predict that older viewers will drift away from the over-the-air networks:

> A recent Pew study showed for the first time more viewers watched the cable networks than the evening news on CBS, NBC or ABC. A closer look at the ratings tells an even more remarkable story. The 55+ demographic group, those born before the baby boom, are watching more television today between 4:30 p.m. and 7:30 p.m., the "news hours," than the corresponding 55+ group was in 1979. The catastrophic drop-off is in viewers born after 1945. In fact, an in-depth look at the ratings suggests that the popularity of the major anchors and of the evening news format is not something that was ever meant to carry over to the Baby Boomers (and the younger generations now entering their prime news-consumption years). The startling conclusion may well be that the evening news was only a transitory phenomenon that had more to do with the particular needs and outlook of the generations born between 1900 and 1945 than anything else. (Alan, 2003, p. 1)

One out of two network news viewers is over age 55 (White, 2001).

BOX 3.1. The Aging Face of CBS News

At age 72, Dan Rather was anchor and managing editor of the "CBS Evening News" and a correspondent for "60 Minutes II." In 2002 and 2003, he traveled to Iraq, Kuwait, Afghanistan, Saudi Arabia, and Israel to cover the war on terrorism. He anchored Election Night 2000, a marathon that kept him on the air continuously for 16 straight hours. Earlier, at age 65, Rather reported from the eye of the storm as Hurricane Opal approached the Florida coast. Two producers "anchored the anchor," clinging to his arms and legs during the ferociously high winds, CBS reported.

Rather began his career in 1950 as an Associated Press reporter in Huntsville, Texas. Later, he was a reporter for KTRH Radio in Houston and the *Houston Chronicle* in 1954–1955. He became news director of KTRH and then news director at KHOU. Rather's competitors were Peter Jennings,

BOX 3.1. *(Continued)*

anchor of "World News Tonight" on ABC, and Tom Brokaw, anchor of the "NBC Nightly News"—both in their mid 60s. Brokaw retired after the 2004 presidential election. Rather was 8 years older than his predecessor Walter Cronkite when he left the CBS anchor desk, and 9 years older than Brokaw. Concern was expressed about Rather's ability to attract the important 25- to 54-year-old demographic group. This group is important to advertisers because each network newscast earns about $100 million per year. As each of the three major network news anchors aged, viewing declined.

CBS planned to eventually shift Rather off the evening anchor desk and onto reporting for "60 Minutes" and "60 Minutes II." These shows have a history of employing older reporters and managers, including:

- Executive Producer Don Hewitt, 80.
- Correspondent Ed Bradley, 62, who had quintuple heart bypass surgery in 2003.
- Mike Wallace, 85, Andy Rooney, 84, and Morley Safer, 71, who all continue to work on "60 Minutes."
- Lesley Stahl, 62, who is one example of an aging female television reporter.

"60 Minutes" draws the oldest audience of any program on broadcast TV, and reporter Steve Kroft, a 57-year-old aging baby boomer, said they should be trying to appeal to younger viewers.

BOX 3.1. *(Continued)*

Mike Wallace, Courtesy CBS.

Sources: Dan Rather, CBS. (2003, December). Retrieved from http://www. cbsnews.com/stories/2002/02/25/eveningnews/main502026. shtml; Steinberg, J. (2003, November 30). At 72, a dogged Rather is not yet ready to yield. *The New York Times*, sec. 1, p. 1; Johnson, P. (2003, August 11). At "60 Minutes," clock ticking on change. *USA TODAY*, p. 3D.

The networks are not predicted to lure younger viewers to the news. Maynard (2001) emphasized, "The audiences for the evening news are probably the people who've always watched it from the time it started, which means they are older" (p. 4). Market fragmentation, or splitting the overall audience across hundreds of cable and satellite TV channels, has also caused problem for network news. Older viewers are more likely than younger viewers to watch programming on CNN, MSNBC, CNBC, and Fox News. In fact, older viewers use their increasing free time during the day to watch the cable news networks (Dorsey, 2003). At the same time, specialty channels such as HGTV, AMC, QVC, C-SPAN, and TV Land are attractive to older viewers.

TELEVISION NEWS CONTENT

There is very little research focusing on television news content targeted toward older people. Recent studies have dealt with how older audience members react to content (Klein, 2003). Content analyses of network and local television newscasts show an absence of stories relating to social issues that might be of importance to elderly people (Stempel, 1988). Adams (1978) conducted an analysis of 10 Pennsylvania television stations and found an emphasis on local politics, not on sensational and human interest stories. Nonpolitical community and organization activity received less than one and a half minutes of coverage, or about 9% of total news time.

Typical television news stories involving the elderly include elderly scams and crime victims; nursing home conditions; elderly drivers; Social Security, Medicare, and prescription drugs; living to age 100 and beyond; Alzheimer's disease; and older daredevils. As baby boomers age, story content may change. For example, coverage of grandparents raising their grandchildren is becoming more common. Likewise, older people who return to the workforce after retirement have attracted news coverage.

Pollack (1989) argued that mass media have done an incomplete job of educating themselves about social policy questions that affect the elderly, and too many editors see the problems of elderly people as boring or depressing.

**BOX 3.2. Network News Coverage
of Older Drivers Stories**
ABC World News Tonight with Peter Jennings
"A Closer Look: Elderly Drivers"
July 17, 2003

One common theme for network news coverage of "older Americans" is the issue of elderly drivers. "This is getting a lot of attention, as you know, after the elderly man in California drove into a crowd of people, or crowds of people, really, killing ten of them," Peter Jennings introduced an ABC News story in 2003.

PETER JENNINGS
(Voice Over) The latest figures from the government show 18.9 million drivers on the road are 70 years old or older. They represent 10 percent of all drivers. Here's ABC's Lisa Stark . . .

LISA STARK, ABC NEWS
(Voice Over) 94 year-old Sylvia Ginsburg still drives everyday. She sees no reason to quit.

SYLVIA GINSBURG, ELDERLY DRIVER
I think that certain old people can still drive, and I feel I am very capable of driving.

BOX 3.1. *(Continued)*

LISA STARK
(Voice Over) In fact, younger drivers, those under 30, are more likely to cause fatal accidents than drivers over 65.

SUSAN FERGUSON, INSURANCE INSTITUTE FOR HIGHWAY SAFETY
Older drivers tend to drive much more cautiously. They don't tend to speed. They don't drink and drive. And, they restrict themselves to situations that are less hazardous.

LISA STARK
(Voice Over) Age alone does not determine whether someone can drive safely.

LISSA KAPUST, BETH ISRAEL DEACONESS MEDICAL CENTER
I think that really is the major dilemma, is trying to red flag which of the drivers are the dangerous drivers.

LISA STARK
(Voice Over) Kapust runs a program at a Boston hospital that puts at-risk drivers through a battery of tests. This one demonstrates brake reaction time. What's really critical, she says, is a road test.

LISSA KAPUST
An actual road test is the best solution to sort out who is safe and who isn't, but that gets back to the difficult issue of time and money.

LISA STARK
(Voice Over) Because of expense and lobbyists for senior citizens, only Illinois and New Hampshire require road tests for elderly drivers when they renew their licenses. Twenty-one states have some extra requirement for older drivers. They may have to renew in person and more frequently. Florida, with the highest percentage of elderly drivers, just passed a law requiring vision tests for those 80 and older when they renew their license.

LISA STARK
(Off Camera) The state of Maryland is trying to develop a simple test to screen elderly drivers. They're looking at everything from vision to memory to attention span, even the ability of drivers to turn their head to see hazards.

LISA STARK
(Voice Over) The problem is only going to get more critical as baby boomers age. By the year 2030, one in four drivers will be 65 or older. Lisa Stark, ABC News, Washington.

LOCAL TELEVISION NEWS AND OLDER PEOPLE

Local television has become a prime source for news and information (Peale & Harmon, 1991). The people responsible for the news decisions that transform everyday events into the sights and sounds of the evening newscast also are held responsible for building the public agenda of issues and events (Berkowitz & Adams, 1990).

However, a substantial number of television news viewers have expressed the concern that local TV news is biased and sensational, often overdramatizes the news, does not look out for ordinary people, manufactures news stories, and overlooks stories that ought to be reported (Hall, 1998). Viewer reactions come from local television news content, which is the product of newsroom employee decisions. In a study of television's effect on adults, Gans (1968) found that one third of the respondents felt that television helped them understand their personal problems and make decisions, particularly when they could identify the situation being presented. Gans' findings suggested that examining television programming to identify messages about human life in general is appropriate, and can be applied to specific categories of individuals, such as older adults.

Journalism research has focused on news reporters and their sources (Sallot, Steinfatt, & Salwen, 1998). However, in local television newsrooms, it is the producer—often a person under age 40—who decides which stories will air in a given newscast, and then writes many of the stories that are broadcast. Producers are responsible for the final content of their newscasts: "Once a decision has been made on which newscast a story will be placed, the reporter will do most of his or her communicating with the producer on questions of story focus, length, etc." (Goedkoop, 1988, p. 72). As much as one half of the overall news content is not written by reporters, but by producers. Producers also decide the order of the stories within a newscast, placing special emphasis on the "lead story of the day, one which the news staff covered in depth" (Fang, 1985, p. 21). Fang's point is that a producer will cut other stories before touching the lead. The research on producers, however, does not address the underlying reasons for selecting a story as the lead. The relatively young age of most producers may influence how they decide and frame news. For example, if older people and issues of importance to them are seen as too boring for news coverage, then younger producers may omit stories or edit them to reflect the desired younger audience.

Research has identified the importance of market forces in organizing the culture of broadcast newsrooms around the need to entertain the audience (McManus, 1994). Gans' (1979) news values have been extended to include concerns such as visual quality, amusement, and topicality

(McManus, 1994, p. 120). In the case of local television news, a consumer-based approach more often has led to commercial pressures and "sensationalism" in the name of ratings, according to Kaniss (1991): "The most common explanation of how economic considerations affect news coverage is that news is selected and presented not so much for its importance as for its ability to entertain. . . . The news media are said to give greater prominence to stories that elicit emotion than to those that inform" (pp. 46–47). Although Kaniss acknowledged the importance of the late evening newscast and its emphasis on timely coverage of crimes, fires, and accidents, she limited her discussion of local television news to station managers, news anchors, and reporters.

Likewise, McManus described a three-stage news production process that is reporter centered. Reporters, too, are hired young and often move on to larger markets. Reporters collaborate with producers, and McManus viewed the producer as an important news manager who selects events to be covered based on similar criteria: "One reason for this orthodoxy is the similar advice given by the major television consultants" (p. 130).

BOX 3.3. Women and Television

The issue of age, women, and television news came to the forefront in 1981 with the Christine Craft case. She was hired with a 2-year contract as a co-anchor at KMBC in Kansas City because of her experience as a CBS sports reporter. She also previously worked at a station in Santa Barbara, California. In July 1981, she was demoted to reporter because audience research was negative about her. Her news director, according to Craft, said: "Christine, our viewer research results are in and they are really devastating. The people of Kansas City don't like watching you anchor the news because you are too old, too unattractive, and you are not sufficiently deferential to men." She was 38 at the time and sued the station.

In a 1983 trial, a Kansas City jury unanimously ruled in favor of Craft, awarding her $500,000 in damages. A federal judge tossed out the verdict. At a second trial in Joplin, Missouri, a jury ruled in Craft's favor, but an appellate court overturned the verdict. The Supreme Court refused to hear the age and sex discrimination case.

In general, women have experienced difficulty in remaining behind the television news anchor desk past age 40. In 1992, 44-year-old Philadelphia TV anchor Diane Allen filed a complaint against WCAU. The Equal Employment Opportunity Commission (EEOC) found in her favor. In 1999, anchor Janet Peckinpaugh sued WFSB, Hartford, Connecticut, for gender discrimination. The case was symbolic for exposing the "older man, younger

BOX 3.3. *(Continued)*

Photo: Christine Craft at the time of the lawsuit, courtesy the Museum of Broadcast Communications and Christine Craft.

woman" model for TV news. Peckinpaugh won a judgment on gender discrimination but lost on the age issue. However, her agent, Ken Lindner, told *Broadcasting & Cable* magazine that age was a factor in the case: "As people get older, and they feel they are wrongfully terminated, they'll look at the case." The magazine's Dan Trigoboff concluded that "female broadcast journalists over 40, regardless of their ability as journalists or communicators, agents and news executives agree, are far less likely to succeed in shifting (to) lucrative positions in other markets."

There are rare exceptions in local television news. In Miami, Florida, WPLG anchor Ann Bishop dominated the market for 30 years. Some consultants and news directors contend that the industry is more open today than it was a generation ago to accepting aging women on the air. The stereotype has been that men may show their age, whereas women must hide it. Former CBS television reporter Marlene Sanders suggested that women are allowed to age on television only if they look "fabulous." She added, "I have a theory—that old people remind others of their mortality—something they do not want to see."

At the network level, there has been increasing interest in keeping older women on the air. Lesley Stahl, Diane Sawyer, Barbara Walters, and Judy Woodruff are a few examples of aging women still in front of the camera. There may be a shift in norms as the overall society ages and media place greater value on experience.

BOX 3.3. *(Continued)*

Sources: Craft, C., The Museum of Broadcast Communications. (2003). Retrieved from http://www.museum.tv/archives/etv/C/htmlC/craftchrist/craftchrist.htm; Trigoboff, D. (1999, April 5). The gender trap. *Broadcasting & Cable*; Tillotson, K. (1997, June 10). Firmly anchored? Television still gives short shrift to women and minority journalists. *Minneapolis Star Tribune*; Lipschultz, J. H. (1994, March). *Craft v. Metromedia, Inc.* and its social-legal progeny. *Communications and the Law*, 16(1), 45–74; Sanders, M. (2002, November). Older women and the media. United Nations Division for the Advancement of Women.

Evidence in the Christine Craft case and others over the years has shown that stations may be concerned about the appearance of older male on-air personalities as well. For men, age may become an issue triggered by weight gain, hair loss, wardrobe selection, and stamina.

BOX 3.4. Former Denver Reporter Won Age Lawsuit

News reporter Dave Minshall was fired in the late 1990s but won a jury award of more than one-half million dollars in an age discrimination case against KMGH-TV 7. Minshall was a veteran reporter with nearly a quarter century in the market and 17 years at the station.

In 1996, a new management team was brought in to reverse sinking ratings—the station was the third rated network affiliate. Two anchors in their early 40s were demoted from the 10 p.m. newscast, and Minshall, 53, was fired after obtaining a 6-month contract renewal. The news director testified during the trial that "she created the news format, 'Real Life, Real News,' with the intention of reaching a younger demographic and that she considered the physical appearance of the on-air anchors and reporters in making overall changes to the news programs" (*Minshall v. McGraw-Hill*, 2003).

In 2003, Minshall won an appeal of the award against McGraw-Hill from the 10th Circuit Court of Appeals. The court affirmed an earlier judgment by the District Court. The company claimed they fired Minshall because of poor work. However, the news director had made several derogatory comments about older people, including a passing remark that "old people should die." More important to the court, she said the station needed a "younger look," the weather person was "too f***ing old," and said she was disgusted when she saw " 'an old fart' on television without a shirt."

Sources: McPhee, M. (2001, September 6). Ex-reporter wins age-bias lawsuit. *DenverPost.com*. Retrieved from http://www.DenverPost.com; *Minshall v. McGraw-Hill*, 323 F.3d 1273 (March 28, 2003).

At local television stations across the country, general managers and news directors set policy affecting news coverage (Goedkoop, 1988), including how older people and their issues are covered. Although the general managers and news directors set policy, it is the producers who make the final decisions about what goes into or is left out of the individual newscasts. As a group, these three players ultimately have strong influence on what viewers see in their nightly local television newscasts. Their interest in targeting a 25- to 54-year-old audience demographic group may help explain some of their decisions.

NEWS STAFF AND OLDER PEOPLE

The Kogan Attitudes Toward Old People scale (1961) has been useful in gathering data about a person's attitudes toward the elderly. The original Kogan scale (OP) consisted of 34 statements—17 phrased positively and 17 phrased negatively. Using this method, a respondent's total or mean score is reflective of a person's attitudes toward elderly people (Hilt & Lipschultz, 1996).

In a revised version of the Kogan scale, the number of statements was reduced to 22 (Hilt & Lipschultz, 1999). A national mail survey in 1997 of local television news producers used the scale (Table 3.1). The research focused on a group of individuals responsible for the writing and editing of local late-night television newscasts. Local television news producers also responded to a series of statements about news coverage. The news producers were compared with previous data collected from television general managers and news directors. In the 1996 study, there were 76

TABLE 3.1
Comparison of Revised Kogan Attitudes Toward Old People Scores

Occupational Groups	N	Score	SD
Producer Study (Hilt & Lipschultz, 1999)			
Television News Producers	76	68.09	12.78
Management Study (Hilt & Lipschultz, 1996)			
Television General Managers	76	95.87	7.84
Television News Directors	81	93.75	9.79

Note. The scores represent summed means for the Revised 22-statement Kogan Attitudes Toward Old People scale. The Likert scale statements were scored from strongly disagree (1) to strongly agree (7). The lower a respondent's score, the more positive were a person's attitudes toward older people. The reliability coefficients for the groups were: producers, $\alpha = .79$; general managers, $\alpha = .46$; news directors, $\alpha = .65$. The overall standardized alpha for the 1994 groups was .58 for the 22 statements, as compared with .81 for the full Kogan list.

general managers and 81 news directors who were asked the original 34 Kogan statements. The three occupation groups were compared on the 22 revised Kogan statements. Index scores for the occupation groups were computed.

A total of 87 of 211 television news producers responded from across the country. This represented a response rate of 41.2%. The respondents came from the largest to the smallest television markets, and everything in between. The typical producer of the late-night television newscast in 1997 was a 29-year-old White (96.5%) female (59.3%) who had completed college (89.6%) with a journalism or mass communication degree (59.3%), and considered herself to be politically independent (39.5%) and middle-of-the-road (65.5%). She was as likely to be married (46.5%) as she was to never have been married (44.2%).

Of 86 usable respondents on this question, only six (7.1%) local television news producers were age 50 or older. In the 1996 study, there were 34 television general managers (44.7%) and 11 news directors (13.6%) in the 50-plus age category. Using the 22-item scores as guideposts, the television news producers in the 1999 study were substantially lower, and thus more positive in their attitudes toward the elderly than general managers and news directors.

The strongest agreement on the revised Kogan scale was with statements that were either neutral about older people, or positive (Table 3.2). There were no statements in which the news producers agreed with a negative statement about the elderly. By contrast, the five strongest statements of disagreement were all negative attitudes about older people. In the 1996 study, six statements yielded statistically significant differences between television general managers and news directors (Table 3.3). The producers in the 1999 study responded in a similar fashion. Overall, the statements yielded slight differences between groups, but the pattern of responses is positive toward older people.

A series of statements yielded statistically significant and strong relations (Table 3.4). The correlations coefficients represented a mix of positive and negative statements about older people, as measured by the revised Kogan scale.

VIEWS ABOUT NEWS COVERAGE

Local television news producers also responded to 10 statements concerning their views about news coverage. Like the general managers and news directors in the 1996 study, the statement with the highest overall mean was "Exciting video helps a story" (6.38). This finding was consistent with later results about local television news coverage (Lipschultz & Hilt, 2002).

TABLE 3.2
Local TV News Producers' Ranked Means

Revised Kogan Attitudes Toward Old People Statements	N	M	SD
The elderly have the same faults as anybody else	83	5.90	1.12
The elderly's accounts of their past experiences are interesting	83	5.70	1.24
Most elderly keep a clean home	83	5.24	1.21
Most elderly seem to be quite clean in their personal appearance	83	5.18	1.41
Most elderly would work as long as possible rather than be dependent	85	5.13	1.35
People grow wiser with the coming of old age	82	5.11	1.44
Most elderly are very different from one another	82	5.05	1.42
Most elderly are cheerful, agreeable, and good humored	83	4.88	1.34
Most elderly respect the privacy of others	83	4.87	1.29
Most elderly are very relaxing to be with	81	4.86	1.29
A nice residential neighborhood has a number of elderly living in it	85	4.66	1.45
Most elderly are as easy to understand as younger people	83	4.60	1.50
Most elderly can adjust when the situation demands it	83	4.36	1.61
The elderly have too little power in business and politics	84	3.57	1.57
Most elderly need no more love and reassurance than anyone else	83	3.42	1.63
It would be better if most elderly lived in residential units that also housed younger people	84	3.25	1.41
The elderly seldom complain about the behavior of younger people	83	3.10	1.34
It is foolish to claim that wisdom comes with old age	85	2.82	1.70
Most elderly bore others by talking about the "good old days"	83	2.45	1.34
Most elderly spend too much time prying into the affairs of others	83	2.37	1.11
Most elderly let their homes become shabby and unattractive	84	2.25	1.18
If the elderly expect to be liked, they should eliminate their irritating faults	83	2.01	1.29

TABLE 3.3
Occupational Group Averages, Six Key Kogan Scale Attitudes

Statements	Producers (1997)	GMs (1994)	NDs (1994)
People grow wiser with the coming of old age	5.11	4.28	4.73
It is foolish to claim that wisdom comes with old age	2.82	3.79	3.22
If the elderly expect to be liked, they should eliminate their irritating faults	2.01	2.79	2.36
Most elderly bore others by talking about the "good old days"	2.45	2.61	2.20
Most elderly spend too much time prying into the affairs of others	2.37	2.43	2.10
Most elderly let their homes become shabby and unattractive	2.25	2.14	1.91

Note. Overall, the six statements had statistically significant *t* values in the 1994 study. For each statement, the scale is: 1 = strongly disagree; 2 = disagree; 3 = slightly disagree; 4 = no response/neutral; 5 = slightly agree; 6 = agree; 7 = strongly agree.

TABLE 3.4
Strongest Correlations Coefficients, Revised Kogan Scale

Statements	r
Most elderly bore others by talking about the "good old days" **with**	
Most elderly spend too much time prying into the affairs of others	.64
Most elderly keep a clean home **with**	
Most elderly seem to be quite clean in their personal appearance	.58
People grow wiser with the coming of old age **with**	
Most elderly are very relaxing to be with	.58
People grow wiser with the coming of old age **with**	
It is foolish to claim that wisdom comes with old age	−.54
If the elderly expect to be liked, they should eliminate their irritating faults **with**	
Most elderly spend too much time prying into the affairs of others	.53
Most elderly are cheerful, agreeable, and good humored **with**	
A nice residential neighborhood has a number of elderly living in it	.53

Again, as with the 1996 study of general managers and news directors, the statement with the lowest overall mean for producers was "Issues about or of concern to older people are hard to explain on TV" (2.84).

It could be argued that what the Kogan scale attempts to measure is not just the respondents' attitudes toward older people, but also a function of positive and negative stereotypes of aging (Barrow, 1996). The responses of local television news producers featured positive, possibly reverse, stereotypes about older people rather than strictly neutral responses. More work needs to be done on how such attitudes by mass media employees affect the portrayal of older people in our society.

Consistent with earlier studies, news producers said they needed "exciting video" in order to tell stories about older people. This professional bias may help explain why more stories about the elderly do not find their way onto the air, regardless of the attitudes of those who make the decisions. In other words, it is not enough for producers to be positive about older people to lead to news coverage. Local TV news' preoccupation with crime stories and its exciting video means we are more likely to see older people portrayed as the victims of crime or scams than we are to see them as prominent newsmakers. It is no wonder that some view the mass media as contributing to the disengagement of older people from society.

TARGETING OLDER PEOPLE THROUGH CRIME COVERAGE

Romer, Jamieson, and Aday (2003) studied how television news cultivates a fear of crime among people. Local television news was one important source for news promoting a fear of crime:

We interpret the relation between local television viewing and fear of crime as particularly consistent with cultivation theory. . . . We find support for the theory primarily in the realm of news reporting, especially at the local level. . . . The focus of local television news on criminal violence may condition audiences to focus on crime and to ignore other problems that are as important but translate less readily to the television news format. (pp. 102–103)

Crime coverage may also affect "perceptions of places where crime is likely to occur and the persons stereotyped as typical perpetrators" (p. 103). For older viewers, the effects may be magnified by their lack of social engagement.

BOX 3.5. Quick Answers: "When I Watch TV I Get the Idea That Older People Really Aren't Safe From Crime. Is That True?"

NO. Although the media may leave the impression that older adults are a major target of violent crime, annual data from the national Crime Victimization Surveys consistently indicate that violent crime, personal theft, and household victimization rates for persons aged 65 and older are the lowest of any age group. Data indicate that this holds true for virtually all categories of criminal victimization: rape, robbery, aggravated assault, simple assault, and personal larceny without contact. Only for the category of personal larceny with contact (e.g., purse snatching and pocket picking) is the victimization rate higher for persons aged 65 and over compared to those aged 25 to 64. Nevertheless, the health and financial consequences may be greater for the older victim.

Source: Breytspraak, L., Kendall, E., and Halpert, B. (2003, December). Center on Aging Studies, University of Missouri–Kansas City. Retrieved from http://missourifamilies.org/quick/agingqa/agingqa10.htm.

Doyle (1997) studied aging and crime. One focus was on the increasing scholarly interest in elderly criminals, as well as victimization of older people. Doyle lamented, "Unfortunately, the mass media as well as the popular and academic literature have disseminated much information about aging and crime that is at best misleading and at worst completely wrong" (p. 342). Doyle found that older people are not very likely to be involved in crime, "either as victims or as perpetrators" (p. 357). Doyle argued that society and researchers have exaggerated the problem of the connection between the elderly and crime.

MARKETING AND TELEVISION NEWS

News managers and producers recognize the need to "please audiences or at least those audiences that advertisers find attractive" because of economic needs: "Market Model journalism is anathema to journalists. . . . It is the model of the business office, not the newsroom. This gives it enduring influence, for instance, it pretty well governs all local television news. But it is the model that any self-respecting journalist fears and loathes" (Schudson, 1998, p. 135). Producers must work in an increasingly competitive environment in which the number of viewers for late evening newscasts has declined dramatically since the 1980s (Jacobs, 1990). Producers could do a better job of recognizing the importance of an older audience, issues related to aging, and take more of a life-span perspective: "The life-span perspective views development as a life-long process" (Williams & Nussbaum, 2001, p. 4). In other words, it should not be assumed that as people age they will automatically fall into decline.

Moreover, do not overgeneralize about older people because there is much individual diversity: "The life-span perspective assumes that the person and the environment are engaged in a transactional relationship influencing and being influenced by each other" (p. 6). So, an older person has a unique set of social and economic conditions related to their lifelong development. Gerontological research and media alike sometimes suffer from stereotyping the plight of older people in physical decline and social disengagement.

CHAPTER SUMMARY

The older population in the United States is increasing dramatically, and has been referred to as the "graying of America" (Barrow, 1996, p. 6). Census projections show that by 2040, the nation could have more people over age 65 than under age 21, and more than 1 in 4 Americans will be age 65 or older (Usdansky, 1992). In the 1990 census figures, adults age 65 and over accounted for 1 out of 8 Americans, as compared to 1 in 25 at the beginning of this century. At the same time, scholarly interest is rapidly increasing in the area of mass media and older adults (Roy & Harwood, 1997).

Radio and television news often attract older listeners and viewers. TV news content sometimes ignores or stereotypes the elderly, even though they are the dominant audience. The portrayal of older people may be influenced by a perception among media people that the elderly and their issues are boring. Producers and reporters tend to be younger than their audience members and may not reflect similar interests. The life-span

perspective challenges traditional gerontology and mass media portrayals by suggesting that individual older people may continue to grow as
they age rather than face physical decline and social disengagement.

REVIEW QUESTIONS

1. Why do older people constitute the majority of the television news
   viewing audience? Why might this be a problem for local and network television news?

2. Why do news people tend to focus on a short list of typical stories
   about older people?

3. Why should there be concern about the tendency of television news
   managers to reassign older women to off-camera jobs?

4. How could media do a better job in responding to the aging of
   America?

5. What are the strengths and weakness of the social disengagement
   theory outlined in chapter 2 versus the life-span perspective introduced in this chapter? How might an understanding of each approach assist broadcasters in their work?

Chapter 4

Print Media and the Elderly

American newspapers are facing a serious challenge as the nation ages. Growth among the coveted 18- to 34-year-old target demographic group of readers has been flat for some time: "It is clear that aging is among the trends that will have the most profound effect on readership" (Somerville, 2001, p. 24). Older readers continue to provide newspapers with their largest gains in readership, but we may be experiencing a change from the findings from the last century. Stone (1987) found that reading patterns remained stable for adults through the working years, but "reading frequency drops slightly after age 65, due possible to health, eyesight, or finances" (p. 109).

Paddon (1995) found that newspapers targeted older readers by publishing special features or sections. For example, the *St. Louis Post-Dispatch* published a "Fifty Plus" series in the early 1990s. Paddon was concerned about the ability of newspapers to sell an older audience to advertisers. However, she predicted the importance of older readers and warned newspapers about taking older readers for granted. Whereas seniors have begun to be seen as a target market, Paddon suggested that newspapers might use national feature stories rather than local content: "As local news staffs shrink and locally generated copy decreases, much more of the editorial content of interest to older readers will likely come from syndicated services" (p. 61).

NEWSPAPER READERSHIP DATA

Newspapers continue to reach out to attract younger readers (Newspaper Association of America, 2003). NAA Senior Vice President and Chief Marketing Officer John E. Kimball said: "In addition to satisfying readers, circulation departments are making great strides in serving adver-tisers with better zoning and other targeting opportunities." Despite the industry's efforts, the largest overall readership gains were among those age 35 and older (Table 4.1). In even more dramatic terms, a whopping 69% (98,634,000) of adult readers were age 35 or older, and 28% (40,165,000) were age 55 or older (Fig. 4.1).

TABLE 4.1
Adult Newspaper Readership 1998–2002

Year	18–24	25 34	35–54	55+	Total
1998	16,197,000	28,166,000	**53,509,000**	**37,120,000**	134,992,000
1999	16,360,000	27,727,000	56,613,000	37,875,000	136,575,000
2000	16,659,000	27,381,000	56,036,000	38,861,000	138,937,000
2001	16,893,000	27,068,000	57,156,000	39,492,000	140,609,000
2002	17,383,000	27,000,000	**58,469,000**	**40,165,000**	143,668,000

Note. Newspaper Association of America (2004). Retrieved from http://www.naa.org.

In the case of average weekday readership, the data suggest that the only large gains were in the 55-plus age category (Table 4.2).

TABLE 4.2
Average Weekday Newspaper Readership 1998–2002

Year	18–24	25–34	35–54	55+	Total
1998	7,052,000	12,930,000	32,588,000	**26,475,000**	79,045,000
1999	6,881,000	12,319,000	31,683,000	26,797,000	77,680,000
2000	6,655,000	11,193,000	31,743,000	27,005,000	76,596,000
2001	6,574,000	10,944,000	31,345,000	27,504,000	76,367,000
2002	7,107,000	11,341,000	32,939,000	**28,251,000**	79,638,000

Note. Newspaper Association of America (2004). Retrieved from http://www.naa.org.

Some newspapers have discovered the importance of "age cohorts," that is, demographic groups of readers and subscribers (Somerville, 2001, p. 25). A Chicago readership project emphasized market forces: "At the heart of that effort was a belief that newspapers needed data and re-search tools to help control their fate by discovering not just how often readers read, or what they read, but which news content is most relevant and useful to them" (p. 26). Specific types of content could increase reader interest for some groups, including older people. Researchers have told newspaper editors: "Focus on the type of local news that has the greatest potential of all topics—intensely local, people-centered news, which is highly relevant to more mature readers" (p. 27).

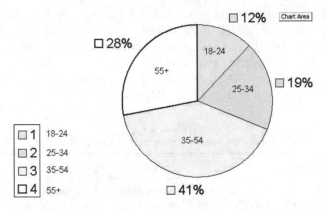

FIG. 4.1. Adult newspaper readership (2002). From Newspaper Association of America (2004). Retrieved from http://www.naa.org.

NEWSPAPER CONTENT AND OLDER PEOPLE

Like broadcasters, print journalists write stories that emphasize a narrow range of themes about older people: the benefits of volunteerism, the dangers of older drivers, the fear of crime, elderly thrill-seekers, and the vulnerability of older people to be victims of scams and rip-offs.

BOX 4.1. One Newspaper's Focus on Seniors

From 1985 until author Al Allen's death in 2001, the *Louisville Courier-Journal* published "Prime Time"—"an excellent example of how a daily newspaper can provide valuable educational information and news to the older adult community it serves" (Nuessel & Van Stewart, 2000, p. 643). Allen's columns sometimes featured community volunteers and provided advice for seniors. In this case, he warned about online scams:

By Al Allen
The Courier-Journal

Learning how a scam works can be instructive for seniors, who often are targeted by swindlers. Here's how one of them works:

For several years, law-enforcement authorities have been warning about a confidence game originating in Africa that seeks to con Americans by gaining access to their bank accounts.

The scam, carried out via e-mail, fax or regular mail, seeks to persuade the victim to make his accounts available for the "transfer" of supposedly huge blocks of money from revolution-torn lands, in return for a sizable commission.

BOX 4.1. *(Continued)*

Recently Robert F. Olinick of Glasgow, Ky., became one of its targets, and he shared two e-mails he received with "Prime Time." It's hard to believe any reasonably intelligent person would be taken in by the clumsiness of the approach—a vague pitch, misspellings and jumbled language, not to mention the sheer incredibility of it all. Here's one of the pitches Olinick received, complete with misspellings and language errors. Hopefully, readers who get a similar one will benefit from his experience and be warned off:

"Thanks to a piece of information I gathered about you through the website, although I did not leave any clue as to the reason for my inquiry bearing in mind the confidentiality required in this absolute risk free business.

"I am Mr. Frank Kwame, the manager of the treasury department of Ecobank head office in Lome-Togo. Recently, we discovered a dormant account with a huge amount of money valued USD 15,000,000.00 (fifteen million U.S. dollars) that belong to one of our numerous customers Mr Duckson Fritz who died in a motor accident in November 1995. During the period of our investigation we discovered that the deceased died along with his family, living no will and nobody behind to come for the claim as next of kin.

"The banking law here stipulates that if such money remain unclaimed for six years, it will be forfeited to the bank treasury as an unclaimed bill.

"A Togolaise cannot stand as a next of kin to a foreigner. It is upon this discovery that I and my colleagues in this department decided to contact you to collaborate with you to pull out this dormant fund.

"We have it in mind to give you a 25% of this total fund of the total money if this proposal meets your interest.

"Urgently reach me through the above stated e-mail, telephone or fax numbers to enable me give you the full details of this transaction and how it is going to work out.

"What I want from you is for you to act as the deceased next of kin. I have in my possession (alone) all necessary document to successfully accomplish this business.

"However it will require that you shall be physically present in Lome-Togo with my assistance to pull act this fund for onward transmission to your account overseas. The next of kin must be present in Lome to sign out this fund, which will take a maximum three working days to conclude.

"Further information will be given to you as soon as I receive your positive response via e-mail or telephone."

A few days later Olinick received a second solicitation from the con artists, with a similar pitch and grammar and spelling just as shaky as the first . . .

Source: E-scams include attempts to access bank accounts (July 8, 2001).

As has already been noted, newspaper readers are overwhelmingly older. It is noteworthy that few newspapers go out of their way to offer columns targeted at an older audience.

In recent years, newspapers have given space to stories about older daredevils. In 2003, for example, the Associated Press reported on Geneva Cranford, celebrating her 80th birthday by skydiving in California. The story began with, "There were no rocking chairs for Geneva Cranford" (Associated Press, July 1, 2003). The newspaper *The Californian* wrote about the event: "She said it's taken about 74 years to fulfill her skydiving dream, mainly because she didn't want to worry other people in her life, particularly her mother, Tessie Edwards, who died in 1995, and her husband, Douglas, who died in 2000" (Lopez, 2003). The newspaper quoted one of her sons: "She's an action-type person."

The Cranford event was not entirely unique. The southern Illinois newspaper *The Carmi Times* published a similar story at about the same time. The newspaper showed 84-year-old Virgie Spurlock of Jonesboro who celebrated her birthday by jumping out of an airplane (http://carmitimes.com/, July 1, 2003). Even former presidents may fit this theme. George H. W. Bush, at age 72, skydived from an airplane and received extensive print and broadcast coverage. These types of stories portray select older people as "rugged individualists," to use Herbert Gans' phrase, appearing to defy the conventional wisdom of elderly disengaging from society in favor of an inactive life. These stories may be a harbinger of future coverage with the assumption that baby boomers will be

Source: http://www.montereybay99s.org/cranford.html

more active as older people. This change in theme, if substantiated, may be related to growing concern about the credibility of our mass media.

BOOMERS AND MEDIA CREDIBILITY

The Internet is a growing source for news and information, but there is conflicting evidence as to whether or not baby boomers continue to have a preference for the hard copy newspaper. A Pew Internet and American Life project found that 60% of people between age 42 and 62 read the daily newspaper, and 44% of this group go online for news. It has been found that older people with an interest in the use of new technologies have a tendency to fall back on traditional behaviors, including newspaper reading. Perhaps some older people continue to view the newspaper as a more credible source for content. Nevertheless, wired aging boomers tend to prefer online business and research: "These tech enthusiasts are the biggest spenders on information technology and seem to welcome the wealth of information the technology enables" (Pew Internet and American Life Project, 2003).

The relation between media use and perceived media credibility is not clear. The traditional finding has been that older people tend to trust their local newspaper—particularly if they subscribe or are regular readers. In one study of Alabama residences, however, there was a drop in newspaper credibility for those people over age 50 (Ibelema & Powell, 2001). Newspaper credibility was lower than broadcast and cable credibility for this age group. The data did not tend to fit a broader national historical trend: "In general, the elderly tend to find the media most credible" (p. 49). The oldest and youngest readers have been found to be least critical in their perception of newspaper image (Burgoon et al., 1986). Although newspaper content sometimes displays the same biases of other media against the elderly, it has been noted that older people may themselves possess negative stereotypical perceptions about the elderly. As boomers age, psychologists have measured how people avoid relating to declining health, nursing homes, and the interests of the elderly.

Newspaper credibility for older people also may be a function of design and layout. In response to the changing nature of newspaper readership, *USA Today* ushered in a new era in which newspaper design and style mimicked the video images seen by baby boomers raised on television. Hartman (1987) discussed how "McPaper" emphasized style over depth (p. 1). The baby boomers appeared to be most satisfied when information was coupled with entertainment. Thus, newspapers were faced with motivating younger readers through meeting psychological needs.

Beyond psychological needs, there are physical issues. For example, older people tend to have diminished ability to read small print. Newspapers have not been very flexible in terms of larger print and layout. Some magazines, however, are easier to read. Nevertheless, magazine content suffers from some of the same limitations as newspapers.

MAGAZINES AND OLDER PEOPLE

Media images of older people contribute to society's perception of aging, and this is particularly true in the case of magazines. Mass media have been charged with failing to capture the reality of being old in America and with creating and reinforcing negative stereotypes about old people (Bramlett-Soloman & Wilson, 1989; Gantz et al., 1980; Schramm, 1969). Some researchers conclude that the media have helped to advance negative stereotypes and a homogenized view of old people in this country (Markson et al., 1989). Barrow (1996) suggested that one way to break the negative stereotypes of age was to "draw attention to people who have made significant contributions in their old age" (p. 39).

Older adults follow the news in both print and broadcast, attend fewer movies, and select messages differently than younger people (DeFleur & Dennis, 1996). The elderly spend more than 40% of their leisure time watching television, reading, going to the movies, listening to the radio, and listening to music (Spring, 1993).

Whereas television and its relationship with older viewers continues to fall under increased scrutiny (Gerbner, 1993; Hilt, 1997a), research into magazines and their portrayal of aging adults traditionally falls into two categories: the readership habits of older adults and their depiction in cartoons and advertising.

The top-rated magazines for the elderly are *Reader's Digest* (including the large print edition), *TV Guide*, *National Geographic*, and *Time*, among others (Robinson & Skill, 1995). One study found that almost 20% of older adults read general interest magazines (Durand et al., 1980). The affluent elderly read many more magazines than their less affluent counterparts (Burnett, 1991). Burnett found that affluent elderly male readers were more likely to read *Newsweek*, *Time*, and *U.S. News & World Report*, as well as other entertainment-oriented publications. Affluent elderly females also read the news magazines, but read other magazines as well. Magazines tend to target the audience that falls under the "well-off, well-educated stratum of the population that the promotion departments of newspapers and magazines like to describe as the 'opinion-makers' " (Grossman & Kumar, 1981, p. 62).

Beyond the reading of magazines, little research has been conducted into the content of magazines. For example, Vasil and Wass (1993) examined nine studies that investigated the portrayal of the elderly in various print media (e.g., magazines cartoons, magazine advertisements, newspapers, and birthday cards). Their evaluation of the quality of the portrayals produced mixed results, and none of the studies under consideration looked at the content of magazine articles. Kent and Shaw (1980) investigated the content of magazine articles. They examined age stereotyping in the news magazine *Time* by conducting a content analysis of named individuals appearing in 1978 issues, and found little age stereotyping. On the whole, however, little attention has been paid to how older adults are portrayed in magazine articles.

JOHN GLENN CASE STUDY

In 1999, a study using a qualitative methodology (Lindlof, 1995; Marshall & Rossman, 1995) examined the January 26, October 26, November 9, and November 16, 1998, issues of *Time*, *Newsweek*, and *U.S. News & World Report* for articles concerning the return of John Glenn to space (Hilt, 2000).

John Glenn was the first American to orbit the earth in 1962 at age 40. Since then, he has served as a U.S. Senator from Ohio and he was a 1984 presidential candidate, but he never returned to space. In January 1998, NASA announced plans for Glenn's return flight aboard the space shuttle *Discovery*. He would be 77 years old when the shuttle launched in late October.

The January 26, 1998, issue of *Time* featured a full-page article (p. 58) on the announced return of John Glenn to space. Two photographs were included—Glenn in his space suit in 1962 and Glenn during the announcement ceremony. The article began with a look back at the 1962 flight, calling him "a rookie pilot in the space agency's Mercury program," and writing that the "40-year-old Marine" had to be able to physically control the spacecraft. The second paragraph moved to the present by giving his age at the time of the announcement (76), and referring to him as "a rookie payload specialist." The paragraph concluded with a listing of some of the things he would have to learn "at an age when most Americans have long since retired."

The story focused on the reasons why Glenn was selected to return to space. "Critics argued that the flight was merely a public relations stunt; NASA insisted it was motivated by good, hard science." Glenn had pushed to a return to space for many years, and viewed it as a "unique opportunity to study the science of aging." Glenn had distinguished himself as "a champion of the elderly." *Time* explained, "It has not escaped his notice that some of the changes the body goes through as it ages—the breakdown of bones and the immune system, for example—are identical to the ones it goes through in zero-G."

The article included criticism of his selection given the fact that other astronauts had been told they were too old to fly. Glenn had been accustomed to being in charge. But, "this time he will be a passenger and scientific subject in a spacecraft piloted by astronauts young enough to be his sons—or daughters."

The January 26 issue of *Newsweek* also featured a full article (p. 32) on the Glenn announcement. The headline "The Ultimate Last Hurrah" was followed by a subhead, "In the Autumn of His Life, John Glenn Goes Home—Back Into Outer Space." This article focused more on his life in between the trips to space. At the announcement news conference, Glenn was described as "balder and more wrinkled" than his 1962 spacesuit photograph. His return to space, according to *Newsweek*, "is ostensibly about studying the common effects of aging and space travel: bone loss, muscle deterioration, sleeplessness, loss of balance." But the article acknowledged that the research was not critical, and the real significance of his mission was to renew interest in the space program.

The January 26 issue of *U.S. News & World Report* did not feature a full article on the announcement. Instead, the information was included in the Outlook column. The two paragraphs focused more on the naming of a teacher for a future shuttle flight than on Glenn's return to space. Glenn was mentioned briefly: "NASA acquiesced last week to Sen. John Glenn's request to fly again in space, where as an astronaut he was the first American to orbit Earth in 1962. The 76-year-old's imminent return to space was of special interest to Barbara Morgan, 46, a third-grade teacher in McCall, Idaho." Nothing else was written about John Glenn.

"THE FLIGHT" ISSUES

The space shuttle *Discovery* took off October 29, 1998, and landed November 7, 1998. Four issues of the magazines under study—the October 26 and November 9 issues of *Newsweek*, the November 9 issue of *Time*, and the November 16 issue of *U.S. News & World Report*—included information about the flight.

The October 26 issue of *Newsweek* was the only news magazine of the four issues under study to feature John Glenn on the cover. The photograph showed Glenn in his shuttle suit with the headline "A New Mission for John Glenn: Exploring the Science of Growing Old." The cover article began on page 30 and was entitled "The Time Traveler." The author, Matt Bai, indicated Glenn's mission was designed "to find out what space can teach us about growing old on Earth." The article described the Johnson Space Center in Houston, and how items from past missions serve as monuments. Bai reported, "Last spring one of NASA's most prized relics, 77-year-old John Glenn, took his friend Bill Clinton on a tour of the cavernous hanger known as Building Nine." The article continued, pointing out differences between Glenn's first flight in *Friendship 7* to this flight in *Discovery*, and concluded with the phrase, "the old man had a lot to learn." Glenn was described as exhausted by 12-hour days in the classroom, and likened to "a grandfather trying to program his VCR."

The article went on to describe the stated reasons behind the mission: how to live longer and better. Some of the experiments that Glenn would endure were detailed, such as the measuring of his sleep patterns and the rate at which his body breaks down proteins. From there the article gave a history of Glenn's involvement with the space program and how he came to be a member of the shuttle flight crew. The article concluded with the sentence, "Whatever Glenn's flight tells scientists about aging, he's already shown the rest of us how to grow old."

This issue contained two other articles concerning the *Discovery* flight. The first article is a two-page look at Glenn's two space flights. It compared the two flights and described some of the experiments that Glenn would undergo. The second article was a two-page examination entitled, "Exploring the Secrets of Age." This article went into more detail about the experiments and the reasons why scientists needed the information: "Scientists hope that by sending people of different ages into space, they'll gain general insights into how the body works and why it fails." This article focused on the experiments, only mentioning Glenn in terms of his contribution to the tests.

The November 9 issue of *Newsweek* featured a two-page picture of the shuttle lift-off with the title "Zero-G and I Feel Fine," a quote from Glenn himself. The relatively short article that followed (three paragraphs) summarized the lift-off and some of the medical tests that Glenn would undergo. References to age were omitted, and the article remained focused on the flight itself.

The November 9 issue of *Time* also focused on the flight and what it might mean for NASA. Entitled "Victory Lap," the article included a photo of the lift-off with an inset picture of Glenn waving as he walked to board the craft. A pull-out poster traced the space agency's progress, from the race to space with the Russians to the shuttle *Discovery* flight. The article recapped Glenn's habit of telling his wife, Annie, that he was just going down to the corner for chewing gum prior to a dangerous flight. Few references to age and aging were included in this article until the last few paragraphs, at which point some of the experiments that Glenn would conduct were detailed.

The November 16 issue of *U.S. News & World Report* included a one-page article entitled "John Glenn's Mixed Message on Aging." This article openly challenged the reasons for sending Glenn back into space. It began with a description of how uncomfortable Glenn was with the title "world's oldest spaceman," but how he began to embrace the description as the launch date approached. From there, the article centered on how people who work with the elderly are beginning to question the adulation of overachievers: "In reality, old age means to live with both vigor and limits."

News magazine coverage of Glenn's trip centered on his return to space and the aging experiments he would undergo. Although comments were made concerning his age and his role as a rookie payload specialist, there were few comments that could be considered ageist or demeaning to older adults. This finding would be in agreement with the conclusions reached by Kent and Shaw (1980). In that research, Kent and Shaw reasoned that the lack of age stereotyping in *Time* is due to the goal of objectivity held by journalists.

For the most part, the same level of objectivity was obtained in the magazines in the present study. However, the November 16 article in *U.S. News & World Report* entitled "John Glenn's Mixed Message on Aging" challenged the reasons for sending Glenn back into space, and suggested that the trip, although well-intentioned, would "gloss over the fact that older hearts, lungs, ears, and eyes do start to wear out." This was the only article in that issue on Glenn's return to space. Barrow (1996) wrote that negative stereotypes must be countered with accurate information. She found that "physical stereotypes are as common as mental ones and are just as false" (p. 40).

The news magazines examined for this study of John Glenn's return to space remained focused on the event itself. The reasons behind his flight were brought forward and analyzed, not in an ageist or stereotypical fashion, but rather to explain why he had been selected. Objective reporting of a worthy news event is, to paraphrase Barrow, one way to break the negative stereotypes of age, and to draw attention to people who make significant contributions in their old age.

RANGE OF CONTENT AND EXPERIENCES

American magazines often portray older people. In one study, a content analysis was done of *Reader's Digest*, *Ladies Home Journal*, *Time*, and *Sports Illustrated* (Gill, 1998). News feature photographs and advertisements revealed a diverse representation and a surprisingly positive image of older adults. The challenge for mass media is to accurately reflect the rich diversity of circumstances that older people face. Because there is wide variation in terms of income, health, education, and other resources, old age may include any combination of positive or negative experiences. Media often find it easier to settle for stereotypical frames rather than struggle with the complexities of aging. A somewhat more detailed portrayal is offered by specialty publications.

SPECIALTY PUBLICATIONS

As boomers age, there has been a proliferation of national and local publications targeted at this age group. The AARP, a primary lobbying group for older Americans, has a number of publications:

- *AARP: The Magazine.* This is a bimonthly magazine featuring articles and columns on money, health, work, travel, and other issues.
- The *Bulletin.* This is a newspaper published 11 times each year. It provides timely information on issues, such as social security, pensions, tax policy, and current legislation.
- *AARP Segunda Juventud.* This is a quarterly bilingual newspaper targeting Hispanics who are age 50 and older.

In local communities, newspapers and magazines have sprung up that feature content aimed at older readers. For example, Omaha, Nebraska, has a monthly magazine called *Generations*, and it describes itself as "Nebraska's Premier Baby Boomer Magazine." The magazine offers stories on gardening, food, retirement, exercise, and finances. The market also has monthly newspapers called *Senior Living* and *New Horizons*. Readers are offered stories on rides to medical appointments, nursing home outings, golf, quilting, and insurance.

CHAPTER SUMMARY

Older readers are particularly important to American newspapers and magazines. The boomer generation has warmed to the Internet for business and research, but they also remain interested in traditional print media. Print media, like their broadcast cousins, tend to offer negative stereotypical portrayals of older people. At times, such as with the coverage of John Glenn's return to space, print media focus on important issues for older Americans. Media may even celebrate old age. In response to the growth of the older boomer demographic group, many new national and local publications were created that target the interests of older readers.

REVIEW QUESTIONS

1. What difficulties might exist for American newspapers in targeting older readers?
2. What strategies would you suggest to assist newspapers in attracting younger readers?
3. Why or why not will younger readers become more interested in newspaper reading as they age?
4. What advantages do magazines have over newspapers in targeting older readers?
5. Why does stereotyping of older people persist in newspaper and magazine content? What can be done about it?

Chapter 5

Entertainment Media

American network television appears to be at a crossroads. The baby boomer age wave is happening in a time of "unsettled" cultural change (Clydesdale, 1997, p. 608). The audience for television is progressively getting older, even as the industry (including advertisers) continues its focus on 18- to 49-year-old viewers. In the fall 2003 season, older viewers helped CBS have "its biggest opening-week audience since 2000" (De Moraes, 2003, p. C7). The network's median viewer age increased 4 years in just 12 months. "Cold Case" (which followed "60 Minutes"), which drew nearly 16 million viewers, became the new "Murder She Wrote" on Sunday night. The network's median age was nearly 60 years old. In an attempt to bank on the trend, CBS claimed that advertisers undervalued older viewers, a group that tends to prefer their network. NBC's president of the entertainment division claimed that CBS was "in danger of becoming a niche network for the 50-plus crowd" (*Omaha World-Herald*, October 2, 2003, p. 8-E).

The uses and gratifications perspective, outlined in chapter 2, helps explain viewer behavior. The desire to be entertained is a motivation for viewers, including the elderly (Palmgreen, Wenner, & Rayburn, 1980). Entertainment television also may offer older people substitution for a lack of interpersonal and social interaction. Particularly for those who are homebound, the video medium provides viewers with people talking to each other and to the viewer through the screen. So-called parasocial interaction occurs when, in the extreme situation, a person has few or no interpersonal opportunities. In such a case, a person may use television to fill the void. Parasocial interaction, an "illusion of intimacy," may also occur with talk radio (Rubin & Step, 2000, p. 639, quoting Horton & Wohl, 1986). This form of media substitution may be related to the concept of social disengagement. As older people disengage from society's activities, the steady stream of entertainment television may serve as a replacement because it is readily available.

Entertainment has been defined functionally as "diversion and amusement," and related to "relaxation and respite" (Wright, 1986, p. 21). Entertainment also is related to "escapism" and the filling of "leisure time" (Severin & Tankard, 2001, p. 323). Media, such as television "may distract people from important social issues and divert them from useful social participation and action" (p. 21). Postman (1986) identified the central importance of entertainment in the study of television: "Entertainment is the supra-ideology of all discourse on television. No matter what is depicted or from what point of view, the overarching presumption is that it is there for our amusement and pleasure" (p. 87). From a cultural and critical perspective, entertainment has come to be related to "genre, narrative, the pleasure of fantasy, and multiple subjectivity" (Tulloch, 2000, p. 65). Entertainment may be ideological. In this chapter, entertainment is considered as a content form of interest to older people

---

BOX 5.1. A Case for Targeting the Older Market

Given that older people like to watch television, and that this group has become increasingly important to the producers of network entertainment television, it is interesting to note that psychographic lifestyle research suggests that there are subgroups of older people worth targeting:

- **Upscale Seniors**—With assets averaging just over $200,000 and incomes over $35,000, Upscale Seniors are living affluent and exciting retirements. They have high usage and high balances in conservative financial investments.

- **Elite Upscale Seniors**—The nation's Elite Upscale Seniors are an active group, with interests including far-flung travel and sophisticated investments. Their premiums on term, universal, and variable insurance are among the highest in the U.S.

- **Affluent Upscale Seniors**—Affluent Upscale Seniors are moderately affluent and preserve their capital by relying on investments such as municipal bonds and treasury notes. Their insurance needs point to annuities and individual long-term care insurance.

Source: Claritas Research, http://www.claritas.com. Retrieved May 17, 2004, from http://www.cluster1.claritas.com/claritas/Default.jsp?main=3&submenu=seg&subcat=seglifepsycle#group3.

for two reasons: their interest as a group in various forms of entertainment and the portrayal of older people in mass media. Both of these factors should be of increasing interest as baby boomers age.

Entertainment is important to the baby boomer crowd. Boomers are immersed in entertainment, particularly television, music/radio, and the movies. Hagevik (1999) outlined important generational distinctions of baby boomers:

- The 81 million births between 1946 and 1960 represented twice as many as their parents' generation;
- Boomers experienced unprecedented economic prosperity and security;
- Baby boomers experienced the Vietnam War personally or through TV;
- TV families (i.e. Ozzie and Harriet) offered insight into nuclear families; and
- Sex, drugs and rock and roll were cultural beacons. (p. 39)

Thus, aging baby boomers come to their retirement years with massive amounts of media experience, including television watching, and a continued desire to redefine life.

Older people may use television for unique purposes. Perloff and Krevans (2001) suggested that psychosocial factors help explain entertainment program preferences, parasocial preferences, and use of television as a companion. Psychosocial factors are those that involve perception of self and environment: "Elderly individuals will be most likely to turn to television entertainment programs and to watch for companionship or for escape purposes when they are lonely and dissatisfied with themselves or their living environments" (pp. 366–367). Thus, media use by older people may be positively related to their degree of social disengagement, if that translates into a feeling of unhappiness about life. In other words, an elderly person living alone may need television to fill psychological and social voids. For example, in the absence of real interpersonal social relationships, parasocial uses of television are those that may exist when the individual is unhappy: "Yet contrary to popular observation, emotional or social loneliness did not significantly predict parasocial program preferences (i.e., watching soap operas). Instead, life dissatisfaction . . . was the best predictor of parasocial preferences" (p. 370). It appears that loneliness is more important, in fact, than the influences of aging. As Grajczyk and Zollner (1998) explained, "TV can be a 'lifeline' and a 'window to the outside world' for people with little opportunity for direct, unmediated social contact, thus possibly raising their satisfaction of life" (p. 181).

Among television viewers, data from 2004 suggested that slightly older males—a group that included 35- to 49-year-olds—watch more network and cable television than other demographic groups. Whereas networks continued to court the younger crowd favored by advertisers, this trend appeared to create a programming conflict (Dobrow, 2004). No data have been found, however, on how program selection and age interact to influence levels of happiness or unhappiness.

ENTERTAINMENT TELEVISION RESEARCH

There is considerable research suggesting that older people are an important aspect of prime-time entertainment television content. In some cases they are portrayed negatively (Davis & Kubey, 1982), and in other cases they are simply ignored (Signorielli & Gerbner, 1978). In the case of older women, former news executive Marlene Sanders told a United Nations group that media influence the rate of advancement: "Certainly the image driven into the minds of TV viewers is not a wonderful vision of aging. This no doubt contributes to many forms of age discrimination, damaging women's progress in the job market. I have a theory—that old people remind others of their mortality—something that they do not want to see" (Sanders, 2002, p. 2). The cultivation perspective contends that television content may influence viewers. For example, content may influence self-perceptions of happiness on the part of older people. Gerbner (1969) offered the example of elderly people portrayed as incompetent or needing help from younger people (Northcott, 1975). This perception might spillover into how people see older people in real life. However, one more recent study indicated that some positive stereotypes had emerged in prime-time television.

TELEVISION PROGRAMMING

Over the years, prime-time television has sometimes successfully featured older women and men. Some prominent examples included "The Golden Girls," "Maude," and "Matlock." These shows helped viewers identify with the likable side of people as they age. Grey hair became acceptable.

"The Golden Girls" won 10 Emmy awards as a highly rated situation comedy. It also succeeded in syndication and cable television. Beatrice Arthur, Betty White, Rue McClanahan, and Estelle Getty were single

Source: Lifetime Cable Channel. Retrieved from http://www.lifetime.com

women living together in Miami. The show, which first aired in 1985, was consistently among the top-rated programs. It remains popular as a show featured on cable channels, such as Lifetime.

H. L. Cohen (2002) used episodes of "The Golden Girls" to study media literacy. Cohen examined how television both reinforces and resists the prevailing images of older women in Western society. Two episodes of "The Golden Girls" were shown to three focus groups of 19 graduate social work students, including 17 women. Four stereotypes in the programs were identified by participants as reinforcing or challenging conventional beliefs:

1. Older women as old fashioned.
2. Older women as losing sexuality.
3. Older women as taking care of self and others.
4. Invisibility of older women (pp. 608–609).

Three recommendations were made: (a) Viewers need critical thinking media literacy skills to challenge stereotypes; (b) television needs to portray a more diverse older population, which represents the aging in society; and (c) portrayals need to accurately reflect complexities of aging (p. 614).

Before "The Golden Girls," Beatrice Arthur starred as a middle–age woman on the 1970s CBS program "Maude." The Norman Lear show tackled difficult political topics such as abortion when Maude learned she was pregnant.

Source: CBS. Retrieved from http://www.cbs.com/primetime/judging_
amy/bio_tdaly.shtml

Another television program that broke the age barrier was "Matlock."
Andy Griffith starred as an Atlanta lawyer specializing in sensational
cases. The aging grey-haired Ben Matlock won nearly all of his cases by
outwitting younger lawyers. Tyne Daly returned to network television
as the aging mother in the series "Judging Amy." The Emmy Award
winner previously starred in "Cagney & Lacey" on CBS. Daly, an experienced Broadway actress, created a role that broke traditional television
boundaries for aging women. In the show, she is portrayed as active, independent, and important.

American network television faces a dilemma about age: Younger
viewers have been attracted to the new reality genre, whereas older viewers are more interested in drama and comedy shows. The problem is that
networks and advertisers remain interested in the younger demographics, even as the average age of viewers increases: "It's pretty clear that 18-
to 34-year-olds have flocked to unscripted reality shows, (while) 25- to
54-year-olds were the mainstays of the comedies and 40-plus were the
mainstays of the dramas," according to NBC entertainment president Jeff
Zucker. Steve Sternberg, an advertising audience analyst for Magna
Global USA, sees a generation gap between younger and older reality television viewers: "Older viewers are actually more likely to watch many of
these reality shows than young-adult/teen dramas like 'Dawson's
Creek.' But since (reality shows) are more likely to replace news mags

BOX 5.2. Older Men Have Prime-Time Entertainment TV Success

Donald Trump hosted a surprise NBC hit reality show "The Apprentice" in the 2003–2004 season. The show featured the 56-year-old Trump considering the employment of 16 youthful candidates, but closing each show with the signature declaration "You're fired!" Frank Rich commented in *The New York Times* that Trump's show is grounded in 1960s-style activities: "That familiarity is comforting. So is the realization that on 'The Apprentice,' we never see Mr. Trump using a computer or a P.D.A.; even his secretary uses an old-fashioned, card-filled Rolodex. The tasks he sets for the contestants are just as retro" (p. 1). In part, the baby boomer culture exhibited by Trump reflects the tension over 1980s yuppie wealth and consumption and 1990s corporate greed.

ABC television, earlier, had success starring Regis Philbin in "Who Wants to Be a Millionaire?" and later "Super Millionaire." These shows featured Philbin, 73, teasing boomer and younger contestants with the opportunity to win large sums of money. Often questions focused on generational knowledge.

Sources: Rich, F. (2004, March 14). Trump is firing as fast as he can. *The New York Times*, sec. 2, p. 1; NBC.com; ABC.com.

TABLE 5.1
Comparison of Network and Syndicated TV Median Age

Program Type	Four Major Networks	Syndication
News magazines	54.4	47.9
Drama	50.1	40.9
Daytime	48.9	45.7
Feature films	48.0	40.2
Late night	44.0	32.8
Sitcoms	43.1	35.1

Note. Data from Chunovick, L. (2004, March 8). Mitch Burg's youth movement. *Broadcasting & Cable*, *134*(10), 10A; Nielsen Media Research.

and movies on the schedule, it does increase the generation gap" (Collins, 2003, p. 1).

When one considers all age groups of viewers, however, the top three network formats for older viewers are newsmagazines, drama, and daytime programming (Table 5.1).

BOX 5.3. Reality TV Show "Survivor"
Featured Older Contestants

CBS television's hit reality show "Survivor" challenged adult contestants to test their skills and wits. Rudy Boesch, 76, finished in third place on "Survivor: Borneo." He then competed again in "Survivor All-Stars." A one-time Navy SEAL, Rudy won the Bronze Star Medal for heroic action in Vietnam. He broke new ground as an older and athletic TV personality.

A third-place finisher on "Survivor: Marquesas," Kathy Vaverick-O'Brien, 50, was the second oldest contestant on the all-star show. She created a foundation focusing on women's self-confidence through outdoor adventure, challenges, and risk taking: "I blew past every known limit I had. The experience demanded it. It was terrifying, eye-opening, and, ultimately, empowering" (www.therealfoundation.com).

Sources: CBS.com; therealfoundation.com.

Entertainment television content, of course, is scripted. One study from the early 1990s found that women were most likely to be cast in minor roles, and their characters were likely to be single, working, childless, and under age 50 (Elasmar, Hasegawa, & Brain, 1999). The portrayal of older characters partially depends on the role being written into the show. Older TV writers, however, have complained that they are "graylisted" out of work after turning 40 (Girion, 2000). Few Hollywood writers have been willing to publicize allegations of ageism. Aaron Spelling countered that Spelling Television employed six people over 40: "No writer should ever be judged by their age" (p. 1).

BOX 5.4. Television Legend Sued for Age Discrimination

"People our age are considered dinosaurs! The business is being run by 'The Next Generation.' "—letter allegedly written by Clark to Andrews.

A 76-year-old game show producer sued Dick Clark . . . alleging the 74-year-old Clark called him a "dinosaur" and refused to hire him because of his age.

Ralph Andrews, who produced the 1960s and '70s game shows "It Takes Two," "By the Numbers" and "You Don't Say," filed the suit in Superior Court.

Andrews' attorney, Phillip R. Maltin, said Clark's actions violated the Fair Employment and Housing Act, which makes it illegal for an employer "to discriminate against a person who applies for a position based upon that person's age" . . .

. . . In the complaint, Andrews said he spoke off and on for more than a year with Clark and other executives about joining the company and was told he would be considered for any openings.

But when he wrote Clark to say he was interested in available positions, Clark wrote back, allegedly turning Andrews down because of his age.

Source: Associated Press Worldstream; Lexis–Nexis (2004, March 2). Dick Clark named in age bias suit.

CABLE TELEVISION

In the highly competitive cable television market, the average age of audience members has been on the rise over the years, even as advertisers desire to reach younger consumers (Table 5.2). "You can see who is getting older, younger," said one media analyst (Romano, 2003, p. 12). Although some of the cable networks have made radical programming shifts, most seem comfortable with adding shows that appeal to younger

TABLE 5.2
Cable Television Prime Time Median Age of Audience

	Median Age
Channels attracting viewers age 50 and older	
CNN	59.6
A&E	58.6
Fox News	58.3
CNBC	57.7
AMC	53.2
MSNBC	52.4
HGTV	51.1
Weather	50.9
Lifetime	50.3
Channels attracting middle-age viewers	
Food Network	49.2
Travel	48.7
Animal Planet	46.7
ESPN2	45.8
TNT	45.2
USA Network	42.7
ESPN	42.0
TLC	40.6
Channels attracting younger viewers	
TBS	39.6
ABC Family	37.1
Spike TV	37.0
VH1	32.3
Comedy	29.4
BET	26.8
MTV	23.3

Note. Magna Global Research: Nielsen Media Research, 2002-03 broadcast season. In Romano, A. (2003, August 25). "Wish you were younger? So do many cable nets." *Broadcasting & Cable, 133*(34), 12.

audiences. Media executives appear to continue to be in denial about the demographic shifts affecting changes in audience composition.

MOVIES, VIDEO RENTALS, AND ENTERTAINMENT AS BOOMER CULTURE

Baby boomers appear to offer a distinct American culture when it comes to combining "work and fun," as well as "generosity and enjoyment" (Mills, 1987, p. 233). Sociologists see baby boomers as an important group to study from a cultural perspective:

This cohort grew up during a period of unequaled U.S. economic growth. It has challenged and supplanted many of the mores of American culture, has found its interests the focus of thousands of businesses, and has alarmed elected officials who must fund its looming retirement. This generational cohort has witnessed, if not participated in, the transformation of nearly every aspect of American society during the five decades of its existence. (Clydesdale, 1997, p. 605)

Clydesdale (1997) suggested that baby boomers are involved in a contest over ideological change in a time when "old strategies continue to characterize action" (p. 629). Sociologists have suggested that baby boomers emerged in a "pivotal era," as their "adulthood" signaled a "harbinger of things to come" in American culture (Sherkat, 1998, p. 1088). Boomers are aware of their generation and the ongoing advertising and marketing targeted at them. There appears to be a level of resentment of the labels (e.g., hippies, materialist yuppies) attached to boomers by media: "The interplay between the media's portrayals and the generation's reactions to them is both constant and intensely personal" (p. 235). There is said to be a "post-boomer culture" in the aftermath of exploring sex, drugs and rock 'n' roll in the 1960s and 1970s (George, 1997).

Aging baby boomers see entertainment in broad terms. From traditional moviegoing, to video rentals, and increasingly to home theater DVD watching, they are changing definitions of mass media. They actively choose from a wide array of delivery options. In terms of content, they offer a unique generational perspective. For example, the movie *Saving Private Ryan* resonated with the boomer who did not serve in World War II but experienced the national trauma of Vietnam: "In post-Vietnam American culture, rhetorical appeals to a mythic American past are constrained by and through traumatic national memory of the war. . . . Significantly, this traumatic memory was constructed, in part, through the visual and discursive practices of popular cinema" (Owen, 2002, p. 251).

There may be an audience among baby boomers for movies featuring older actors and actresses. In the 2004 Golden Globe awards, four of five actresses nominated for Best Actress in a Comedy were near age 40 or older (Holson, 2004): "It is older female moviegoers, a group largely ignored in the late 1990's, who are driving the popularity of these movies" (p. 12). One explanation is that baby boomers enjoy watching stars they have known for years. Older actresses, from Meg Ryan to Diane Keaton, have played roles with sexual scenes. Susan Sarandon has been identified as one of the first actresses in modern moviemaking to play sexual roles into her 50s (Smith, 2003). Movies are a part of a larger American culture, which has been driven by a demanding baby boomer generation for more than a quarter century. This is perhaps seen no more clearly than in the music and radio industries.

MUSIC AND RADIO ENTERTAINMENT

The radio industry has been challenged by aging rock and rollers (Sutel, 2003). It has been argued that baby boomers have remained consumers into their 50s and beyond, and this is unlike previous generations. Likewise, their preferences for music may be grounded in a generational identity. G. Burns (1996) identified three reasons for the baby boomers' attachment to the music from their youth: the clear identification as members of the boomer generation, their refusal to part with childhood, and mass media reinforcement through marketing and advertising (pp. 129–130). With this in mind, advertisers may be willing to support programming targeted at the boomer age group. Initially, radio formats such as Top 40, adult contemporary, and classic rock catered to boomers as they moved through their 20s and 30s (George, 1997). Later, as boomers aged, talk formats proliferated:

> Members of the generation of 1946 to 1964 were bound by the strands of the culture they created—everything from communes to a common language inaccessible to adults—and their elderculture is likely to reflect that same innovative spirit, if not an actual restoration of some old familiar practices. . . . The widespread popularity of radio talk shows among our current older population provides a hint of what is to come. Only a minority of people actually call in, but even those who just listen seem to get a sense of participation and, at the very least, a feeling that they've got company in the house. (Gerber et al., 1989, p. 240)

Industry researchers describe the challenge for radio stations as keeping the boomers while also attracting younger audiences. *Inside Radio* newsletter editor Tom Taylor said the industry would adapt: "Boomers are still rewriting the rules. . . . They're still trading up houses, still working, and they're not ready to ship off to Florida and play shuffleboard. It's at the crux of a major advertising issue" (Sutel, 2003, p. 1). Reilly (1999) suggested that boomers strongly influenced the rock concert entertainment industry by demanding better food, bathrooms, and amenities at concert venues. Rock music itself exploits generational identity by its focus on time: "Time has served as a *sensitizing concept*" (Kotarba, 2002, p. 398). For example, the Top 40 music format provided emphasis on the week's top songs and established "the 'week' as a crucial time frame" for baby boomers as they grew into adulthood (p. 403).

The change also is affecting the music industry. The Recording Industry Association of America (RIAA) has found that more than one third of all purchases are made by buyers over age 40. RIAA's 2002 consumer report found "a larger increase in the share purchased by buyers over age 45 in the past year compared with purchasing patterns of other age groups" (RIAA, 2003, p. 1).

As baby boomers age, radio may become increasing important as a parasocial substitute for interpersonal interaction. Music formats may become less important to the generation, and radio talk could well emerge as a dominant format. Rubin and Step (2000) concluded that radio talk show listeners find rewards in their relationships with talk show hosts. Host credibility relates to motivation to be a regular listener.

GAMES AND TRENDS

Media usage by aging baby boomers involves substantial amounts of time, which may keep the generation from a level of physical fitness suggested by health experts (Hansen, Stevens, & Coast, 2001; The Robert Wood Johnson Foundation, 2001). Whether older people use free time reading entertainment-oriented publications or playing games, the time commitment is in direct competition with other activities. Older people increasingly use computer and video games. For example, 13% of people age 50 or older were found to regularly play such games: "Overall, 60% of all Americans, or about 145,000,000 people, say they play interactive games, exploding the myth that most gamers are teenage boys alone in their rooms" (USA Today Magazine, 2001, p. 6). In fact, one commentator noted that older men can be found using realistic video games located in shopping mall arcades. Freedman (1995) explained, "What struck me most about this impressively realistic driving game was that the people lined up to play it were all men in their thirties and forties—men who presumably had real cars parked nearby on real roads" (p. 136). Freedman believed that male baby boomers enjoy virtual reality games that simulate what they do in real life. It is projected that as baby boomers age, they will show "a renewed interest in leisure and entertainment" (Schonfeld & Furth, 1995, p. 78). With more freedom on their hands, media technology, entertainment activities, and a variety of ways to spend their time will become increasingly important.

CHAPTER SUMMARY

Entertainment is important to most baby boomers. Other media have challenged American network television's role as the principle provider of entertainment. Nevertheless, television remains the dominant entertainment medium—one that "must suppress the content of ideas in order to accommodate the requirements of visual interests; that is to say, to accommodate the values of show business" (Postman, 1986, p. 92).

The boomer age wave is happening in a time of "unsettled" cultural change. Entertainment may offer older people substitution for a lack of interpersonal and social interaction. Parasocial interaction occurs when in the extreme situation a person has few or no interpersonal opportunities. Elderly people, as well as soon-to-be boomers, may use entertainment for companionship or for escape purposes when they are lonely and dissatisfied with themselves or their living environments. However, some upscale seniors, rather than facing social disengagement, live affluent and exciting retirements. Baby boomers appear to offer a distinct American culture when it comes to combining "work and fun," as well as "generosity and enjoyment." Baby boomers may favor active use of free time in their later years, and media may be especially important to them.

REVIEW QUESTIONS

1. Why is entertainment important to consider when studying aging baby boomers?
2. What is parasocial interaction? Why is it important?
3. What difference might it make if more baby boomers come to their retirement years with wealth and an interest in remaining active?
4. What are the recent trends in the baby boomers' pursuit of entertainment?
5. How does the current baby boomer culture compare to earlier generations and their expectations of entertainment?

Chapter 6

Advertising, Public Relations, and Advocacy

Hugh J. Reilly
University of Nebraska at Omaha

Marketers, advertisers, and public relations professionals are accustomed to separating their target audiences into neat little segments. Whereas every target audience has diversity, perhaps none is as diverse as older consumers. If we are to believe the AARP, then the older consumer segment begins at age 50 and stretches all the way to centenarians.

Thompson (1990) grouped seniors into three broad categories: "active seniors" (ages 50–64), "less active seniors" (ages 65–74), and "seniors" (age 75 and older) (pp. 28–30). Herzbrun (1991) also split seniors into three segments: preretirement years, where people are still working but planning for their retirement; active retirement years, when grandchildren's needs and concerns about health become more important; and the "elderly" years, when seniors become more sedentary (pp. 15–16). What is important is not how older consumers are labeled, but that the marketer or communicator recognizes there are distinct differences in this target audience. These differences help to determine the methods, media, and mind-set used to effectively reach these disparate groups of seniors.

DEMOGRAPHICS AND PSYCHOGRAPHICS

The 2000 U.S. Census reported that approximately 12.3% of American males and 15.2% of American females were age 50 or older. The Census Bureau projected that those figures would rise to 16.6% of all American males and 19.5% of all American females by 2025. By 1998, someone age 55 or older headed 35% of all American households, and another 22%

were headed by someone age 65 or older. Older Americans remain a unique group from a marketing perspective.

Experiencing the Great Depression and World War II shaped the attitudes of people born in the 1920s and 1930s. This generation generally believed in working, saving money, and planning ahead. The sedentary lifestyle of older consumers traditionally made them good prospects for books, hobby supplies, movies, and health aids (Herzbrun, 1991). However, Underwood (1990) found that "older consumers" had only marginally more brand loyalty than other segments of the population (p. 30).

There are many other factors influencing the buying behaviors of older Americans. Bone (1991) narrowed it to five major characteristics:

1. Disposable income—approximately 33% of older Americans had a significantly higher level of disposable income than the average American.
2. Health—nearly 40% were in poor health.
3. Activity level—approximately 60% still considered themselves "active."
4. Free time—80% had heavily scheduled days leaving little free time.
5. Social time—most older consumers, 60%, were "Sociables," choosing to spend the bulk of their time in groups. (pp. 47–49)

Other researchers have found that older Americans are more passive than active. Dychtwald (2003b), for example, estimated that 40 million retirees spend an average of 43 hours a week watching television and that, as a group, they have the lowest rate of volunteerism of any age group (pp. 6–12).

Thomas and Sullivan (1989) found that "the mature customer is healthier, wealthier and wiser, especially about money matters, than any other group of this age in our history" (pp. 32–34). Older customers fit one of two groups: pre- and postretirees. Two basic fears for retirees may be that they would outlive their savings and that they would become sick and have to be cared for by family or health care professionals. These twin fears may tend to influence many of their buying decisions (Thomas & Sullivan, 1989, pp. 32–34). Older consumers may be cautious spenders, in part, because of the dramatic effect of declining available income in retirement. Alan (2003) found that the homogenous view of older consumers should be revised:

> Marketing, advertising and, yes, my field, public opinion research, all use age as the principal basis to anticipate everything from who will watch which television program to who is the target market for various products.

But we're all finding that the predictive power of age is diminishing because North Americans aren't behaving as past generations did at the same stages of life. (p. 45)

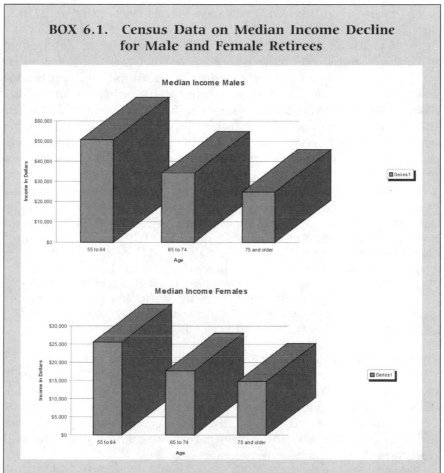

BOX 6.1. **Census Data on Median Income Decline for Male and Female Retirees**

The median income for both males and females from age 55 to 64 compared favorably to the average per capita income. However, at age 65, median income dropped below the national average. The census listed the median income for those from age 55 to 64 as $44,776, which was 6% higher than the median income for all Americans. However, for households age 65 and older, median income dropped to an average of $23,118, which was 46% lower than the national average. The median household income for all Americans was $42,228.

Source: U.S. Census Bureau (2000–2002). The data depict the decline in median income as men and women age and retire.

Income, however, does not tell the entire story. In many cases, mortgages have been paid off, and large items may be paid for with cash. Living expenses, with the notable exception of medical expenses, are often lower.

Older consumers between age 50 and 64 tend to be healthy and in their peak earning years (Waldrop, 1992). Men at age 55 can expect to live another 22 years, and women can expect to live for another 27 years. Some members of this group retire before age 65, but even those few often work part-time somewhere else once they retire. Among "mature householders" over age 65, Social Security becomes the primary source of income (p. 24). Unfortunately, workers whose incomes were modest when they were employed paid less into the system and will have lower incomes. The median incomes for "mature householders" are lowest among older women who had little or no employment experience. These women make up 65% of householders over age 85 (p. 28).

The group that is likely to have the single biggest impact on joining the older consumers is the baby boomers, born between 1946 and 1964. The vanguard of this group, those born between 1946 and 1954, has already become part of AARP's target market. According to Dychtwald (2003b):

> The assumption that boomers would migrate through life's stages in exactly the same way as the smaller and more traditional generations before them proved to be way off-base. More indulged as children, boomers were also more inclined to question the status quo and more willing to speak out and challenge authority than members of any previous generation. (p. 7)

Dychtwald added that at every stage of their lives, boomers have had to "fight through the bottleneck that their own numbers have caused" (p. 8). They have received more attention than any other group, but the odds against receiving the services and benefits they want has always been an uphill challenge: "As boomers migrate into maturity, their vast influence over the economy, social policy and culture in general will transform America into a gerontocracy" (p. 8).

Boomers are predicted to try to postpone old age, and their desire for personal growth and new lifestyle challenges will "render obsolete the traditional 'linear life' paradigm" (p. 9). Boomers may not follow the traditional pattern of education, career, retirement, and leisure: "It will become normal for 50-year-olds to go back to school and for 70-year-olds to reinvent themselves through new careers. Phased retirements, part-time and flex-time work, and 'rehirements' will become common options for elder boomers who either need or want to continue working" (p. 9).

In the end, the "50 plus" crowd is difficult to categorize either demographically or psychographically. According to the AARP, the group spent more than $400 billion on apparel and entertainment in 2003, making them a true economic force. However, although those between age 50 and 65 have much higher average incomes than the national average, average incomes drop rapidly after age 65, which is the traditional retirement age.

There is also a great disparity between the psychographics of seniors from the World War II generation and the vanguard of baby boomers who are just reaching their 50s. Those that are older than 75 had their values shaped by the twin forges of the Great Depression and World War II. In contrast, baby boomers had their values shaped by the rapidly changing society of the 1950s and 1960s. It seems that it may be more helpful to use the demographics and psychographics of this age group to determine what marketing tactics to avoid rather than what marketing tactics to adopt. The diversity of baby boomers may be their most distinctive quality (Smart & Pethokoukis, 2001): "Despite attempts by marketers and the media to brand them as one, perhaps the most common trait of the generation born between 1946 and 1964 is its individuality" (p. 54). Smart and Pethokoukis quoted Milken Institute demographer William Frey: "The boomers have been a very distinct generation all the way. They have broken the mold in every conceivable way. I can't imagine them really changing as they age" (p. 54).

MARKETING AND AGING

Older consumers are the fastest growing segment of our overall population. They account for more than 40% of total demand (Lewis, 1996). The 50-plus age group accounts for more than 50% of discretionary income, the majority of the personal assets in the United States, and 70% of the net worth of U.S. households (Thompson, 1990).

The biggest mistake made by most marketers is to lump all those over age 50 into one homogenous group. However, despite attempts by greeting card manufacturers and the AARP, there is nothing magical about age 50. Most workers still have many productive years left in their career. What is significant is whether a person is retired or still working. Lifestyle is more important than actual age. Szmigin and Carrigan (2001) argued that the lives of people over age 50 today are significantly different than the lives of their parents and grandparents: "Most importantly for marketing, they all belong to generations which are adept consumers, brought up on television, changing brands and continued product innovation and development. . . . They are a wide and varied group with a huge range of differences, both in terms of their spending power and circumstances and also in the way they are using their time" (p. 31).

Stephens (1991) wrote extensively on the concept of "cognitive age"—the idea that older people may have a cognitive age that is 10 to 15 years younger than their actual age (p. 37). That is, their values more closely match the interests of younger people and may have great impact on planning for marketers and advertisers trying to reach this age group. Older consumers, who are cognitively young, can be reached by many of the same methods employed to reach younger audiences. They are active. They need many of the same goods and services. They may be good prospects for travel services, cars, and other leisure activities.

In contrast, consumers who are cognitively old may be more interested in products and services that are a better fit to more sedentary lives (Stephens, 1991). They may be more interested in products and services "which help them to cope with a future that is likely to be seen by them as negative" (p. 45). Cognitive age can also have an effect on how marketers reach older consumers. Stephens (1991) suggested that those who are cognitively young are easier to reach because they are more likely to be seeking new information. By targeting younger markets, media may also be effectively used to reach those that are cognitively young: "On the other hand, those that are cognitively old appear to be harder to reach. They apparently do not seek information for its own sake and probably stick to media vehicles that are known and familiar to them" (Stephens, 1991, p. 46). Thompson (1990) supported Stephens' idea of cognitive age:

> The comparative vitality of today's 50-plus consumers creates younger, healthier self-perceptions. Some experts contend that today's older Americans generally feel as much as 15 years younger than people did at the same age a generation ago. Communicators should always address this segment in a tone consistent with this positive, upbeat, younger self-image. Emphasizing the negative aspects of aging will only reflect negatively on the message. (p. 29)

Thompson (1990, p. 29) suggested a 5-point strategy to effectively reach older consumers:

1. Segment the message. Realize that baby boomers just reaching the 50-plus age group have a much different outlook than do those consumers already past age 75.

2. Use the Time Factor. Seniors have more time or perhaps just know how to use it more efficiently. Many marketers use this fact to create exhibits or build interactive relationships with seniors. Many older consumers also have more flexibility than their younger counterparts. This can also work to the advantage of marketers. Thompson listed fast food

restaurants and movie theaters as two kinds of businesses that have been successful in attracting older consumers during traditional down times.

3. Provide detailed information because older consumers are more willing to read labels, do comparative shopping, and carefully evaluate a product or service.

4. Take advantage of seniors' inclination to join groups. Marketers should network with these organizations. Marketers whose products or services benefit these organization's members might find these organizations willing to endorse their products. In addition, many marketers, notably financial institutions, have created their own clubs or membership organizations specifically designed to offer discounts and other product benefits to their members.

5. Use the concept of "added value" to attract older consumers. This is often done through providing better service. It might be something as simple as printing brochures in larger typefaces or adding phone lines to answer customer's questions. Added value can also be reinforced by marketers adding benefits to club memberships. An example would be banks that offer discounts on trips to local sites and special events for their members.

Many conventional marketers take their cue from advertisers when devising a marketing plan. Advertisers have long been in love with the 25- to 49-year-old target market. That group is their priority, and every other group is secondary. This made perfect sense when the baby boom generation fell into the younger age group. However, now that the baby boomers have begun to move past age 50, it is not so clear-cut. Despite the growth in the numbers of older consumers, traditional prejudices against age still flourish. Carrigan and Szmigin (2000) contended that when marketers feature older people in their mainstream media ads, they usually feature them as caricatures. The only ads that commonly feature older consumers are for products that have traditionally been used exclusively by those over age 50.

For years, marketers ignored the older consumer unless they were selling a product or service specifically targeted at seniors, such as dentures or nursing homes. Now it has become one of the hottest of all target markets. According to the 2000 Census figures, although they make up just 30% of the population, they control 75% of the nation's financial assets and more than one half of the discretionary income. However, this does not mean that everyone should make older consumers the top priority. There is a "great deal of variance of wealth" among members of the mature market (Miller, 1991, p. 11). Although some may have high levels of discretionary income, as well as home equity, many would still fall below the poverty line without their Social Security checks. People age 50 and older represent 37% of the adult U.S. population, and they control most of the money in the country—accounting for $2 trillion in income and 50% of all discretionary income. Unlike their parents, Kelly (2000) pointed out that these folks are spending instead of saving: "They're out there spending and enjoying themselves. They travel several times a year. They spend more on entertainment than any other age group" (p. 8).

Businesses may see opportunities in the 50-plus market, but they are not always sure how to approach it. Products (e.g., cars, health and beauty aids, and airlines) may have a lot of appeal to older consumers, but they are rarely featured in ads for these products. As an example, a content analysis of newspaper advertisements for banks looked at the way senior citizens were used as models in those ads. Peterson (1995) found that older consumers were not shown as often as their younger counterparts, especially when taking into account the percentage of older consumers that use bank services. In addition, seniors tended to be shown in a less favorable light than their younger counterparts. Not surprisingly, this phenomenon is not as pronounced in the ads of banks focusing specifically on older consumers (Peterson, 1995).

There are many advertisers not looking beyond basic demographic data when examining older consumers. Adler (1996) suggested that there are a few simple rules to follow in developing an effective marketing campaign for seniors: avoid stereotypes, accentuate the positive, empower the consumer, divide and conquer, and draw on life-stage events and issues (p. 32). *The Economist* (2002) suggested that "the most successful advertising campaigns targeted at mature consumers focus instead on active and healthy lifestyles and introduce positive role models. Rejuvenated patients cycling with their grandchildren or practicing tai chi are far more effective that the stereotype of a frail arthritis sufferer" (p. 51). There are some industries and companies that, by the 1980s and 1990s, were the first to focus on older consumers. United Airlines was one example. In 1985, they launched "Silver Wings Plus," which, for a membership fee, allowed people age 55 and older to receive discounts on hotels, car rentals, and United fares. The average Silver Wings Plus member was 72 years old and had an annual income of around $70,000 (Miller, 1991, p. 13). SunAmerica, a mutual funds company, targets baby boomers with a TV ad campaign that asks, "Where do you want to be?" It features shots of leisure activities like skiing and surfing and lets consumers know that SunAmerica mutual funds can "help get you there" (Cardona, 2000, p. 69).

Boomtown Casino Westbank in New Orleans targeted their ads at women age 25 to 54 with household incomes below $50,000, as well as people over age 65. Their ads ran on daytime soaps, "Wheel of Fortune," and "Entertainment Tonight" (Weissman, 1999). Simmons Market Research found that people age 55 to 64 were 19% more likely to say they had been to a casino some time in the past year than the average population. A 1998–1999 analysis of television programs on which the top 10 casinos advertised revealed that men and the over-65 crowd were the primary targets (Weissman, 1999).

The alcohol industry also focused some of its attention on seniors. E. & J. Gallo Winery advertised a wine called Livingston Cellars in *Modern Maturity*. Gordon's Dry Gin used a picture of an unshaven Humphrey Bogart from "The African Queen" on its label. A collector's edition showed Bogart cracking open a crate of Gordon's (O'Connell, 1998, p. B1). Chura (2002), in an article on baby boomers and beer consumption, quoted a beer distributor on baby boomer buying habits: "Baby boomers as they age up are going to be an even better consumer demographic than their parents were for us. They already have been used to a really fun lifestyle their whole lives. They've never sacrificed anything the way their parents have. . . . They're indulgent and they're impetuous in their spending habits" (p. 4).

Some other examples included Buick, which gave its older customers special service. Hyatt opened a chain called Classic Residence. The travel inn, geared toward the retired, offered group activities aimed at the 50-plus market (Underwood, 1990). Other marketers focus on older women. Diesel Marketing created a billboard ad showing an older woman sitting on the hood of an MG with a tagline that read, "The road ahead's all mine." A Shoppers Drug Mart TV spot, created by TBWA/Chiat/Day, featured a 40-something woman warning her peers to take care of their health, stating, "I want my hair to turn grey; I want to be a grandmother." A Lubriderm moisturizing lotion campaign, aimed at women from age 35 to 50, showed images of women in their 70s talking about how they lived and are living their lives—the importance of taking some time for themselves. The tag line is, "Feel good from the outside in" (Gardiner, 2001, p. 2).

Perhaps the most common campaigns aimed at those over age 50 are pharmaceutical ads for products, such as Viagra and Cialis (Fig. 6.1). The industry has used a variety of approaches. They have used famous older men (i.e., former senator Bob Dole and former football coach Mike Ditka) to tout their products on television, and ad campaigns have been reinforced on the Web. Pfizer has developed an ad campaign aimed at baby boomers (Langreth, 2000). One of the ads begins with a handsome man in his early 40s preparing for a date, while a voice-over begins with, "I'm ready. Ready as anyone can be." He then runs down the steps and drives to his doctor for a free sample of Viagra.

Source: www.viagra.com

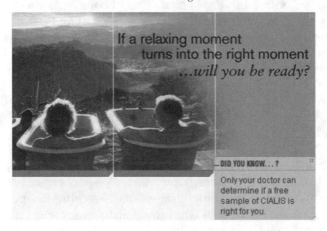

Source: www.cialis.com

Source: www.levitra.com

FIG. 6.1.   Images of male enhancement drug Internet advertisements.

Advertisers and marketers are beginning to focus more on older consumers, but the overuse of stereotypes and reliance on myths about aging continues to hamper the effectiveness of marketing campaigns aimed at older Americans.

CORPORATE COMMUNICATION

Seniors are inundated by hundreds of messages at home and at work. It is their task to decide what is important and what can be ignored. As the number of messages increase, that job becomes increasingly difficult. Technological advances have had a great impact on corporate communication. Video teleconferences, desktop publishing, vast phone systems, and intranets all have had an impact on corporate communication.

Many larger organizations have developed a company intranet to help them communicate with their employees. Debra Miller, former national president of the Public Relations Society of America (PRSA) believed that some organizations created an intranet because they felt the need to stay competitive: "Some companies do not have a strategy for using electronic communications. They simply put everything they've done on paper into a computer" (Miller, 2001, p. 36).

For seniors, this flood of new technology can be intimidating and frustrating. In contrast to younger employees who may be unable to recall a time without e-mail, older workers might miss the bygone days where they gathered around the water cooler to hear the latest news. They may miss the face-to-face interaction they had earlier in their careers. Sanchez (1999) suggested that "advances in technology have fundamentally altered both the nature of production, causing a shift in focus from products to services, and the very nature of communication. It cannot be assumed that messages and methods, no matter how well-crafted will convey the sender's message and meaning to diverse audiences" (p. 9).

Dychtwald addressed the issue of the baby boomer generation's desire to stay young, even as they grow older in the workplace. He suggested that the graying of traditional male and female roles in the workplace will lead to workers taking time off for midlife and midcareer sabbaticals and returning to school (Schlossberg, 1992). Of course, all of this complicates corporate communication at a time when communication technology impacts all aspects of life.

Kelly (2000) found that older people are becoming more comfortable with the use of technologies:

Half of those 50-plus have PC's at home and 70% of those have Internet access. Our research shows that people 50 and older are comfortable with technology (57%) and 60% say, "technology makes my life easier." The ma–

ture market is one of the fastest growing segments on the Internet, and the biggest spending demographic. In 1998, they spent three times the average. (p. 8)

Perhaps no form of internal communication has had more of an impact than the advent of e-mail. It has become a ubiquitous form of communication. Ninety percent of the respondents from one study cited e-mail as the most frequently used medium of employee communication. However, despite e-mail's popularity, it was not considered the most effective medium for communication:

> Employees are bombarded with e-mail all day and they do not take the time to process and understand much of e-mail messages that aim to communicate valuable information. Study results show that, in fact, ongoing publications for all employees are the most effective medium for in-depth and complex communication (70 percent), followed by group meetings (60 percent) and only then by electronic mail (55 percent). . . . The lure of e-mail can be deceiving. Organizations should evaluate what communication methods, or combination of methods, are the most effective in reaching their employee populations. (Sanchez, 1999, p. 12)

The study concluded that the most effective means of communication are traditional forms, those which senior workers are already most comfortable. Corporate communication methods will continue to evolve and be affected by technology. However, to effectively reach all age groups, employers will need to use a variety of methods to be successful.

NONPROFIT AGENCY COMMUNICATION

Charities large and small have traditionally depended on older consumers for the bulk of their gifts. Although these donors may not always give large gifts, they are consistent and loyal in their giving. The world famous Father Flanagan's Boys' Home, better known as Boys Town, described their typical donor as a woman, 60 years old or older, who gave two to three gifts a year of $10 or more.

Most nonprofits communicate with older consumers via direct mail. For several reasons, this is a proven method to communicate to this group. First, generally they are a more stable group. They are less likely to move or change their address. Second, they are comfortable with receiving offers through the mail and trust it far more than they trust telemarketing, e-mail, or traditional mass media advertising. Third, they enjoy the personal nature of a letter, often developing strong relationships with the charities they support.

Boys Town crafted their appeal letters to appeal to older consumers, especially women. As a charity that helps children, they appealed to maternal feelings and offered them an opportunity to help in a personal way. Many animal protection charities appeal to the same target group using the same techniques. A small gift, called a "premium" (e.g., a prayer card, stickers, mailing labels etc.), is often included in the mailing to entice the donor to open the letter.

Boys Town's formula is to focus on one or two individuals in each letter and tell their story, relating how their experience at Boys Town has improved their lives. The letters often start with a powerful quote and then briefly tell the child's story of abuse and neglect. Somewhere in the first quarter of the letter, a specific "ask" is made of the donor. This "ask" is repeated toward the end of the letter and always in the postscript. Direct mail studies have shown that the first sentence and the postscript are more likely to be read than any other parts of the letter.

These nonprofit direct mail techniques can also be successfully used by for-profits. *Bank Marketing* editors suggested a number of tactics (Price, 1989). When targeting senior citizens, banks should begin with their existing database, and understand how that list was compiled. They should provide a high quality readable package, offer a premium, emphasize product benefits and not features, allow responses to come in a variety of ways, give readers a specific name of someone to talk to, and focus on retaining customers with high quality service. Petrecca (2002) suggested that baby boomers are very health conscious. They seek health information for themselves and are a prime market for the role they play as caregivers to aging parents. The specific nature of most health information makes them a good target market for direct marketing.

It is ironic that the factors that make direct mail so effective in reaching seniors also make them susceptible to con artists. It is that sense of intimacy and trust for direct mail that enables con artists to successfully scam seniors into believing deceptive claims or phony notifications that they are grand-prize winners. Fortunately, a coalition of federal, state, and local law enforcement officials as well as the AARP, the Federal Trade Commission (FTC), and the U.S. Postal Service have banded together to combat the targeting of seniors by direct mail scammers.

OPINION FORMATION

Opinion formation is driven by many factors, but is heavily influenced by experience and environment. Lunsford and Burnett (1992) found that seniors may resist new products for a variety of reasons. There may be physical limitations, such as packages that are difficult for arthritic hands to open or products that are difficult to use. Their resistance may also be because they see no clear benefit in the product, because they do not identify with the product's brand image, or because use of the product seems risky (Lunsford & Burnett, 1992). Lunsford and Burnett (1992) indicated that marketers might overcome this resistance by making their products "intergenerational" (p. 53). They suggested using adult children of older consumers as opinion leaders in a word-of-mouth campaign and segmenting seniors into discernable age groups. They also suggested using elderly models to advertise the product, make information on the products easy to obtain, offer product trials and samples, and focus on new uses for the products rather than simply replacing older products (Lunsford & Burnett, 1992).

Wolfe (1992) echoed the claim that older consumers have a more complex cognitive structure and are more introspective than younger consumers due to the maturing process. Older people have been found to respond better to ads that suggest a product's value, than to ads with unambiguous claims. In fact, Wolfe foresaw a time when American advertising will begin to resemble Japanese advertising, which focuses more on subjective values and moods than on hard sell techniques.

Schewe (1991) recommended a 7-point approach to communicating with older consumers:

1. Keep the message simple. Aging may lead people to react more slowly and less accurately, so message information should not be overloaded.
2. Make the message familiar. The more complex a message is, the more important it is to keep it in familiar territory.
3. Make the message concrete. Emotional appeals tend to be vague. Make the message hard-hitting and precise.
4. Take it point-by-point. Let the reader concentrate on each section before moving on.
5. Give preference to the print media. Older consumers need more time to process the information.
6. Supply memory aids. Use visual cues. Help older people remember what the earlier product looked like before introducing the new product.
7. Make good use of context. Attach the message to pleasant memories. Involve the audience in a personal way, and invoke images of family and friends. (p. 53)

A Yankelovich, Clancy, and Schulman survey found that consumers over age 50 make more trips to the supermarket, purchase convenience foods in bulk quantities, and favor quality over price more than younger consumers (Kornreich, 1991). Some of the conventional wisdom about how older consumers form opinions about products (i.e., that they are very price conscious) may not be true.

Older consumers' body image also figures into opinion formation. Greco (1988) suggested that older people are used most effectively in ads when they promote a product or service consumed primarily by the elderly (especially travel, health care, financial services, and insurance). However, if it is a product that appeals to both younger and older people, it is often best to use a younger person in the ad.

Although older consumers use many of the same opinion formation techniques as their younger counterparts, there are some key differences. Lumpkin and Festervand (1988) believed that older consumers would rely more heavily on advertiser-supplied information than other groups. They theorized that, due to a lack of mobility or because of reduced income, older consumers take time to be better informed before making a purchase. Older consumers are also more likely to be persuaded by guarantees or the positive reputation of a product or a store. The researchers also found they rely more heavily on salespeople than younger people and will pay a little more to shop in a store that caters to their age group (Lumpkin & Festervand, 1988).

Ebenkamp (2002) described baby boomers as "indulgent" (p. 23). Analysts do not believe the "gimme-gimme generation" will limit spending in old age, so they may continue to "spend on small luxuries" (p. 23). Ebenkamp (2002) suggested that although boomers' bodies are winding down, they will shun marketing that implies they are ready for the rocking chair. They recognize that there are changes in their bodies, but they are not going to be that stereotypical "old person" (p. 23).

Lewis (1996) claimed that as people age, they become more subjective—often viewing information through the prism of "What does this mean to me?" In order to effectively communicate with older consumers, Lewis recommended using "touchstones," tying what is being sold to a known and accepted base (pp. 20-25). For seniors, one of the best ways to do this is to use testimonials. Peer testimonials are often used by mature resorts and assisted living communities. Group testimonials, complete with names, city, and state, are used to help shape opinions about a variety of products and services. Celebrity testimonials have been used to sell products ranging from denture cream to Viagra. The use of celebrities is controversial, because it is so subjective. For example, a celebrity that appeals to one person may offend others.

CHAPTER SUMMARY

Perhaps the cardinal error made in communicating with seniors is to assume that once people reach age 50 they all can be classified in a category that extends to centenarians. Thompson (1990) separated seniors into three broad categories: "active seniors" (age 50–64), "less active seniors" (age 65–74), and "elderly" (age 75+). Despite the efforts of Hallmark and American Association of Retired People (AARP), there is nothing magical about age 50 or 65. It is significant if individuals are still working. Lifestyle is far more important than actual age.

When the baby boomers (born between 1946 and 1964) join the older consumers group en masse, they are expected to have a powerful impact on the behaviors and lifestyle choices of seniors. Dychtwald (2003b) believed that boomers will try to postpone their old age and their desire for personal growth, and new lifestyle changes will disrupt the traditional patterns of education, career, retirement, and then leisure. These new seniors may be making many nontraditional choices, such as going back to school and starting new businesses after they retire.

Another variable is the influence of new technologies. These can be intimidating to older consumers. They have been much more comfortable with direct mail than with e-mail. Previous studies showed that regular newsletters were the most effective way to transmit in-depth and complex information, group meetings were second, and e-mail was third (Sanchez, 1999). However, this appears to be changing as baby boomers enter the senior population. The next chapter examines how boomers are more likely to be comfortable with the online world.

REVIEW QUESTIONS

1. Given that marketers should segment the older consumer target audience, how should this be done?
2. What are some of the challenges that marketers face when trying to communicate with older consumers?
3. What are some of the techniques that can be used to effectively reach older consumers?
4. What should be kept in mind if a company wanted to advertise the following products to older consumers?
   a. Retirement Resort Village
   b. Automobiles
   c. Alcohol
   d. Travel
5. Considering that older people tend to rely on their years of experience, why might baby boomers be a challenging target market as they age?

Chapter 7

Internet and New Media

Aging baby boomers have been enthusiastic about use of the Internet and other new media. Unlike some of their parents' generation, boomers learned to use computers and the World Wide Web in the workplace. Browne (2000) concluded that older people, including aging baby boomers, are quickly accepting new technologies:

> Thus, the idea that age-related "technophobia" or lack of interest are the main obstacles to elderly computer and Internet usage seem to be disappearing. In fact, many argue that one of the main reasons that elderly users have been underrepresented in computing is that until recently, hardware and software design, particularly interfaces, have simply not been designed to accommodate them. (p. 1)

At the same time, researchers have had a general interest in how older people adopt and use new technologies.

Kubeck, Miller-Albrecht, and Murphy (1999) compared 29 older adults (mean age 70.6) recruited from senior centers without computers with 30 younger adult college students (mean age 21.8). Participants were required to be Web users. Older adults were less efficient and less accurate in searching for information: "With brief but well-designed training, novice older adults were successful in their Web searches and they had very positive reactions to the Web experience" (p. 167). Kubeck et al. "had expected older adults to be more negative before and after the Web search, but the stereotype of computer-phobic, disinterested older adults was not supported in this study" (p. 181). Among aging baby boomers, 74.3%

TABLE 7.1
NORC GSS (2002) Computer Use by Age Category

AGECAT * R USE COMPUTER Crosstabulation

			R USE COMPUTER		
			Yes	No	Total
AGECAT	18–36	Count	785	227	1012
	Young	Expected Count	675.5	336.5	1012.0
		% within AGECAT	77.6%	22.4%	100.0%
		% within R USE COMPUTER	43.0%	24.9%	37.0%
		% of Total	28.7%	8.3%	37.0%
	37–57	Count	751	260	1011
	Boomers	Expected Count	674.9	336.1	1011.0
		% within AGECAT	74.3%	25.7%	100.0%
		% within R USE COMPUTER	41.1%	28.6%	36.9%
		% of Total	27.4%	9.5%	36.9%
	58–95	Count	291	423	714
	Elderly	Expected Count	476.6	237.4	714.0
		% within AGECAT	40.8%	59.2%	100.0%
		% within R USE COMPUTER	15.9%	46.5%	26.1%
		% of Total	10.6%	15.5%	26.1%
Total		Count	1827	910	2737
		Expected Count	1827.0	910.0	2737.0
		% within AGECAT	66.8%	33.2%	100.0%
		% within R USE COMPUTER	100.0%	100.0%	100.0%
		% of Total	66.8%	33.2%	100.0%

$\chi^2 = 296.59$; $p < .001$.
Source: National Opinion Research Center, General Social Survey (2002).

used computers, making their portrait similar to younger people (77.6%) and not at all like the elderly (40.8%) (see Table 7.1).

DeGraves and Denesiuk (2000) were also interested in how older people use the Web: "Seniors are embracing computer technology and the Internet with growing confidence, destroying agist myths about their reluctance to use computers, and agencies like CRM (Creative Retirement Manitoba) are struggling to meet their needs" (p. 354). White and Weatherall (2000) purported that adults' usage of information technology is in need of data-based theory-building: "Some older adults are not merely comfortable interacting with IT but are using it to facilitate their own interests and goals. . . . Specific interests such as genealogy and communication with family are assisted greatly by the use of IT" (p. 383). Participants tended to use the Internet for communication with family and friends, and grandparent–grandchildren interaction was particularly important:

The efficiency and speed of e-mail, combined with the absence of geographic barriers, make IT an extremely useful tool for communication. This specific use of IT appears to be an area of importance for older adults, and it warrants further investigation. In particular, the effect of computer-mediated communication on patterns of intergenerational communication is an area worth pursuing further. (pp. 383–384)

In 2001, the Pew Interest and American Life Project published an extensive examination of the use of the Internet by older people (Table 7.2). "Wired Seniors: A Fervent Few, Inspired by Family Ties" found that 50- to 64-year-olds were three times more likely to use the Internet than people age 65 and older. These "pre-retirement" Web users were more similar to the overall Internet population in that they were active with e-mail, news and information, and research for their work (p. 3). In a follow-up to the 2001 study, Pew found that the margin between the two age groups had decreased (Pew Internet and American Life Project, 2004):

- By 2004, older women—previously less likely to use the Internet—became as likely as older men to be online.
- More seniors log on from home than all other age groups.
- Relatives, including grandchildren, often motivate seniors to go online.
- By far, e-mail is the top use of the Internet.
- Web sites offering information about hobbies, finances, and health are the most popular for older Americans, and these are "sharp growth areas."
- Seniors also use the Web for news, weather, and fun browsing. (pp. 3–9)

In an 8-year span, the percentage of Americans age 65 or older who used the Internet jumped from 2% to 22%: "Wired seniors are often as enthusiastic as younger users in the major activities that define online life such as email and the use of search engines to answer a specific question" (Pew Internet and American Life Project, 2004, p. i).

For aging baby boomers, 75% reported getting news online, 55% searched for jobs online, and 31% used instant messaging: "There is a burgeoning group of Americans who are slightly younger than retirees and who are vastly more attached to the online world" (p. ii). In other words, there was empirical support for the idea that as boomers age, there will be a "silver tsunami" of Internet users: "They are unlikely to give up their wired ways and therefore transform the wired senior stereotype" (p. iii).

TABLE 7.2
Pew Internet and American Life Project: "Wired Seniors" (2001)

Select Activities	Percent 50- to 64-year-olds
E-mail	
Send and read e-mail	94%
Fun	
Get hobby information	72%
Browse Internet for fun	53
Check sports scores	31
Information seeking topics	
Travel	66%
Weather	62
News	60
Finances	50
Political	39
Religious	18
Major life activities	
Health information	60%
Work research	50
Transactions	
Online shopping	45%
Online banking	16
Buy/sell stocks	15
Auctions	13

Note. From Pew Internet and American Life Project. (2001, September 9). *Wired seniors: A fervent few, inspired by family ties*, p. 9.

In a study of older adults using SeniorNet and other Web sites, it was found that the higher the Internet usage, the higher the level of satisfaction with computer-mediated communication for support (Wright, 2000). The use of larger online groups appeared to be related to lower life stress. "For those individuals who spend less time on the Internet, the supportive relationships may be perceived as too insignificant to exhibit costs or rewards" (p. 115). Coulson (2000) studied technological challenges facing gerontologists in the new century: "The World Wide Web has enabled senior citizens to develop complex networks to discuss various topics, ranging from self-help groups to platforms for interactive socialization" (p. 308).

Chen and Persson (2002) studied 218 older people (mean age 75.6) and compared them to 178 college students (mean age 19.8). The study also compared Internet users and nonusers on psychological well-being. There is an emerging literature that suggests the positive effects of Internet usage on older adults. Older Internet users tended to score higher on measures of personal growth and life purpose. As Chen and Persson

BOX 7.1.   An Instrumental Elder Web Community
By John Dillon

With the widespread availability of Internet access, computer-mediated communication has become, for many mature adults, a means of conducting life's business and for negotiating social support. In particular, the "young old"—those 55 to 69—represent an escalating Internet subpopulation. This is due to the relatively ample amount of leisure time they enjoy, improvements in health care that extend "middle age," and the desire among many within this group to use new technologies to help maintain a vital life style.

Sociologists have denoted several psychological components of well-being and contentment among older adults. Botwinick's (1984) tripartite model outlines the levels of income and income management, health and health awareness, and social support (family and friendship). This model points to three of the notable strengths of the World Wide Web as a personal information agent.

A variety of interactive chat and e-mail avenues are available for social support, in areas ranging from romance to bereavement. Social linkages in the form of e-mail, chat groups, and posted "bulletin boards" have grown explosively in the past decade, ushering in a "new . . . relational world" being created through Internet discussion groups that in many ways is not much different from face-to-face interaction (Parks & Floyd, 1996, p. 80).

Mass media allow elderly people to keep up with the ever-changing world around them, a clear tie to the "surveillance function" suggested by uses and gratifications research (Palmgreen et al., 1985; Rosengren, 1985). Internet communities may also be used as surrogates for interpersonal "interaction" and relationships (Nussbaum et al., 2000, p. 64).

Among younger populations, Papacharissi and Rubin (2000) found that motives to use the Internet are accounted for by "interpersonal utility" variables (e.g., belonging to a group, meeting new people, and expressing

BOX 7.1. *(Continued)*

oneself freely); "passing time" (diversion from boredom); "information seeking" (e.g., to find solutions to problems, or to get free advice); "convenience" (particularly e-mail and e-shopping); and pure "entertainment" (p. 185).

Essential to many theories concerning media use is the concept that media offer predicted and expected rewards. Within this uses and gratifications approach, the audience is expected to be active and goal directed. Expectancy-value theory extends this construct to suggest that the determinants of gratifications sought are one's belief about what media will provide and one's evaluation of that choice. On the whole, both the uses and gratifications and expectancy-value frameworks apply well to Internet use, given that Internet use is relatively purposive compared to other media platforms. Instrumental media consumption suggests an active user who makes choices about media channels and who shows goal-directedness in pursuit of gratifications. Papacharissi and Rubin (2001) found that one salient use of the Internet reflected an instrumental orientation, which has been denoted as active and purposive, often having to do with information seeking, and characterized by utility, intention, selectivity, and involvement.

SeniorNet is a nonprofit online community of more than 40,000, welcoming those age 50 and above to engage in discussions, to access databases of specific interest to them, and to encourage usage of computer technology. A study of one year of discussion forum postings at SeniorNet.org found that 39% of sampled messages contained strongly instrumental characteristics. The postings with the greatest percentage of instrumental bearing were: Announcements and Requests, Computer and Online Internet Q&A, Computer Lessons and Projects, Consumer Education, Financial Topics, and Leadership Exchange. The Leadership Exchange area is a place to call for and provide assistance to people in leadership and volunteer situations (Dillon, 2003).

Emblematic of the purpose-bearing potential of SeniorNet was the posting: "Chatting is social but I, for one, want some interactional knowledge (from my communication)."

Binomial categories were identified within instrumental postings: Expression and Connection, and Strategy and Empowerment. Expression and Connection suggests the instrumental desire to affiliate; to seek support, advice, or even rescue; as well as to show need to projects one's skills or affections. Expression and Connection was notable for a relatively high frequency of support providing and support seeking. There were, in fact, more postings providing support than seeking it, generally meaning that when someone listed a concern and requested assistance, more than one person responded.

BOX 7.1. *(Continued)*

The most frequent "rescue"-classified support variable had to do with technology, where people wanted help with their computer problems. But another concerned illness or personal tragedy, where users asked for prayer, or responded that they were providing prayer to another SeniorNet member. The pursuit of companionship and networking also scored high in the expressive vein.

Many who posted tended to project their affections as a means of providing context for self-presentation. That is, a common means of putting "a face on their message" was for people to define themselves by their likes and dislikes.

Strategy and Empowerment strongly concerned health information, finance questions, and direct advice, including how to achieve financial objectives and how to avoid financial rip-offs, topics concerning civilian or military service, travel experiences, and learning. By far, the strongest Strategy and Empowerment classification proved to be learning, both technical (usually concerning computerization) and humanistic (often marked by free exchange of pertinent life stories and life wisdom).

Indeed, the "young old," who consider themselves SeniorNet's core clientele, are very Net-aware and active. They show strong indications that they use the Internet toward fulfillment of life contentment issues, as well as for interpersonal utility and information seeking. Perhaps echoing the spirit of our times, where "old age" is seemingly forestalled, learning issues are an important component of senior activity. There are indications that cyber-communication among these individuals does assist successful aging, and further, that a substantial component of such communication is deliberate and goal directed (instrumental use).

As opposed to undirected and ritualistic chit-chat, SeniorNet postings demonstrated a marked capacity for focused, intentional communication. It may be that older persons have less "time to kill" than younger people, or it may be that the perspective of age lends itself less toward frivolous exchange and empty dances. And the providing of support (answering questions, the giving of encouragement or prayer) actually exceeds the amount of petitioning for support—a wonderful hallmark for a community of elders.

Dr. Dillon is a professor of journalism and mass communications, Murray State University.

pointed out, "In a sense, older Internet users were more like young adults than non-users. This conclusion was further supported by group differences in personal characteristics between older Internet users and non-users. Older users tended to be younger, healthier, better educated, and had more financial resources than older non-users" (p. 741).

INTERNET USE, OLDER MEDIA,
AND AGING IN AMERICA

Older adults' use of the Internet reflects their interest in news and information. As a group, older people spend far more time watching television
than reading newspapers, watch more television than any other age
group (Media Literacy, 2003), and give television news higher credibility
ratings (Folkerts & Lacy, 2001, p. 233). Older viewers are major consumers of television news, preferring news to other programming (Scales,
1996). However, Goodman (1990) found that older men and women favored television for their national news and information, but preferred
newspapers for local news. At the same time, the elderly are increasingly
among the most enthusiastic consumers of online information (Cole,
2003). The UCLA Internet study also suggested that higher percentages
of elderly people than teens use the Internet. However, not much is
known about whether or not older people have an interest in news-
oriented Web sites. It has been found that wired seniors, in a study of
Internet users around the globe, watched less television than nonusers
(UCLA World Internet Project, 2004).

Use of online information is important because of the statistical
trends. A United Nations report noted that 16% of the U.S. population is
age 60 or older, and predicts that this will rise to 27% by 2050 (Chamie,
2003). The U.N. report also predicts that, by 2050, in developed nations
"the proportion of older persons is expected to be double that of children
(32 per cent versus 16 per cent). As a result of these changes, the median
age in the more developed regions, which rose from 28.6 years in 1950 to
37.3 in 2000, is projected to reach the unprecedented level of 45.2 years
in 2050" (p. 15).

The elderly are increasingly among the new consumers of online information. The UCLA Center for Communication Policy found that
Internet use was more popular among the 56 and older crowd than
among teens (Cole, 2003). Internet users watch less television than non-
users. The Pew Internet and American Life Project found that wired seniors are inspired by information and social contacts, particularly those
related to family and health (Associated Press, 2001). At the same time,
however, older people—particularly some older women—are reluctant to
use the Internet (Adler, 2003).

CMC, E-MAIL, WEB SURFING,
AND ONLINE NEWS AND INFORMATION

The computer-mediated communication literature has explored the important influence of new media technology in creating interaction, online
communities, and a sense of identity for various groups (Barnes, 2001).

For older people, information Web sites appear to be important (Burnett & Marshall, 2003). Internet technology may be particularly important in addressing social change with respect to American families (Surratt, 2001). Personal and family web usage allows people to share information over great distances (Barnes, 2003). Ferguson and Perse (2000) suggested that the Web is becoming a functional alternative to TV for many. Hindman (2000) found that Internet adoption is affected, not only by rural–urban divides, but also age, education, and income.

Technology and new media also have been studied from the perspective of its uses (Pavlik, 1996), gratifications (Lin, 1993), and media richness (i.e., lack of nonverbal cues in e-mail; Kahai & Cooper, 2003), as well as its cultural importance (Stevenson, 1995). The use of online media, most recently, has been addressed as cyberculture—focusing on communities and individual identities (Bell, 2001; du Gay, Evans, & Redman, 2000; Jones, 1997). Communities and identities suggest the importance of local news and information, as well as the influence of online news.

Local newspaper Web sites had an initial advantage over local television Web sites as a source for online news and information. Media Audit (2002) found that some local television newsrooms had made inroads in attracting audiences: "A few are making a formidable challenge to the newspapers in their markets, but the others seem to be uncommitted" (p. 1).

National news organizations, particularly those that have older audiences, have had success focusing content and attracting aging baby boomers to their Web sites.

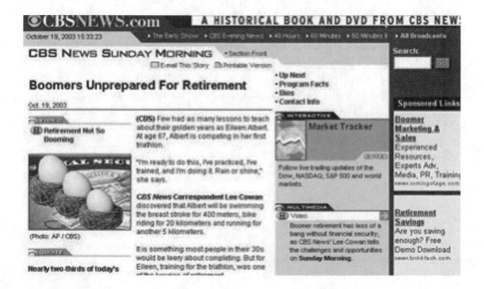

Overall, people inclined toward active information seeking are most likely to look at all types of medium for content (Stempel, Hargrove, & Bernt, 2000).

The elderly offer a unique group to study. For example, researchers have examined the training and evaluation of Internet use among the elderly (Cody & Dunn, 1999; White, 2002) and computer usage in nursing homes and assisted living centers (Namazi & McClintic, 2003; Pepper, 2002). For middle-age and older adults, World Wide Web usage may vary by interest (Morrell, 2000). The popular press has highlighted usage by grandparents to communicate with distant family members (Katz, 2001; Segan, 2002). Increasingly, older people are being studied in a variety of contexts: "New issues about work and technology are being raised for discussion" (Riggs, 2004, p. 17). The literature suggests the need for detailed study of older people and their motivation for having an interest in the use of technology.

CASE STUDY: OLDER PEOPLE AND THE WEB

A qualitative, descriptive, and ethnographic case study involving elderly residents of one midsize American city offered insight into why older people are enthusiastic about online information. The data explored how this group was reached by traditional broadcast and other mass media. The community-based study of all socioeconomic groups examined the importance of media use and interpersonal influence as they relate to consumer behavior and cyberculture.

In-depth interviews with the elderly have been found to be a useful method for studying media consumption (Riggs, 1998). In spring 2003, qualitative and ethnographic interviews of older Americans were conducted to ascertain their Internet usage. The study followed earlier methods (Hine, 2000; Miller & Slater, 2000). Observations were made at computer training labs in a midsize midwestern city.[1] Diffusion theory, which explores how ideas, innovation, and change spread through society, informed the investigation (Rogers, 1995). Information may be described by the pattern of its flow through various communication channels. The interviews yielded a wide range of interest and usage among the

---

[1]Researchers observed and interviewed people age 50 and older in one midwestern, midsize market. First, populations in retirement communities, villages, and facilities were identified. Cooperation from as wide as possible a range of socioeconomic conditions was sought. Specifically, the study targeted upscale, middle, and lower income retirement communities and facilities; individual homeowners in a range of socioeconomic conditions; apartment dwellers; and others.

elderly. Older women and men were interviewed as they used the Internet. The youngest was 55 years old, and the oldest was 84 years old.

John, Age 71

John first used a personal computer about 7 years ago. He has had a home computer for about 3 years. He took a summer noncredit university writing class, and he needed to learn word processing to do course work. He first learned computing and Internet research at a senior center computer lab. Now, he visits 15–20 Web sites each day, and he checks his e-mail several times a day. John has used Yahoo e-mail for his part-time job and for personal correspondence.

John has an interest in astronomy and uses the Web to keep up with the latest NASA and scientific information. Also, he visits the local newspaper Web site, *USA Today*, and the *New York Times* for news. He visits local television news Web sites for weather and "developing stories." He sometimes visits CNN and ABC for news and science links. He has listened to college football games on the Web, and he occasionally has visited magazine Web sites. He tracks college sports scores online. And, he views movie trailers and listens to classical music.

John says he has sometimes been prompted to visit a Web site because of a television story, but he does not watch TV while surfing the Web. John is enthusiastic about the Internet: "It's like the whole world opens up to a person online." He added, "I think back to what my father would have thought of this. And he would have said, 'Wow, this is great!' . . . It would be have been unbelievable to him that all of this is available right at hand, with a couple of clicks here and there, and there it is."

John perceives himself as using the Internet more than anyone he knows because he likes the immediacy: "I can know right now. I don't have to wait until the 10 o'clock news or the morning newspaper." As much as he likes the Internet, he dislikes the pop-up advertising (Table 7.3).

TABLE 7.3
Pop-Up Advertising Usage by Industry

Industry	Percent Share of Pop-Ups
Entertainment	9.9
Hardware and electronics	7.8
Public services	7.0
Software	6.9
Travel	6.1

Source: Nielsen//NetRatings, fourth quarter (2002).

John now helps other seniors learn about the Internet.

Although you cannot force someone to be interested, he believes there is something for everyone on the Internet: "Something that would invigorate the mind a little bit. . . . Help you if not physically to get out of that chair, mentally to get out of that chair."

Jeanette, Age 67

Jeanette had very basic data entry computer experience from work, but she began using it more in 2002. She purchased a computer and used it to play games. At the library, she learned about computer classes. She first learned computer basics and then began to e-mail her son in Florida. She still does not use the computer as much as she wants to because she is busy with other activities, particularly church and gardening.

She has 10 hours per month of free e-mail, but she plans to subscribe for more time. She checks her e-mail every other day. She likes e-mail because she can take her time, "but you can't beat face-to-face" communication. When she gets online, she sometimes checks weather information and tries to search. "I don't really know what I'm doing; I just get on there and try to find something." She likes MSN, Yahoo, and NetZero for e-mail. She sometimes visits the local newspaper for "front-page" news: "I don't go into it because I really don't know how to go into it." She sometimes visits health and weather Web sites. She has watched TV and used the Internet at the same time. She notices and is interested in web addresses shown on TV, but generally is not able to access them.

Jeanette also finds pop-up advertising on the Internet confusing. She has trouble navigating on the Web, and the ads direct her away from what she is trying to do.

Jeanette is very interested in playing games, and she has "tried" online games. Sometimes she has had difficulty getting online games to work. She would like to do more in this area. She gets confused between her access via the Internet Service Provider and the software used to access the Web. She is more likely to play games loaded on the hard drive of her computer than to go to an online game site.

Sister Joan, Age 76

In 1997, Joan purchased her first computer for letter writing. She "pretty much taught herself" with help from friends and classes. In 1998, she began using e-mail. Now, she regularly visits her Dominican Sisters' Web site and Yahoo for "headlines." She has a dial-up connection and avoids using the Internet when she is expecting a telephone call. Sometimes, she plays an offline game. Sister Joan explains, "I can't talk on the phone and be on the computer at the same time. So, when other people are trying to call me, that's a bit of a problem." She would prefer to have a constant Internet connection, but those options are too expensive. For now, she spends offline computer time working on a family tree or making greeting cards.

She likes the timeliness of e-mail delivery. She checks e-mail as often as twice each day. Most e-mail between the Sisters and other family are brief. When reading e-mail, she says she can "picture" the person writing a note.

She checks the local newspaper Web site but also continues to subscribe. "Once in a while" she checks local TV station Web sites. She "sometimes" checks a network TV news Web site for additional information on a story of interest. She is a registered nurse and "sometimes" visits health Web sites. She has book-marked favorites but usually just uses a search engine to find information. She infrequently visits magazine, weather, and auction sites.

Eunice, Age 84

Eunice first used a computer when she was 80 years old. A friend advised her to take a class to learn how to use the computer given to her by a daughter living in another state. Within 6 weeks, she was on the Internet and then purchased a new computer. Four years later, she was maintaining her own Web site.

She has relatives across the country and wants to communicate with them. The password protected family Web site allows them to share personal information and photographs. When a family member adds content to the Web site, each participant gets an e-mail prompt; this happens regularly. She checks e-mail once each day. She gets e-mail from family, friends, and online merchants.

She visits a variety of Web sites: the local newspaper, the *New York Times* (daily), network television, radio stations, weather, sports, and shopping. Her television is in a different room. She sometimes turns it on and *listens* to TV while checking e-mail. Also, she listens to a lot of radio during the day.

She calls herself a "shopaholic," frequently visiting name brand online stores, such as Eddie Bauer. She likes not paying sales tax and saving money on sale items. Eunice overcame her fears of online shopping because of "secure" Web sites. Sometimes the online price is less than the in-store price. Also, she likes specialty shoes from Canada and buys online. She has bid and purchased items on e-Bay. She learned about it in a class.

Eunice has installed Real Player on her computer but does not know how to use multimedia files. She is interested in learning how to access audio and video files. She has downloaded games and played them.

Eunice sees the Internet as a "source of information." The volume of information is what she likes most. However, she worries about spending too much time online: "I think maybe it draws me there too often. It takes up too much of my time, but I said after I retired, 'I'll never be lonesome.' Because if I'm bored, I can go there, and the time just passes." She finds the Internet "remarkable." Before the Internet, she spent more time volunteering at a local university health office.

Joe, Age 79

Joe purchased a computer in late 2000, knowing "absolutely nothing about" how to use it. For years, he had no interest, but his children convinced him. He revealed, "I think it has extended my life. It's a constant challenge. I think I'm on the verge of Alzheimer's . . . the mental exercise is fabulous." He began in 2001 with a dial-up Internet connection. He experienced many problems, so he switched to a high speed cable modem and his problems disappeared.

He has a daily Internet conversation with a friend in New Zealand. He reads his friend's local daily newspaper online so that he has something to talk about. He has an interest in amateur "Ham Radio," and he has seen some of those transmissions migrate to the Web. Also, he reads a lot of e-mail. He forwards items to a group of friends he worked with 30 years ago.

Joe does not use the Internet for American mass media sites of any kind. He remains a local newspaper subscriber and reads the hard-copy edition. He does use Web sites for checking on severe weather conditions. He has purchased a couple of items online from Wal-Mart.

For the most part, Joe uses his computer for digital photography projects, including a slide show promoting his interest in a downtown trolley car line. Overall, he says, "I'm not an Internet type person."

Charlie, Age 69

Charlie first used a personal computer 3 years ago. He wanted to learn because he felt "totally illiterate," and he began using the Internet within 4 months to follow the stock market. He continues to check his stock prices daily on Excite and Yahoo. A European vacation prompted him to visit Web sites featuring the places he had been on his trip.

He has purchased a second computer and continues to use a dial-up connection. He uses e-mail each evening to communicate with family, friends, and business associates. He is an instructor in a computer lab for senior citizens and thinks that the activity is important to them. He shows people how to access the local newspaper. He reads the online version rather than subscribing. Also, he reads *USA Today* and *PC World* online. He likes to forward articles to friends: "I like the idea that it's so fast. It's almost instant. . . . It's almost like being there." He continues to listen to local radio during the day and watches television at night, but he does not read newspapers as much as he once did.

Charlie, like other interviewees, most dislikes pop-up advertisements. However, they are no more than an annoyance for him. He saw his previous electronics experience as a personal advantage (he repaired musical organs) because he was not afraid of the keyboard or computer.

Charlie concluded that the computer and Internet are "the most important invention" in his lifetime: "It gives me or anyone else the advantage of reaching out. I can go anywhere. It's an information source. Without it, what would I do?" Overall, Charlie sees the Internet as a replacement for newspaper and library reading—a superior and faster way to obtain information about any of his special interests.

Mary, Age 70, and Margaret, Age 70

Mary and Margaret are twin sisters, and they were interviewed together at Mary's apartment in a housing authority low-income building for seniors. Margaret owns a house.

Mary first became interested in computers in about 1997, but she was not using a computer at the time of the interview. She was concerned about being able to receive telephone calls. She experimented with WebTV but did not like it. He granddaughter helped her. Mary used the Internet for e-mail, movie reviews, and checking health Web sites. At first, she liked WebTV but says it changed over time. She had difficulty disconnecting from the subscription service. At the time of the interview, Margaret was urging Mary to buy a computer and get back on the Internet. She even offered to give her a free monitor: "I want to get in on things. Find out stuff that's going on. I want to try some of this eBay stuff. I want to see some of the big garage sale stuff. I like a lot of the current stuff coming on. . . . If you know how to get into these different places, you can get a lot of information on that."

Margaret was using computer bulletin boards 20 years ago. Her son took an electronics course and sparked her interest. Also, she worked at a cemetery and worked with computerized records. Over time, the Internet captured her interest. Margaret explained, "Well, I don't think there's anything you can't do on the Internet anymore. There's games. There's jokes. You find lost relatives. You talk to people overseas."

Margaret said 90% of her use is e-mail. She checks it four times each day on an inexpensive dial-up service. She volunteers at the library and stills works with computerized records. She uses the Internet to trace genealogy, check weather, preview movies, and buy on eBay. She visits the local newspaper Web site, and uses Google to look for other information: "If you think it a little differently in your head, you can come up with different websites on it, too. It's just marvelous. 'Cause you can go to bed at night and all of the sudden something will pop in your head and you'll wonder if I can find that. It's amazing what you can come up with. . . . Things you've always wondered about, and there it is." Margaret finds Web URLs difficult to type, and Google is easier to use than Yahoo.

Margaret also appeared to be very enthusiastic about the potential of eBay. She had just purchased several items online, including a digital camera. She also was planning to become an eBay seller.

The twins compared the Internet to when they were schoolchildren, and the librarian would not let them touch certain books. Now, Margaret enjoys Internet jokes: "You can't stay depressed on e-mail." Both said they had visited Web sites suggested on television. They disliked pop-up advertising on the Internet. Despite the annoyance, Margaret said it still seems like magic: "It's foolish not to get into it. Especially for older people. On a cloudy afternoon, you can sit there and talk to people all over the world. And no charge. That's the sweet part. And the jokes that come across. Oh, wow! Somebody thinks them all up." Although Mary enjoys the Internet, she remains concerned with being able to do it without support from "kids." Margaret believes older people need to have friends using the Internet—people who can help answer questions and interpret instructions. "We speak a different language than you guys." Asked if the Internet is better than television, Margaret responded forcefully: "Get real. There's no comparison." The twins no longer watch daytime television, and Margaret says she sleeps less to have more time online.

Judy, Age 65

Judy started using a computer at work in the 1980s. Her brother-in-law gave her a computer in 2000. At first, she called him "every other day" for help. She mainly checks e-mail and does word processing. She uses the Web to check her bank statement, cartoons, the Mayo Clinic, and other health sites. She checks information on prescription drugs. She explained, "New diagnosis, or whatever. I do it more for research than anything else."

Judy checks e-mail daily. She reveals, "It keeps me in touch without having to go out. When you get to be my age, you don't want to go out that much anymore." She loves jokes and cartoons. She wishes everyone had e-mail because she enjoys keeping in touch with family members who do use it.

She subscribes to the local newspaper and also checks that Web site before it is delivered. She watches cable television for weather. Her concerns for security keep her from shopping online or doing online banking: "It scares me." She uses the Web to visit religious sites. She reads online movie reviews.

Judy likes the convenience of the Internet: "It's just there. You don't have to go to a library and look it up in a reference book." She dislikes the slow dial-up speed of Juno, but she cannot afford a cable modem service.

Liz, Age 55

She began using a personal computer in 1998. Her husband set up and maintains the home computer. Liz uses it mainly for word processing and e-mail. He husband accesses the Internet regularly. She prefers reading and watching cable television channels.

Liz is a retired schoolteacher and teacher union president. She never had a computer in the classroom, but the union office was computerized. She learned Word and acquired an e-mail address. When asked about her use of the Internet, she responded:

> I haven't really. No. No, and I've taken classes. . . . I went to two or three of them. Whatever I signed up for. And they said, "Here's how you use the Internet." Well, I haven't done it. This is not my first interest, and so I don't. I'm still back with reading a good book and highlighting the hell out of parts I want to remember. And writing letters to people, and sending it snail mail.

She does use e-mail for political action. She has friends and relatives in nearby cities and uses e-mail every other day for communication. She and her husband use an economical, low-speed dial-up service, which is commercial free.

Marge, Age 71, and Cindi, Age 62

Marge and Cindi were interviewed at a senior wellness center computer lab. Cindi had been using a computer for 3 years. Marge, a retired secretary, had used a computer for 20 years, and she began using the Internet about 6 years ago. Marge's daughter encouraged her to connect to a high-speed cable modem, but she found it to expensive and changed to dial-up. Marge uses the Internet for e-mail and some information, but she said she does not "surf" the Web. Cindi also has e-mail with family and friends, and she checks but does not do banking online. Marge checks e-mail daily, but Cindi checks it less frequently. Marge and Cindi both have received photographs of grandchildren. Neither of the women was enthusiastic about the Internet as a source of news, but they sometimes checked the Web for entertainment, weather, and special interest items. Cindi has used her America Online account to listen to music. Both women have seen Web sites mentioned on morning network television, and they have checked, for example, online recipes.

Both women mentioned book reviews, movie reviews, and health Web sites. Marge reads about preventive health and prescription drugs, and she plays bridge online. Cindi has watched her son buy and sell on eBay, but she has not used it. She elaborated, "I look it up on there, and then I turn around and call them. I'm nervous about putting my credit card on there. I know that's stupid because it's just as stupid to do it over the telephone." Cindi is a regular viewer and buyer from QVC, the cable TV shopping network. She has looked at items on their Web site, but she calls to buy. Cindi goes online while watching TV. Both women like the convenience of timeliness of online information. Both women complained about "spam" e-mail and pop-up Web advertising. After an 11-day hospital stay, Marge had 293 junk e-mails. Marge found the Internet useful when she needed to obtain her Pennsylvania birth certificate. She was able to pay for it online and received it a few days later. Cindi, at the urging of a friend, went online to get her Missouri birth certificate. She found it easier than struggling with an automated telephone system.

Bob, Age 83

Bob, at his son's urging, got a computer about a year ago. His church gave him the used computer. A friend connected it for him to Juno. He has learned e-mail and word processing. Bob has never surfed the Web: "I haven't seen anything that I was really interested in to do that, and besides, if I was interested, I wouldn't know how to do it."

He checks his e-mail everyday. "It's fun for me to do." He writes short notes of "a line or two," but he does not find it "essential." He prefers to use local and long distance telephone calls as an easier way to speak with his children. Bob has had occasional trouble getting his computer to work. He has a friend who helps get it working again. His e-mail is with family members, a few church members, and people from his old neighborhood.

Overall, Bob does not anticipate increased use of the computer. At 83, he says he is just not very interested in online information. He prefers television reruns, local television news, network television news, morning radio, the local newspaper, *Reader's Digest*, *Prevention*, and *Men's Health*. He has a collection of 10 compact disks, and he enjoys listening to music.

Older Americans, like other groups, vary in their use of the Internet. The subjects for this study all used e-mail, and it was most important to them. When this group of older people did surf the Web, they were more likely to seek information about their special interests rather than mass media. Some were interested in online shopping and auctions. They were most likely to use Google or Yahoo to find sites dealing with weather, health, games, jokes, and entertainment information.

The subjects for this study were observed having a lot of difficulty navigating the Web, and they relied on search engines to guide them. For most, a search engine was their starting home page. E-mailing with family and friends was a regular and often daily part of their lives. Although some had been in a chat room, none continued to participate.

The results of this exploratory study were not promising for traditional mass media on the Web. Local television news sites, for example, would need to be redesigned as portals of information about health, entertainment, and weather to be of great use to older Americans. Overall, they expressed little interest in what media offered. They saw the Internet as a functional replacement for the library rather than mass media. They tended to be newspaper subscribers, radio listeners, and television viewers rather than Web surfers.

Programmers, sales managers, and advertisers face an enormous challenge with respect to the Internet. On vital health information, for example, the Mayo Clinic offers source and message credibility that is difficult to match. If media partnered with such sites, these older people would still go directly to the sites they trust. Further, mechanisms such as pop-up advertising tend to be annoying to this group. However, humorous advertising has been found to be effective when targeting older Americans: "The image of seniors as frail and humorless is outdated, and . . . humor is in fact among the best ways to reach them" (Norton, 2001, p. 6).

These individuals sometimes belonged to online communities of friends, family, and interest groups, but they did not recognize them as such. Most often, they shared regular e-mail with a small number of people.

This study validated the difficulties in getting older people to adopt new technologies. It takes family members, friends, local groups, and computer classes to overcome apprehension and confusion. Older people found computer jargon difficult, and they were easily stalled by a simple problem. At the same time, the older people in this study expressed great enthusiasm for their access to massive amounts of information.

There is a need to go beyond studying a pilot group of older Internet users. Future research needs to explore issues related to those who have not been online. Age is one variable that influences use. Other influences include work experiences, technical aptitude, supportive atmosphere for learning, and the limitation of being on a fixed income.

During the past decade, the first group of older Americans went online. This picture will change dramatically as the baby boomers reach retirement age. In the future, it will be more likely that older people will be comfortable with the Internet and online media. The task facing mass media organizations is to meet the needs and interests of this diverse group, which already constitutes the bulk of their current audience. The Internet has opened a large doorway to information. Inevitably, older people's interest in Web sites takes time away from traditional media use.

OLDER PEOPLE AND THE ONLINE WORLD

Vann (2003) suggested that older people have begun to turn to "armchair shopping" as an alternative to fighting crowds, weather, and traffic (p. D4). Online shopping allows older people with medical problems or physical limitations to remain active. AARP has counted more than 36 million seniors using e-mail, online banking, and shopping. For some older people, the transition from mail order catalog shopping to online shopping was natural. Older consumers have been warned to be careful in their online shopping by going only to Web sites of well-known companies. Shea (2003) highlighted the fact that older seniors may be different from aging baby boomers; they may be less inclined to use the Internet in general and online shopping in particular. The same may be the case for the use of online information, and they may have a particular interest in sharing humor.

BOX 7.2.   Forwarded E-Mail Joke

> Sent: Tuesday, July 22, 2003 1:33 PM
> Subject: How Old?
>
> E-mail message
>
> How Old Is Grandma?
> Stay with this — the answer is at the end — it will blow you away.
> Different!!!
> One evening a grandson was talking to his grandmother about current
> events. The grandson asked his grandmother what she thought about
> the shootings at schools, the computer age, and just things in general.
> The Grandma replied, "Well, let me think a minute, I was born,
> before television, penicillin, polio shots, frozen foods, Xerox, contact
> lenses, Frisbees and the pill.
> There were no credit cards, laser beams or ball-point pens. Man had not
> invented pantyhose, air conditioners, dishwashers, clothes dryers, and
> the clothes were hung out to dry in the fresh air and man had yet to walk
> on the moon.
> Your Grandfather and I got married first and then lived together.
> Every family had a father and a mother. Until I was 25, I called every
> man older than I, "Sir"- - and after I turned 25, I still called policemen and
> every man with a title, "Sir".
> We were before gay-rights, computer-dating, dual careers, daycare
> centers, and group therapy. Our lives were governed by the Ten
> Commandments, good judgment, and common sense. We were taught to
> know the difference between right and wrong and to stand up and take
> responsibility for our actions.
> Serving your country was a privilege; living in this country was a
> bigger privilege. We thought fast food was what people ate during Lent.
> Having a meaningful relationship meant getting along with your cousins.
> Draft dodgers were people who closed their front doors when the evening
> breeze started.
> Time-sharing meant time the family spent together in the evenings and
> weekends-not purchasing condominiums.

BOX 7.2.　*(Continued)*

> We never heard of FM radios, tape decks, CDs, electric typewriters,
> yogurt, or guys wearing earrings. We listened to the Big Bands, Jack Benny,
> and the President's speeches on our radios. And I don't ever remember
> any kid blowing his brains out listening to Tommy Dorsey.
> If you saw anything with 'Made in Japan' on it, it was junk. The
> term 'making out' referred to how you did on your school exam. Pizza
> Hut, McDonald's, and instant coffee were unheard of. We had 5 & 10-cent
> store where you could actually buy things for 5 and 10 cents. Ice-cream cones,
> phone calls, rides on a streetcar, and a Pepsi were all a nickel. And if you
> didn't want to splurge, you could spend your nickel on enough stamps to
> mail one letter and two postcards.
> You could buy a new Chevy Coupe for $600 but who could afford one?
> Too bad, because gas was 11 cents a gallon. In my day, "grass" was mowed,
> "coke" was a cold drink, "pot" was something your mother cooked in, and
> "rock music" was your grandmother's lullaby. "Aids" were helpers in the
> Principal's office, "chip" meant a piece of wood, "hardware" was found in a
> hardwares tore, and "software" wasn't even a word.
> And we were the last generation to actually believe that a lady
> needed a husband to have a baby. No wonder people call us "old
> and confused" and say there is a generation gap.....
> and how old do you think I am???..... Read on to see—pretty scary if you
> think about it and pretty sad at the same time.
> *
> This Woman would be only 58 years old!

Source: Anonymous forwarded e-mail (July 22, 2003).

An important sector of online information for older people is health
care. The elderly may be trained to use the Internet for health care information, and this may reduce anxiety (Campbell & Wabb, 2003). The Pew
Internet and American Life Project found that more than two thirds
(69%) of wired seniors were daily users of the Internet, and researching
health information was a popular activity (Jesdanun, 2001). Eighty percent of all Internet users have searched for online health information
(Weaver, 2003).

WEB SITES OF INTEREST
TO AGING BABY BOOMERS

The following Web sites may offer insight into issues of importance to
older people:

Alive & Kicking Magazine. "Magazine for adults 50 plus." http://www.aliveandkicking
magazine.com.
Baby Boomer Bistro. "About the chat site." http://www.babyboomerbistro.org.uk/bbb/
copystore.nsf/httphomepage?readform.
BabyBoomers.com. "Baby boomer news." http://www.babyboomers.com/news.htm.
Baby Boomers at Suite101.com. "Real people helping real people." http://www.suite101.
com/articles.cfm/baby_boomers/1-20.
BoomerCafe. "It's your place." http://www.boomercafe.com.
Boomernet. "The baby boomers' surfing center." http://www.boomernet.com/.
Boomers International. "The sandwich generation." http://boomersint.org/parents.htm.
Center for Aging Services and Technologies. "Welcome." http://www.agingtech.org/index.
aspx.
The Seniors World Network. "Welcome boomers and seniors." http://www. seniorsworld
network.us.

CHAPTER SUMMARY

Aging baby boomers, an enthusiastic group of Internet users, are unlike
their parents' generation—boomers learned to use computers and the
World Wide Web in the workplace. Older adults' use of the Internet reflects their interest in news, information, hobbies, and family. They use
the Internet for communication with family and friends. Grandparent–grandchildren interactions are particularly important. For middle-
age and older adults, World Wide Web usage may vary by interest. AARP
has counted more than 36 million seniors using e-mail, online banking,
and shopping. Older people use online technologies to acquire health care
information.

REVIEW QUESTIONS

1. Why do baby boomers have greater interest in the Internet than
   their parents?
2. What types of Web content would be of interest to aging baby
   boomers? Why?
3. What is SeniorNet? Why is it important?
4. How can the Internet be used to bring families closer together?
   What intergenerational communication problems might limit
   meaningful interaction?
5. Why would you think health care information would be of growing importance to baby boomers?

Chapter 8

Health and Sexual Media Content

David E. Corbin
University of Nebraska at Omaha

Americans have long had a great ambivalence about growing old. We want to live longer but somehow stay "younger." As James Taylor sang: "Never give up, never slow down, never grow old, never ever die young." Both Rod Stewart and Joan Baez sang songs entitled "Forever Young," which helped popularize a youth obsession that built on Frank Sinatra's "Young at Heart" and "You Make Me Feel So Young." This chapter explores the importance of health and sexuality of older people as a media issue.

NO SEX, MANY LIES, AND NOT MUCH VIDEOTAPE: AGING, HEALTH, SEX, AND THE MEDIA

Fascination with youth is, of course, not a new concept. It has resonated from Ponce de Leon's quest for the Fountain of Youth to Goethe's *Faust* to Oscar Wilde's *The Picture of Dorian Gray* (Dorian declares that he would give his soul if he were to stay young forever if instead the portrait would grow old). In James M. Barrie's *The Adventures of Peter Pan*, the character never wants to grow up. Michael Jackson named his ranch "Neverland" after Neverland in *Peter Pan*. Actually, Barrie's notes listed Peter as "a demon boy (villain of story)" (Miller, 2003, p. 35). Jackson's painful attempts to stay "young" have come to demonstrate why it is Peter and not Hook who is the villain of the story and why we should not necessarily try to tinker with our bells to stay young.

Being surrounded by phrases such as "forever young" and "young at heart," which both imply that young is automatically good and healthy and old is bad and sick, contributes to a self-loathing, self-fulfilling prophecy for many older adults. Even older people may discriminate against other older people, thus becoming their own worst enemies. Consider the aphorism: When the ax came into the woods, the trees said, "Don't worry, the handle is one of us."

AGEISM

Ageism, whether by older adults themselves, mass media, or the public at large, is unhealthy and unwise—it is the wood handle on the ax. Ageism is unhealthy because it encourages people to expect dementia, incontinence, and loss of libido in old age, and it is unwise because it discriminates against what most of us will be in the future.

Levy, Slade, Kunkel, and Kasl (2002) found "that older individuals with more positive self-perceptions of aging, measured up to 23 years earlier, lived 7.5 years longer than those with less positive self-perceptions of aging" (p. 261). This is a strong statement about why we need to stop the negative stereotypes related to growing older. The question is, how do we shed the stereotype that aging is unhealthy, unhappy, and unacceptable, especially when media are so often unfriendly to older adults?

Starr (1997), speaking to the American Society on Aging, concluded that commercial pressures promote the negative stereotype of older people:

> The simple fact is, ad agencies don't like old people. They don't like their looks, their interests, their needs, their preferences, and more important, they don't want to know who they are. . . . In a sense the relationship of the media and ad agencies to the elderly is like the fabled zipless sex act. "Give us your money and we'll give you our services—but no names and certainly no kissing—we don't really want to know who you are." (p. 3)

On September 4, 2002, at a Senate Special Committee on Aging entitled "Image of Aging in Media and Marketing," actress Doris Roberts (in her 70s) from the hit television program "Everybody Loves Raymond" testified to the following:

> Society considers me discard-able: my opinions irrelevant, my needs comical and my tastes not worth attention in the marketplace. My peers and I are portrayed as dependent, helpless, unproductive and demanding rather than deserving. In reality the majority of seniors are self-sufficient, middle-

BOX 8.1. Health Communication Theory

Public health communication campaigns are one important aspect of public communication campaigns. Atkin (2001) made the point that targeted health campaigns may be effective, but only to a limited degree: "Due to the wide variety of pitfalls, audience members are lost at each stage of message response" (p. 51). For example, it may be difficult to capture attention from people who are in denial that the message is for them. The degree to which people seek information on their health appears to have an effect on their willingness to absorb and process new information.

In the United States, public health campaigns in such areas as mammography has been successful by communicating to early adopters of the medical technique: "The rate of mammography for breast cancer detection has tripled over the past thirty years" (Rogers, 2003, p. 64). The diffusion of new ideas spreads among older people through mass and interpersonal communication channels.

Frey, Adelman, Flint, and Query (2000) examined how communication constructs symbolic collective meanings about health and community. Emotional and physical health may be related to health practices and perceived outcomes of treatments.

Health is a highly personal matter for people. The health communication literature, grounded in classic studies of persuasion and adoption, is cautious in its expectation of promoting dramatic change over a brief period of time. However, well-funded and long-term campaigns, such as those aimed at getting people to stop smoking, have demonstrated some slight decreases but not uniform effects among people young and old. People may or may not communicate with friends and family about health conditions, and mass media present conflicting messages.

Public campaigns may involve media advocacy, involving traditional political communication efforts to change policy through agenda setting and framing (Wallack & Dorfman, 2001). Aging baby boomers have experienced a lifetime of media messages advocating various health messages, and tune-out is a problem. Older Americans may be skeptical of dramatic social change. Likewise, in their personal lives, aging baby boomers may have experienced successes and failures at changing their behaviors. Public health communication campaigns, then, exist within this complex social context.

Sources: Atkin, C. K. (2001). Theory and principles of media health campaigns. In R. E. Rice & C. K. Atkin (Eds.), *Public communication campaigns* (3rd ed., pp. 49–68). Thousand Oaks, CA: Sage; Frey, L. R., Adelman, M. B., Flint, L. J., & Query, J. L. (2000). Weaving meanings together in an AIDS residence: Communicative practices, perceived health outcomes, and the symbolic construction of community. *Journal of Health Communication,* 5(1), 53-72; Rogers, E. M. (2003). *Diffusion of innovations* (5th ed.). New York: The Free Press; Wallack, L., & Dorfman, L. (2001). Putting policy into health communication. In R. E. Rice & C. K. Atkin (Eds.), *Public communication campaigns* (3rd ed., pp. 389–401). Thousand Oaks, CA: Sage.

class consumers with more assets than most young couples and substantial time and talent to offer society. This is not just a sad situation, Mr. Chairman. This is a crime. I'm here to urge you to address the devastation, cost and loss that we as a nation suffer because of age discrimination.

Age discrimination negates the value of wisdom and experience, robs us of our dignity and denies us the chance to continue to grow and to flourish. We all know that medical advances have changed the length and quality of life for us today. We have not, however, changed our attitudes about aging or addressed the disabling myths that disempower us. (Roberts, 2002)

The program "Everybody Loves Raymond" has addressed sexuality issues among Roberts' character and her on-screen husband, played by Peter Boyle, but it has also perpetuated the stereotypical, meddling mother-in-law. Of course, the writers of sitcoms generally write for humor, not education. The cheap laugh will almost always win the day at the expense of changing stereotypes. Writers believe that they are satisfying the marketers who pay the bills.

The AARP has launched a campaign saying, "These days, doctors don't pronounce you dead. Marketers do" (Ives, 2004, p. 8). This view is the opposite of that put forth by Alice Roosevelt Longworth, who said: "The secret of eternal youth is arrested development." Many of the ad executives and media moguls seem to be among those with arrested development. These executives cannot seem to break out of their infatuation with youth.

What if Madison Avenue catchphrases and slogans (e.g., "for those who think young," "age defying," and "rejuvenating") were replaced by wiser interpretations (e.g., "age is opportunity," Henry Wadsworth Longfellow; "How old would you be if you didn't know how old you was?," Satchel Paige; "The older you are, the freer you are," David Brower; or "to everything there is a season," Ecclesiastes)? For every positive image of older adults in the media, there are probably as least 10 negative images.

LEXICON

Even dictionaries weigh in on the ageism issue. The 11th edition of *Merriam-Webster's Collegiate Dictionary* reflects our aging society. John M. Morse, president and publisher of Merriam-Webster, said:

While new words in the dictionary reflect language changes over the last 10 years, the editors consider which words will have staying power and are likely to be encountered by future readers. . . . What's in the dictionary is important beyond just looking up words. It's a sign—or warning—for advertisers and even politicians who have to appeal to the public. Significant changes in society create significant changes in the lexicon. And a dictionary is telling us where change is taking place. (Brock, 2003, p. 9)

For example, Pfizer, the manufacturers of Viagra, created the term "erectile dysfunction" (ED) for the medical condition that used to be called impotence. The very word "Viagra" is now part of the American lexicon.

The popularization of Viagra and its recent pharmaceutical competitors and the marketing of products for ED makes many people believe that ED is inevitable. The same can be said for the advertising of adult diapers; it makes the general public think that incontinence is definitely going to happen. A simple analogy might help to illustrate how good health practices can change our expectations.

THE CHANGING FACE OF AGING

People once believed that losing most or all of their teeth was a natural consequence of aging. Through preventative dental care, flossing, brushing, and fluoride, we now know that most people will not lose their teeth as they age. It is important, therefore, to distinguish between aging, environment, and poor health behaviors.

Famous comedian George Burns went to the doctor when he was in his 90s to inquire about his bad right knee. His doctor said: "George you've got to expect things like this at your age." Burns responded by saying: "My left knee is the same age." The message is, of course, that we often attribute things to aging that are really due to something else.

Ken Dychtwald, president of Age Wave, accused the AARP of reinforcing the coupling of aging with illness. He said, "AARP is in an interesting paradox because they have built a lot of their character and political clout based on the proposition that older adults were frail and needed protection because they were powerless" (Ives, 2004, p. 8). Jim Fishman, group publisher at AARP Publications, disagreed: "Essentially what AARP is trying to do is help everyone who have very real needs, but there are also people who want to enjoy the benefits of their longer, healthier lives" (Ives, 2004, p. 8). Will America change as the baby boomers become older adults? According to Brock (2003):

What cannot be escaped is influence that the 70 million baby boomers will have on society. They have distorted everything as they have moved along. We're about to see the last, but greatest, example of this as they become old. If you thought they were troublesome as teenagers and obnoxious as young adults, you ain't seen nothing yet. They are going to demand a level of health care at least consistent with what their parents, a much smaller group, received. The boomers will force us to become more focused on health care for the elderly, and this is a good thing; the issue should have been raised years ago. "The dictionary is telling us that we are going to get educated in gerontology over the next decade or so, whether we want to or not." (p. 9)

John F. Zweig, CEO of WPP Group–USA, the parent company of media giants J. Walter Thompson, Ogilvey & Mather, and Young & Rubicam said that corporate advertising or marketing plans generally include at least a paragraph on the increasing importance of the mature market. "It's not lost on these people that this 25% of the population [55 or older] controls 70% of the purchasing power," Zweig said. "Yet, despite this there are countless examples of ageist or just plain stupid exclusions of this incredibly important market" (Kleyman, 2004).

The *Chicago Sun-Times* reported that the program director of Chicago's ABC-owned news/talk radio station instructed his staff to screen out "any old sounding callers," because the station's target market is the 25- to 54-year-old age group. The message was, "We do not want to air any callers who sound over 54." The rationale, apparently, is that these old-sounding folks will scare off the younger listeners that advertisers are trying to reach (Kelley, 2002).

RELUCTANT COVERAGE

Whereas some markets eschew older adults, other markets are beginning to recognize their importance, albeit, with an emphasis on health costs and disease:

> In major newspapers, hardly a day passes without a prominent piece on age related subjects. And the pace is quickening. But the skewed focus is more telling. Take away stories on Medicare and Social Security and what do you have left? In the next tier is mostly Alzheimer's, nursing home abuses, some elder abuse, and related issues of sick, helpless, and dependent older adults. Now let's be clear on what I am saying. These topics are certainly important, even vital to our economic and social survival into the 21st century, as the explosive growth of the elderly population plays itself out. But there is more, much more. (Starr, 1997)

MYTHS OF AGING

Rowe and Kahn (1999) wrote about the six myths of aging, many of which are perpetuated by the media. As you analyze the media, look for examples of these myths:

Myth 1: *To Be Old Is to Be Sick*. Aging is not a disease. The trend is for people to live longer, healthier.

Myth 2: *You Can't Teach an Old Dog New Tricks*. Older adults have many more years to remember, so it may take longer to retrieve some memories or to learn new skills, but older adults learn well. The vast number of older adults who are using computers is testimony to their ability to learn new skills.

Myth 3: *The Horse Is Out of the Barn*. Many people wrongly believe that you might as well continue long-practiced bad behaviors because the damage is already done. Smoking is one example. In reality, stopping smoking after many years can still produce positive health outcomes.

Myth 4: *The Secret to Successful Aging Is to Choose Your Parents Wisely*. Genetics are important, but health behavior and environment are just as important, if not more important, for good health and a long life.

Myth 5: *The Lights May Be On, But the Voltage Is Low*. Physical, mental, and sexual abilities can be maintained throughout the life cycle. A general rule of thumb, is, if you don't use it, you lose it.

Myth 6: *The Elderly Don't Pull Their Weight*. One problem with our society is that it too often measures worth by paid work and because many older adults are retired the assumption is that they are not doing anything. The fact is, almost a third of older adults work for pay; another third serve as volunteers in churches, hospitals, or charities; and countless others provide help and service to family members, friends, and neighbors. Research shows that the current older generation exhibits more social capital (i.e., joining organizations, volunteering, voting, etc.). Some researchers are concerned that the next generations will not be as involved in social capital to the detriment of society and their health. For example, over the last 25 years, attending club meetings is down 58%, being at family dinners is down 33%, and having friends over is down 45%. According to Putnam (2004), "Joining one group cuts in half your odds of dying next year." It is not just the content of watching television that can perpetuate aging stereotypes, but the hours that people spend watching television cuts back on the time people spend in activities that build social capital (p. 1).

BIASED TREATMENT

Ageism may be considered unpleasant but relatively innocuous. However, the frightening findings of the Alliance for Aging Research's "Ageism: How Healthcare Fails the Elderly" (2003) suggest the following:

- Health care professionals do not receive enough training in geriatrics to properly care for many older patients.
- Older patients are less likely than younger people to receive preventative care.
- Older patients are less likely to be tested or screened for diseases and other health problems.
- Proven medical interventions for older patients are often ignored, leading to inappropriate or incomplete treatment.
- Older people are consistently excluded from clinical trials, even though they are the largest users of approved drugs.

Given the discrimination against older adults in health care, there should be more attention given to truly important health topics. Headlines like the following should be reaching larger audiences, but are not:

- "Shortage of Geriatricians Compromising Care for Nation's Elderly"
- "Many Medical Journal Pharmaceutical Ads Misleading"
- "Physicians Often Give Patients Requested Drugs"
- "More Than 25% of Drug Errors Among Elderly Outpatients Preventable"
- "One Quarter of Outpatients Suffer Drug Side Effects"
- "Physician House Calls Reduce Costs, Improve Care for Medicare Patients"

HEALTHY PEOPLE 2010

Healthy People 2010: Leading Health Indicators, which is the health plan for the nation, calls attention to the following health needs, which apply to all ages. Listed next are the main categories of national concern with an example of a special concern for older adults.

- Physical Activity (extremely important throughout the life cycle)

Source: David E. Corbin. Staying fit at age 78, like this man, defies some of the stereotypes of the frail elderly.

- Overweight and Obesity (a growing problem in America)
- Tobacco Use (still a problem, but less of a problem among baby boomers than the current older generation)
- Substance Abuse (prescription drug abuse and misuse is a big problem among older adults)
- Responsible Sexual Behavior (although sexually transmitted diseases are much less common among older adults, the incidence in older adults is increasing)
- Mental Health (depression is a major concern among older adults)
- Injury and Violence (preventing falls is an important concern)
- Environmental Quality (older adults are more vulnerable to air and water pollution)
- Immunizations (it is very important for older adults to get their flu and pneumonia shots)
- Access to Health Care (national debates will continue relative to what Medicare can and should cover)

Older adults need to be made aware of these major health problems instead of dwelling predominately on the minority of older adults who will go into nursing homes or require adult diapers.

PERCEPTIONS OF AGING

Mass media have distorted the reality of growing older. Older people know what it is like to be younger and older. Younger people only know what it is like to be younger, so they do not have a perception of growing older. It rarely occurs to younger people that a large segment of the older population is happy with their present age. It is often shocking to younger people that a sizable percentage of older people do not envy youth. Dorothy Parker, that famous American wit, said: "Paradoxical as it may seem, to believe in youth is to look backward; to look forward we must believe in age."

Forty-four percent of Americans age 65 and older describe the present as the best years of their lives, according to a study conducted by the National Council on the Aging (NCOA). In addition and contrary to some persistent misperceptions about aging, 84% of all Americans say they would be happy to live to be 90 years old. *Time* magazine (Paul, 2003) reported that 79% of baby boomers "see no serious limits on activity until they are 70+." Fifty percent "plan to be active and going strong beyond 80" and 83% "expect treatment for the ills of aging to improve" (p. 78).

Morrie Schwartz (the subject of national bestseller *Tuesdays with Morrie*) and the artist Elizabeth Layton (who took up art at age 68) believed that there is another, less stereotypical, way to view aging. Schwartz did not lament growing old because: "If you've found meaning in life, you don't want to go back." In Layton's self-portrait, "Buttons: Her Strength Is in Her Principles," she depicts herself wearing a button that proclaims: "How dare you assume that I'd rather be younger." Walt Whitman, the great American poet, said: "Youth large, lusty loving—youth full of grace, force fascination. Do you know that Old Age may come after you with equal grace, force fascination?"

Unfortunately, it is the negative, not the positive, stereotypes of aging that persist. From a health standpoint, what is scary is that health care providers seem to mirror the general public's aversion to growing old. On May 19, 2003, there was a Senate Special Committee on Aging called, "Ageism in the Health Care System: Short Shrifting Seniors?" At that hearing, Dr. Robert Butler recommended that all physicians should be introduced to the field of geriatric medicine in medical schools to help dispel the myths among medical students toward aging. In addition, medical schools and drug companies should be encouraged to conduct more and better research among older adults.

AGING AND SEXUALITY

If our youth-oriented culture and media are squeamish about old people, then they are extremely squeamish when it comes to sexuality among older Americans. This topic is viewed like Mr. Cellophane in the musical "Chicago," that is, people look right through them—older adults are not even on younger people's radar screens. The fact is, about one half of Americans age 60 or older engage in sexual activity at least once a month, and 4 out of 10 respondents wish to have sex more frequently than they currently do (National Council on the Aging, 1998).

A good sexual relationship is viewed as important to quality of life for a majority of older adults, but the quality of interpersonal relationships is even more important (AARP, 2004a). I. B. Singer, Nobel Laureate, said: "Literature has neglected the old and their emotions. The novelists never told us that in love, as in other matters, the young are just beginners and that the art of loving matures with age and experience."

The release of the movies "Something's Gotta Give" and "Calendar Girls" have received considerable press coverage because they portrayed older adults who were not socially or sexually retired. Indeed, the AARP established the "Best Movies for Grownups Awards" and "Something's Gotta Give" was a winner of the Best Grownup Love Story in 2003 (Newcott & the Editors, 2004).

If sex among older people pushes younger people over the edge, then imagine what happens when they find out about older gays and lesbians who are sexually active. A search of the Internet revealed many dating services, bulletin boards, and chat rooms for older adults to find partners—both straight and gay.

Cafe Central	Online Dating Tips	Love Stories

Read dating tips, get advice and learn how to find a mate that's right for you.

The 12 Mistakes of Dating Again
Most men and women who re-enter the dating world are nervous and make mistakes. Here are the most common slip-ups.

Are You Involved in a Negative Attraction?
Beware these warning signs that you're attached to someone who is emotionally unreliable.

Let Your Body Do the Talking
Your gestures, expressions, eye contact and touch are sending a message. But what is it?

Get Back in the Mix!
- Pick a Nickname for Your Honey
- 11 Questions to Ask When Seeking a Mate
- Find Love on Vacation

Dating Again 101
- Eight First-Date Should's and Shouldn'ts
- Do You Have a Healthy Dating Attitude?
- 10 Ways to Increase Your Confidence

Ask the Expert
- How to Go From E-mail to Soul Mate
- Dating, Sex and Disability: What's Myth, What's Reality?
- What Are the New Rules of Dating?

Source: ThirdAge (2004). This is a sample web page relating to relationships, sexuality, and older adults. www.thirdage.com

ONLINE INFORMATION

Fortunately nonmainstream media are emerging to overcome ageism and to provide sound health information such as Aging and Health online, the many health-related pages and stories from AARP (AARP, 2004c), and ThirdAge online (ThirdAge, 2004). There are, however, many Internet sites that give questionable or downright dangerous health advice. Hence, the AARP has developed a web page to inform older adults about how to separate the good from the bad information (AARP, 2004b).

LIGHT AT THE END OF THE TUNNEL?

Some ads are beginning to show older adults in a more positive light. As Kelley (2002) pointed out, "My favorite ad is a print campaign for Eileen Fisher clothing. The slogan, 'Women change the world every day,' accompanies a portrait of women of varied ages, including a gray-haired woman with wrinkles. Each is beautiful, but not in a glamour-model way. Kind of makes you want go out and buy the clothes." If we want a healthier and less stereotypical old age, then we need to stop seeing age as the enemy and start taking better care of ourselves while demanding that the media grows up from their perpetual adolescence. Society can create a healthier society and demand that the media gives a more balanced view of aging, health, and sexuality. The baby boomers have generally gotten their way. But, will they demand a society that denies age or one that embraces successful aging?

CHAPTER SUMMARY

There is a link between media views on aging and health. People who view aging as positive are more likely to live longer than people who view aging negatively. In addition, ageism among health care professionals negatively affects the care that older adults receive. Mass media, whether through advertising, television, movies, music, or newspapers, help to perpetuate negative stereotypes of aging, and therefore perpetuate ill health. Nevertheless, people are living longer and better than ever before, and as the baby boomers move into old age they will probably put a new face on marketing, the media, and health in America.

REVIEW QUESTIONS

1. What evidence is there that positive attitudes toward growing older can influence health in later life?

2. What are two ways in which the media helps to perpetuate negative stereotypes of aging?

3. How would you counter the myth of aging that older people do not "pull their own weight"?

4. What evidence is there that older adults are interested in being sexually active?

5. What evidence is there that views toward health and aging are beginning to improve?

Chapter 9

Political Issues of Media and Gerontology

This chapter deals with the importance of political issues related to mass media and gerontology. According to the AARP (1998), "When they begin to retire in large numbers in 2008 (when the oldest boomers turn 62), they will create pressures on private and public retirement systems as they begin to withdraw from the labor force, and they may in the process redefine retirement" (p. iii). By 2030, all of the baby boomers will have reached age 65, and this will have political implications. For example, the sharp rise in the number of Alzheimer's disease cases will mean that, by 2050, more than 13 million Americans will suffer serious cognitive impairment (Hodes, 2004). Mass media coverage of the issue is projected to increase and the subsequent political response to the problem will impact the country.

THE POLITICS OF AGING

The demographic shift in the United States as baby boomers reach retirement age inevitably raises political issues. The distribution of scarce federal dollars means that fewer workers will be asked to pay for the increasing costs of Social Security, Medicare, and other health-related costs:

> A story about older Americans takes on a different perspective when it's looked at from the eyes of those who will have to pay for the Boomers—today's kids. There are fewer of them because the Boomers had fewer children. Time spent climbing the corporate ladder, along with high rates of di-

vorce, cut down the time to have that second or third baby. Lawrence Kotlikoff, the Jeremiah who worried about who was going to support future retirees, says some government economists predict if you add in Medicare, the coming shortage is even worse. (Associated Press, 2004, p. 4)

The aging trend will be seen throughout the industrial world, influencing economies inside and outside the United States:

Don't look around for evidence. You won't see it. We're in a quiet period. While the number of senior citizens rises each year, growth in the number of possible workers has been keeping pace since 1985. It will continue to keep up until the boomers start to retire in 2008, just one presidential election in the future. The bumper crop of boomers born in 1946 will be reaching the age at which most people start taking Social Security, 62, in 2008. (Kotlikoff & Burns, 2004, p. B6)

On political issues, such as Medicare and Social Security, it is likely that the coming conflicts between generations will be portrayed in media as complex and difficult to solve (Cohen, Adoni, & Bantz, 1990).

BOX 9.1. Assisted Suicide Media Coverage Promoted Ageism

Brogden (2001) contended, "Geronticide means the death of the elderly person as a consequence of the actions or inactions of others—by direct coercion, or by a mix of social, psychological and economic pressures" (p. 155). Media coverage of Dr. Jack Kevorkian's highly publicized assisted suicides during the 1980s and 1990s led to much public discussion on the issue.

Photo Source: CNN (November 8, 1995).

> **BOX 4.1.**   *(Continued)*
>
> Such coverage may have contributed to stereotypes and attitudes—negative and positive—about the elderly (Palmore, 1999). Brogden continued, "There is evident danger here that in that final act advantage may be taken against those elderly with least power, least access to economic resources, and least relevant knowledge. Ageism, in whatever form, has a continuing history in disposing of those on the socio-economic periphery" (pp. 180–181).
>
> Source: Brogden, M. (2001). *Geronticide: Killing the elderly.* London: Jessica Kingsley.

SOCIAL SECURITY

By 2030, nearly 70 million Americans will be age 65 and older. This is significant because the ratio of workers to retirees will have shrunk to two to one. There is debate among economists whether or not this change will plunge the country into crisis. Galbraith (2004) suggested that the Social Security shortfall should not be viewed as a crisis:

> As the baby boomers retire, the revenues we're banking on will fall short of benefits due. That's no crisis. It merely means that there will be, for a time, more old people and fewer young. The economy will simply have to adjust.
> . . . The solution is obvious. Raise taxes on the part of the population that can afford to pay—the wealthy. Transfer funds from the wealthy to the non-wealthy elderly. . . . When the baby boomers pass on, so will the need for these measures. In the meantime, it's only logical and ethical that those who can afford it keep the promises we've made. (p. 1)

However, any proposal to raise taxes on workers, wealthy or not, will be guaranteed to produce political squabbles and fairly intense media coverage. Some economists fear that the younger generation will not be able to afford paying for the costs of the aging baby boomers.

MEDICARE

The AARP, once called the American Association of Retired Persons, has used issues such as Medicare reform to appeal to aging baby boomers. Bill Novelli, AARP's executive director and CEO, has focused on how to help the United States prepare for demographic changes. AARP has promoted policies that would help maintain the financial viability of programs like Medicare. Novelli, a former advertising executive, told National Public Radio that he tried to strengthen AARP's political power by helping shape a prescription drug benefit for seniors: "It's really interesting. Younger members, let's say people 45 to 60, they are even more in favor of Medicare drug coverage than older people. And I think the reason is, that as boomers go into care-giving, as they care for their parents, they help to pay for their parents' drugs and as they see the future, they understand that we need drug coverage in Medicare" (Shapiro, 2003, p. 1). Novelli and AARP's support helped drive a bill through Congress (U.S. Newswire, 2003). Speaker of the House J. Dennis Hastert told a Washington press conference that Medicare, because of advancements in the pharmaceutical industry, faces new challenges that were not imagined at its inception in 1965. Lower percentages of funding now go to doctors and hospitals, and higher percentages pay for prescription drugs.

OTHER RETIREMENT WORRIES

There are a number of other concerns about aging baby boomers, and mass media are likely to be reporting these stories in the coming years. Krout and Coward (1998), for example, emphasized "commonly held myths or beliefs" held about aging in rural America (p. 5). The rural elderly are believed to retire to carefree small-town settings. Additionally, society assumes strong family support and high levels of health and satisfaction. Rural life is portrayed as lived in integrated communities with plentiful services. The assumption is a lower cost of living allows the elderly to get by on less money. Krout and Coward suggested that the elderly myths assume too much similarity among rural people.

In one sense, baby boomers may be thought of as the first generation of "free agents" as they face retirement (Russell, 1993, p. 175). Faced with delayed retirement, perhaps into their 70s or even later, boomers have not fully recognized the impact of a financially stretched national retirement system in a nation with too few workers. As Russell indicated, "Employers may not want boomers to retire early because there are too few people to replace them, since the generations that follow the baby boom are much smaller" (p. 177):

> The constructions of old age and the linkage to aging to crisis in the United States have promoted both politics and social policies that not only reflect but also reproduce and exacerbate preexisting social class, gender, and racial and ethnic disparities among the old. . . . A critical question for old age policy, indeed for domestic social policy, is who will pay and who will benefit? (Estes, 2001, p. 117)

In the larger political context, there is evidence that baby boomers face this domestic social policy challenge with a turn away from independence and, for some, toward political conservatism:

> Over most of the past thirty years, the baby boomers have been among the least politically active, at least in terms of voting in presidential elections, but in recent years this has changed. In 1968, less than 60 percent of eligible baby boomers reported having voted, which was among the lowest rates of turnout, whereas in 1992 more than 75 percent reported voting, among the highest turnouts. However, even if their relative contribution to public opinion and electoral politics increases, it may be a mistake to assume that their impact will be to move the country in a more "liberal" direction. With respect to party preferences, the baby boom cohorts have steadily increased their level of identification with the Republican party, from roughly 12 percent in the early 1970s to about 30 percent in 1994. This increase has been at the expense, not of their Democratic party affiliation (which has remained fairly constant), but of heavy declines in their self-identification as "independent." More than 55 percent of baby boomers identified themselves as "independent" in 1968, whereas in 1994, the figure was less than 40 percent. (Alwin, 1998, p. 52)

There is political interest in the issues of aging, but scholars suggest that affluent baby boomers may be more likely to focus on individual pocketbook issues rather than wholesale protests (e.g., the Gray Panthers in the 1970s; Williamson, 1998). The affluent aging baby boomers are those individuals that AARP had in mind as coverage of the 2000 elections began.

AARP CASE STUDY: ELECTION 2000

The 2000 U.S. presidential election was one of the closest in history (Kranish & Johnson, 2000). Additionally, throughout summer and fall 2000, poll data suggested a split electorate (Whitman, 2000). Issues of importance to older Americans—such as social security, prescription drugs, and taxes—were front and center in the national debate (Benedetto, 2000). This case study examined how AARP portrayed the candidates and issues through its two publications: *AARP Bulletin* and *Modern Maturity*. The presidential election cycle is viewed as an important time for public discussion to determine which social issues deserve to be at the top of the political agenda. Often, important issues do not receive adequate media attention in the periods between national elections. Therefore, during a presidential race, it is crucial to observe which social issues are given the most attention. In the case of AARP media, it should be valuable to know whether or not the most widely circulated publications to older people function as an alternative source of information.

AARP AND ITS PUBLICATIONS

AARP is an association that targets individuals age 50 and older, and focuses attention on issues of importance to older Americans. Its publications may be studied within a larger context of print media research and the field of gerontology. The study of mass media content that is targeted at older people requires a synthesis of disparate research because of the emerging nature of the communication gerontology field.

AARP describes itself as a nonpartisan association that promotes social welfare and education for older Americans. It was founded in 1958 and now has more than 30 million members:

> AARP membership is open to anyone age 50 or older, whether working or retired. Members receive *Modern Maturity*, a full-color bimonthly magazine that features health, consumer, and financial news and information, as well as entertainment and travel updates and a nationwide calendar of events. Members also receive the monthly *AARP Bulletin*, which offers late-breaking news and feature stories on a wide range of issues that affect midlife and older persons. (http://www.aarp.org)

Modern Maturity is the bimonthly flagship publication for AARP. Its circulation of 20.4 million is the largest of any magazine in the nation and reflects "the graying of America" (Vivian, 2001, p. 56). AARP mails *Modern Maturity* and *AARP Bulletin* to members, and they are archived on its Web site (www.aarp.org). AARP's huge membership offers a large *potential* readership base. The next closest magazines in terms of circulation are *Reader's Digest* (12.6 million), *TV Guide* (11.1 million), and *National Geographic* (8.5 million), which are publications that do not routinely focus on political issues. News magazines, such as *Time* (4.1 million) and *Newsweek* (3.1 million), reach broader but considerably smaller audiences than *Modern Maturity* (Vivian, 2001, p. 57).

RELEVANT PRINT MEDIA STUDIES

Research into magazines and their portrayal of aging adults is less common than studies about television (Gerbner, 1993; Hilt, 1997a). Print media studies traditionally fall into two categories—the readership habits of older adults and their depiction in cartoons and advertising.

Among top-rated general circulation magazines, *Reader's Digest*, *TV Guide*, *National Geographic*, and *Time* are popular among older readers (Robinson & Skill, 1995). One study found that almost 20% of older adults read general interest magazines (Durand et al., 1980). The affluent elderly read many more magazines than their less affluent counterparts (Burnett, 1991). Burnett found that affluent elderly male readers were more likely to read *Newsweek*, *Time*, and *U.S. News & World Report* for news and information. News magazines also target content toward affluent elderly females—an audience that falls under the "well-off, well-educated stratum of the population that the promotion departments of newspapers and magazines like to describe as the 'opinion-makers' " (Grossman & Kumar, 1981, p. 62).

Affluent older readers may have been likely to read *Time*, *Newsweek*, and *U.S. News & World Report* coverage of John Glenn's return to space in 1998, as reported in chapter 4. There were "few comments that could be considered ageist or demeaning to older adults" (Hilt, 2000, p. 167). On the whole, however, little attention has been paid to how older adults are portrayed in magazine articles. Pollack (1989) argued that mass media have done an incomplete job of educating themselves about social policy questions that affect the elderly, and too many editors see the problems of elderly people as too boring or depressing for regular coverage.

Numerous studies show that use of mass media increases during middle age through the retirement years (Dimmick et al., 1979). Thanks to health care improvements, the elderly are living longer and have more disposable income than ever before. One study found that 90% of people at retirement age or over said keeping up with the news is extremely important (Lieberman & McCray, 1994).

Williams and Nussbaum (2001) generalized from the research that there are three factors explaining the increased use of television by older people: an increase in leisure time available, an interest in news and public affairs, and the impact of age, gender, and income. However, these factors have the opposite effect on radio listening. Reading is a special case: "The reading of books and magazines remains a popular activity throughout life, with a sharp decline starting around 65 years of age if eyesight begins to fail. The reading habits of older adults are also different from the reading habits of younger adults" (p. 257). Among older adults, the most popular magazines appear to be *Reader's Digest*, *TV Guide*, and *Better Homes and Gardens*. Unlike the general circulation magazines, *Modern Maturity* has the luxury of being able to focus content on issues directly of interest to seniors.

Modern Maturity has been studied, but only in the context of its advertising. Baker and Goggin's (1994) content analysis of *Modern Maturity* advertisements revealed an emphasis on the natural effects of aging as decreasing sexual attractiveness and intimacy. No studies have been found of the magazine's news content or political coverage. This case study used the 2000 presidential election cycle and the first 100 days of the Bush administration as a context for examining issue and event coverage. The study used qualitative research in careful description of the coverage of elderly issues. The goal was to preserve the form and content of AARP publications and analyze their qualities (Lindlof, 1995). The description of the social reality created by AARP content was studied within the context of the 2000 presidential election. As such, this study was "exploratory" and "descriptive" (Marshall & Rossman, 1995, p. 39).

The case study examined two AARP publications, *Modern Maturity* magazine (bimonthly) and *AARP Bulletin* newspaper (monthly), from January 2000 through April 2001. This period covered the presidential primary election, the general election, the election aftermath, and the first 100 days of the George W. Bush administration. The focus was on coverage of candidates and national political issues of importance to older Americans—defined in this study as people age 50 and older receiving AARP publications. Specifically:

- Only stories focusing on the presidential candidates and issues were analyzed;
- Political coverage was defined as content that either dealt directly with the election or those specific issues associated with it;
- No attempt was made to distinguish between social and political issues about aging;
- Each article that covered political candidates, social or political issues were read in search of themes and patterns in topics and coverage; and
- By definition, issues covered within the two AARP publications were assumed to be issues to importance to the elderly.

Each edition of the two publications was analyzed within this framework. In some cases, a particular story might highlight the candidates and specific issues, including those issues of importance to people age 50 and older. In other cases, an article might focus on simply elderly issues or the candidates themselves.

AARP PUBLICATION CONTENT

Most of the AARP's focus on the 2000 election coverage was in the *AARP Bulletin* rather than the more feature-oriented *Modern Maturity*. The *AARP Bulletin*, because it was a monthly tabloid-appearance newspaper, was able to be more timely in developing coverage of candidates and issues.

AARP Bulletin

Between January 2000 and April 2001, the *AARP Bulletin* had extensive coverage of the campaign and its result (Table 9.1). An examination of cover story topics revealed that one fourth dealt with health and medicine. The remaining cover stories focused on the presidential campaign, the economy, and technology issues.

In a January 2000 article titled, "Big Issues Hostage to Election," prescription drug legislation, Medicare, and Social Security were described to seniors in a page 3 story as difficult issues likely to be avoided: "But with the 2000 presidential election nearing, observers think it's unlikely that lawmakers will make major headway on these and many other tough issues in what is likely to be a highly partisan Congress" (p. 3). Such reporting, especially for a publication targeting elderly people, appeared to tell older Americans that the election was placing them on the sidelines. In the same issue, Social Security was also addressed in an interview (p. 6) with a Brookings Institution economist. Finally, an editorial (p. 28) urged readers to get involved in the election.

In the February 2000 issue, the cover story (p. 1) was, "We Want You! Presidential Hopefuls Target Older Voters." This article focused on the leading candidates: John McCain, George W. Bush, Al Gore, and Bill Bradley. Typical of horse-race style coverage, AARP followed the major media model of "giving uniformly skimpy treatment to all candidates except for those designated as front-runners" (Graber, 1993, p. 273). A cartoon showed the four in a race—McCain on a skateboard, Bush in cowboy boots, Gore in roller-blades, and Bradley in high-top basketball shoes (carrying a ball). The article was titled, "Watch Out: They're After You! Older Voters Loom Big as 2000 Target" (p. 3). The article was meant to trivialize the election in terms of important senior issues. Readers were

TABLE 9.1
AARP Bulletin Cover Story Topics, January 2000–April 2001

Topic	Frequency
Health and medicine	4 (26.6%)
Presidential campaign	3 (20.0%)
Economy	3 (20.0%)
Technology, Internet, and privacy	3 (20.0%)
Other (lifestyle, scams)	2 (13.3%)
Total	15 (100%)

Note. The cover stories were counted utilizing dominant and manifest categories. The purpose was to provide a simple frame of reference for the qualitative analysis. See Krippendorff, K. (1980). *Content analysis: An introduction to its methodology.* Beverly Hills, CA: Sage.

told that whereas candidates were interested in their vote, the horserace was more important than their issues. In another article (p. 10), McCain was shown fielding questions at an AARP sponsored event in New Hampshire. The audience questions at the forum provided some focus on the need to control health care costs. Veteran broadcast journalist Daniel Schorr was profiled (p. 14) and lamented the influence of television on the campaign as focusing on personality and appearance. The issue also featured a "Where the Candidates Stand" (p. 29), listing the positions of Bush, McCain, Gore, and Bradley on Social Security, Medicare, long-term care, and managed-care patient protections. This feature came closest to describing issue positions by reporting direct quotes from the candidates on each major issue: Social Security, Medicare, long-term care, and managed-care patient protections. Clearly, these four items establish a senior agenda. *AARP Bulletin* also listed the candidates' Web sites.

In March, a story was titled, "In Iowa, Bradley Puts Focus on Health Care" (p. 12). The Democrat had spoken to an AARP gathering. He identified himself as the presidential candidate that would do the most about the health care problem. However, the story mentioned Bradley had lost both the Iowa caucuses and New Hampshire primary to Al Gore. On the next page, John McCain was featured in an article titled, " 'Earnings Test' Decried." McCain told more than 600 AARP members that he would push for a repeal of the earnings test for Social Security beneficiaries. An *AARP Bulletin* editorial in that issue agreed: "Time to end the earnings limit on Social Security" (p. 28). McCain surprised George W. Bush in New Hampshire, and was shown campaigning in South Carolina. The next month, the publication reported on a U.S. House vote (422–0) to repeal the Social Security limit. The story featured an interview with House Speaker Dennis Hastert.

The only campaign material in the April 2000 issue was an editorial titled, "Voters Need to Look Beyond Sound Bites" (p. 31). The editorial directed readers to the AARP Web site. The earnings test legislation was signed into law, and AARP reported on this in the May issue. In that same issue, there was just one campaign story: "Bush and Gore Joust Over Social Security" (p. 31). The article identified the likely major party nominees. Bush said, "I happen to think it's broke, and I think this country needs to elect somebody who will spend the [political] capital to fix it." Gore responded to the proposal to cut taxes by calling it a "risky tax scheme." Overall, AARP had left the primary season and politics behind for the time being. Instead of politics, AARP turned to other concerns such as telephone scams and hormone replacement therapy.

In June, two stories ("Gore Tells AARP Bush Plan Would Imperil SS" and "Bush Unveils Social Security Retirement Account Plans," p. 2) again focused on the Social Security issue, which was clearly judged as the important senior citizen issue by AARP. The stories featured color photographs of each: Gore speaking to 9,000 AARP members in Florida and Bush speaking to an unidentified number of voters in California. In the July–August issue, two more Social Security articles and an editorial were featured. In "Voters Face Clear Choice on Social Security Plans," a public policy expert noted that the 2000 campaign was unique in that voters had "a clear-cut choice" (pp. 6-7). In "Social Security Emerges as a Key Campaign Issue," AARP Executive Director Horace B. Deets wrote, "While AARP has not endorsed either candidate's position on Social Security, we have developed a set of principles" (p. 28):

- AARP supported protecting Social Security funds and using budget surpluses to extend solvency.
- AARP supported creation and expansion of Individual Retirement Accounts (IRAs) as an addition but not replacement for Social Security benefits.
- AARP opposed further raising of the retirement age for full benefits.
- AARP supported a continued contribution-based formula for benefits.

In an editorial, the *AARP Bulletin* urged voters to be informed and get out to vote for all races, not just the presidential contest. The AARP principles could be used by voters planning to judge candidates in the fall election, but it is not clear how they might do that given the limited media attention provided on Social Security.

For the first time since February, the campaign was the cover story in September. In the page 1 story, " 'A Lot Is at Stake,' Bush, Gore Collide Over Social Security's Future," the election was called "a referendum on the future direction of Social Security." The story continued on page 3: "Hot Debate on Social Security's Future." The publication showed two campaign-style signs representing the two positions. One read, "PERSONAL ACCOUNTS ARE RISKY BUSINESS" with the word "risky" in red letters. The other sign read, "IT'S OUR MONEY: LET US INVEST IT!" with the words "our" and "us" in red letters. The signs roughly reflected the Gore (risky) and Bush (invest) positions. The same article continued on page 25 with specifics about each plan and campaign Web site addresses. In another article, the *AARP Bulletin* listed a host of campaign, issue, and political party Web sites (pp. 3, 31). In another story, "Social Security Debate Raises Many Questions," the Bush and Gore plans were compared in terms of whether they would solve the long-term problem, how the rival plans affect average people, and how retirement accounts in each plan differ (pp. 24, 26). In the final election story in this issue, "AARP

Launches Voter Campaign," survey results were reported. The poll asked adults which issues were most important in choosing a president. Respondents said family values (27%), education (24%), Social Security (18%), prescription drugs/Medicare (10%), and tax cuts (9%) were most important (p. 29). It was interesting to note that a majority of AARP's own readers thought issues other than Social Security were most important in choosing a president. The other concerns listed reflected issues highlighted by mainstream national media covering the campaign— largely a candidate-driven agenda.

In October 2000, the presidential candidates were on the cover in an article titled " 'Where I Stand,' Presidential Contenders Speak Directly to *AARP Bulletin* Readers." There were two articles beginning on page 3 ("Gore, Bush Speak Out on Issues; Vice President Offers Details on Drug Proposal," and "GOP Nominee States Case for His Drug Plan"). The focus of both stories, continued on pages 10–11, was the Medicare prescription drug coverage. In addition to extensive quoting of both candidates, the publication used a box comparing each plan. In a separate story, the *AARP Bulletin* reported that issues affecting older Americans had become more important than in previous elections. At the same time, another story reported that Americans were not sure how to fix Social Security. In a page 20 column, AARP's Deets wrote that "for many American families, Election 2000 will be nothing less than a referendum on their economic futures" (p. 20). Whereas AARP clearly had a position on Social Security reform, the organization's coverage adopted an objective journalism tone—perhaps in fear of alienating Republican readers.

With Election Day approaching, the November issue featured two "What if . . ." articles on the future of the nation under Bush or Gore (pp. 3, 30–31). AARP forecasted that if Bush were elected, then the likely outcome would be retirement reform; if Gore were elected, then the likely outcome would be a prescription drug plan. A page 28 editorial again urged people to vote, however, AARP never endorsed a candidate in the 2000 election.

In December, with the election result in doubt because of the Florida recount, the AARP story was titled, "Americans Stay 'Cool' While They Wait, Eyes Are on Florida as Recount Proceeds" (pp. 3, 10). The article described the confusion with the so-called butterfly ballot, which led some voters to inadvertently vote for Reform Party candidate Pat Buchanan rather than Gore: "Because many of those complaining about the ballot were elderly, some critics singled out older voters for blame, charging they were the problem rather than the ballots" (p. 10). However, AARP Executive Director Horace B. Deets responded by saying that the issue affects voters of all ages, not just older people. Given the amount of national attention afforded the voter confusion story, it is clear that AARP's limited reporting on it gave readers the impression that it was time to move forward.

On page 10, the *AARP Bulletin* wrote, "Older voters make a difference." Among voters age 60 and older, 51% voted for Gore and 47% voted for Bush. The story added that older voters in Iowa and Wisconsin kept Gore in the race. In its page 20 editorial, the paper urged bipartisan cooperation, regardless of the result. AARP took a decidedly noncontroversial tone.

By January 2001, it was finally known that George W. Bush would be America's 43rd president. The page 3 story was entitled, "Bush Puts National Unity at the Top of His Agenda" (pp. 3, 12). Bush restated his interest in education, tax relief, and Social Security reform. The *AARP Bulletin* also interviewed political analyst David Gergen on page 24 about Bush's priorities. He said the prolonged election fight did not diminish the institution of the presidency, but he did not relate the outcome to its effect on older Americans.

With President Bush in office, the first 100 days of his administration received substantial attention. In February 2001, the page 1 cover story was about cutting taxes. The *AARP Bulletin* also discussed the privacy of medical records as an important issue on the political agenda. The Deets page 20 column that month urged responsible use of the budget surplus. By March, the focus on tax cuts continued: "Debate Over Tax Cut Plan Will Shape U.S. Agenda" (p. 4). The editorial addressed Bush's prescription drug plan, saying that there should be a bipartisan measure that would include coverage for all beneficiaries. Finally, in April 2001, the *AARP Bulletin* again focused on the Bush agenda: "Tax Cuts: What They Could Mean for You" (pp. 8–9). The story offered hypothetical tax cut figures. A box summarized the Bush plan.

Modern Maturity

Between January 2000 and April 2001, there was limited coverage of presidential politics in *Modern Maturity*. Not until the September–October issue of the magazine did the election surface, but it was not the cover story. There was a "Presidential Voters Guide." The Bush and Gore positions were given on Social Security, Medicare, long-term care, and managed care patient protections. AARP also targeted the guide to provide readers with the positions of U.S. Senate candidates in *their* states. The magazine issue also listed political Web sites.

In the November–December issue, the election was the cover story. A panel of writers and cartoonists offered open letters to the next president. For example, columnist Ellen Goodman wrote that the next president should "think family." She emphasized the needs of older people. A

"Talking Heads" cartoon feature quoted Ed Asner, Tom Brokaw, Lauren Hutton, and others. Mary Tyler Moore urged the next president to "bring scientific advances from the animal lab to the patient's bedside" (pp. 48–49). A final article contemplated what qualities the nation's first woman president would need to have. Overall, the election coverage in the magazine was feature oriented.

In the months following the disputed election, *Modern Maturity* never returned to the subject. The magazine, which already had begun to target baby boomers, was renamed *mm* beginning with the March–April 2001 issue. The name changed again with the March–April 2002 issue to *AARP Modern Maturity* to better reflect reader perceptions. During the period under study, the magazine featured entertainers such as Sean Connery, Paul McCartney, Paul Newman, Judge Judy, Steve and Cokie Roberts, Shirley MacLaine, and Clint Eastwood—all on the cover in 2000–2001.

PATTERNS AND THEMES

Overall, AARP had a consistent pattern of placing Election 2000 within the context of many other ongoing concerns of elderly people. Clearly, the election was defined in terms of its potential effect on Social Security, first and foremost, as well as Medicare and other policy issues. These issues overshadowed other campaign issues—foreign policy, education, and taxes. An observable pattern during the period under study was that the election was one among many important concerns for older Americans.

The language employed by AARP throughout the period under study fit a theme of the importance of seniors and their issues in society. The AARP agenda placed a fair amount of importance on, for example, Social Security. It did so with a tone suggesting that readers need to be realistic in their expectations for reform. The message seemed to be that their vote was important, but their voices may or may not be heard. Even as the controversial Florida recount occurred, the AARP message was to stay cool and move on. This fit a theme of conservative advocacy—one apparently utilized by AARP in its lobbying efforts. This pragmatism leads coverage to lean toward noncontroversial positions.

INTERPRETING AARP PUBLICATION CONTENT

The *AARP Bulletin* offered the only detailed coverage of the 2000 presidential election and its aftermath. *Modern Maturity*, on the other hand, was entertainment oriented and downplayed the election. The *AARP Bulletin* focused on health and medicine, the presidential campaign, the economy, technology, Internet and privacy, and other lifestyle issues. The *AARP Bulletin* featured much coverage of Social Security and prescription drug costs in its election reporting. By contrast, *Modern Maturity* appeared to avoid looking like a magazine targeted only at the elderly population. Most of the coverage during the period was focused on candidates and elderly issues—not broader social issues. Clearly, AARP did target messages to its 55-plus age group.

The AARP's focus on concerns of older people, along with a large circulation of its publications, means that the organization plays a potentially more important role than general mass media in coverage of select social issues (Pollack, 1989). AARP may fill gaps in media reporting on the problems of elderly people, seen by some as too boring or depressing for regular coverage. However, *Modern Maturity* failed to offer a serious alternative for political coverage. Although the lesser-known *AARP Bulletin* did a better job, it may receive less attention from readers. The impact of both publications has not been established in research on AARP. It is not known what effect, if any, the publication had on the election through influence on older readers.

It is known that AARP has had difficulty in attracting the attention of baby boomers, and the organization has made adjustments in its publications. *Modern Maturity* was changed to *mm* for the March–April 2001 issue as one way to deemphasize the word "maturity" for those age 55 and older. Additionally, for those age 50 to 55, AARP offered a publication called *My Generation* to hook younger readers (Nohlgren, 2001; O'Briant, 2001). One study suggested that boomers would not consider themselves old until age 70 (Hall & Tian, 2001). In response, *mm* was renamed *AARP The Magazine*, which began to focus on younger readers. *My Generation* was discontinued. Another new publication placed emphasis on Spanish language readers with *AARP Segunda Juventud*—by 2025 AARP estimated that the over-50 Hispanic population would reach 17 million (Kong, 2002).

It may be that AARP's lobbying role means that its publications serve that function as much or more than reader needs. A broader study might include the perceptions of policymakers on AARP coverage. Further, the nature of elderly issues needs to be studied in the broader mass media and compared to AARP positions. For example, although AARP said the election was a referendum on Social Security, during the honeymoon period that followed their publications accepted President Bush's top agenda item, cutting taxes, as the most important issue. However, in the February 2002 *AARP Bulletin*, there was a return to concern about Social Security. In a cover story Special Report, AARP said, "Americans learn the truth about privatization: 'There's no free lunch.' "

Agenda setting remained an important concept when studying publications during an election cycle. AARP's horserace-style coverage mirrored the mass media model, which lacked in-depth treatment of issues and candidates. The 2000 election year appeared to spawn discussion on Social Security and other issues important to older people. In the case of AARP, it is not clear that their publications served as an alternative source of information to mainstream media.

The 2000 presidential election served as the backdrop for this study. It would be valuable to also study AARP outside of the election context. Given the direction of AARP's *Modern Maturity* as an entertainment magazine, the *AARP Bulletin* is likely to be the publication focusing, in the future, on serious issues. Increasingly, AARP's Web site also may have the potential to be influential in formation of political orientations and public opinion. Regardless, it is clear that AARP and its constituency will be increasingly important in the years ahead as America grows older.

The social disengagement literature offers potential in this area. It could be argued that disengaged older Americans may be satisfied with a message from a group, such as AARP, that it is okay to be marginally involved in politics and political issues. The theme of conservative advocacy fits nicely within this frame. Communication between AARP and its readers, in this sense, is likely to reflect the context of an older population where some members are more active than others.

THE FUTURE OF BABY BOOMERS' ISSUES

As baby boomers age, there is concern about the potential impact of social disengagement on political activities. However, because boomers may not behave similarly to previous generations, some suggest that they will remain politically involved and engaged, for example:

> Alarm about declining citizen engagement and dwindling "social capital" in the country may be overstated, based on an in-depth survey of the experiences and attitudes of Philadelphia area residents. Most Philadelphians are active participants in the social and civic lives of their neighborhoods and communities. Many volunteer their time and give their money to charitable causes. Moreover, there is little indication of social isolationism. Residents of the Philadelphia area engage in a variety of informal social activities that are the basis of interpersonal support networks. Merely one in ten, mostly the poor and elderly, say they have virtually no one to whom to turn for personal support. (Kohut, 1997, p. 2)

Age, further, may influence trust and confidence in government, and this seems crucial to sustained civic involvement in community affairs:

Distrust of institutions is so pervasive that, in and of itself, it does not bear a particularly sharp relationship to civic engagement. The demographic factors that strongly correlate with interpersonal trust—race and education—also relate to confidence in institutions. Generational differences are also clearly evident. People under 50 years of age are less trusting than the pre-war generations, and of the post war generations, those under 30 are generally more cynical than Baby Boomers 30 to 49 years old. As with interpersonal trust, the survey found that whites are more trusting of many institutions than non-whites, and the well educated more than the less educated. (Kohut, 1997, p. 4)

For baby boomer-age Internet uses, there may be a relation between seeking public affairs information and their existing engagement in local civic activities (Jennings & Zeitner, 2003). Thus, baby boomers seeking activity in their later years may opt for alternative lifestyles, which would lead to expanding uses of mass media that fit nonlinear lifestyle patterns:

In addition to their desire to postpone old age, the boomers' propensity for personal growth and new lifestyle challenges will also render obsolete the traditional "linear life" paradigm—in which people migrate in lockstep first through education, then work, then leisure/retirement. In its place, a new "cyclic life" paradigm in which education, work and leisure are interspersed repeatedly throughout the life span is emerging. It will become normal for 50 year olds to go back to school and for 70 year olds to re-invent themselves through new careers. Phased retirements, part-time and flex-time work and "rehirements" will become common options for elder boomers who'll either need to or want to continue working. (Dychtwald, 1999, p. 6)

It may be that as baby boomers break the aging mold, their diverse activities and increasing levels of social engagement will challenge mass media stereotypes about the elderly. If so, traditional portrayals could be replaced or transformed into new social constructions of reality about older people—particularly as the wave of aging boomers transforms the social landscape of the nation (Gamson, Croteau, Hoynes, & Sasson, 1992).

CHAPTER SUMMARY

During the next quarter century, all of the baby boomers in the United States will have reached retirement age. This demographic shift will create political challenges as the nation struggles to pay for rising Social Security, Medicare, and health-related costs. Organizations, such as AARP, are predicted to have growing influence as they target aging boomers.

This generation, because of its nontraditional lifestyle patterns, may dramatically influence mass media portrayals of political issues.

REVIEW QUESTIONS

1. As baby boomers retire, how might this change politics in the United States?
2. How might this demographic shift affect you, your friends, and family?
3. How would you predict that mass media will cover stories about funding of Social Security, Medicare, and health care?
4. What examples can you think of today that might suggest media are already breaking from traditional stereotypes about the elderly?
5. Why is AARP an important player in the politics of aging?

Chapter 10

Aging Americans, Mass Media, and the Future

Mass media continue to be important in understanding perspectives about older people. The term *elderly* may conjure images of sick, decrepit, or easily bilked people because of the content of constant media coverage. However, baby boomers appear to be treated differently by mass media. Boomers are the subject of stories on newfound health and activity. At the same time, the American Society on Aging, the National Council on the Aging, and groups such as Civic Ventures (http://www.civicventures.org) are now focusing on aging baby boomers. Older boomers will need more options for activity and civic engagement, and this will alter programming at social, educational, and health-related facilities. This trend is bound to grow, as policymakers, media, and agendasetters themselves face their retirement years. The 77 million baby boomers born between 1946 and 1964 clearly have become the focus of aging discussions, media coverage, and social policy. Improvements in health care, longer life expectancies, and innovative use of new technologies all have combined to create new opportunities and challenges.

AARP is at the forefront of the coming age wave. Each year, as four million Americans turn 50, there is added reason to pay attention. As baby boomers become elderly, there will be increased interest in marketing to them: In 2003, "consumers over age 50 spent nearly $400 billion" (Ives, 2004, p. 8). The historic concern about protecting the elderly because they were viewed as "frail" and "powerless" may be problematic because aging baby boomers have been portrayed in media as strong rather than weak (p. 8). For example, the Experience Corps program has enlisted over 1,000 volunteers to tutor and mentor urban public schoolchildren. As older boomers remain active, and as media begin to cover their activities, we may expect a change in traditional notions about what it means to be old.

Conventional wisdom held that the natural aging process brought decline in physical "vigor" and financial resources, and that some (but not all) activities are affected: "Activities, such as reading, sitting and thinking, and gardening, as well as interaction with family and friends, do not decline with age; however, active participation in sports and strenuous activities and travel and participation in activities outside the home do" (Osgood, 1995, p. 545). The baby boom generation, however, appeared ready to push the physical limitations of age. At the same time, they come to their elder years with, in many cases, significant financial resources and a willingness to keep working. Even in retirement, boomers are likely to view leisure in new ways.

In Arizona, for example, *The Arizona Republic* reported on how traditional retirement communities such as Scottsdale are bracing for a new kind of retiree: "Unlike generations before, boomers can expect to be healthy and active participants in their communities during a retirement that will average 30 years" (Rau, 2004, p. 1). Boomers are viewed as different and more diverse than their parents, and this is said to produce new needs in a retirement community. Boomers will demand the latest technologies in their homes, and retirement activities will shift, according to predictions: "They grew up in an environment of hip music, earrings and tattoos" (p. 2). Beyond lifestyle differences, aging boomers are predicted to keep working—"not just for money and health benefits, but for the fulfillment they get from working" (Sergent, 2002, p. 1).

It is somewhat difficult to separate mass media coverage of trends affecting older Americans from actual social change. The optimism about aging baby boomers that is often seen in mass media is tempered by the reality of potential crises suggested by Dychtwald (1999):

1. By living longer, boomers will stress the social entitlement system. One possible solution is to delay retirement age.
2. Epidemics of chronic disease could be costly to society. More resources need to be targeted at research.
3. Caring for the elderly is a social and economic drain. Long-term insurance programs need to be restructured.
4. Boomers have had a tendency to avoid saving for old age. There is a need to increase awareness and change financial behavior.
5. Young may be pitted against the old. Society to need to take advantage of skills, value and wisdom of the aging boomers.

Media coverage of aging baby boomers, however, tends to be limited to simple themes. Complex social problems and solutions tend to be avoided as boring. Media are beginning to embrace the life-span perspective, which offers an alternative paradigm about aging that allows us to view some older people as using their education, income, health, experience, and time as tools for lifelong development, activity, and social engagement. Media portrayals about aging baby boomers, then, may be more positive than the stereotypical negative images of the elderly.

To some extent, what media say about the elderly or baby boomers is accepted as factual through the construction of social realities about life and death. Achenbaum (2001) explained, "The *media* is an important temporal force. Creative artists can use technology in ways that transport us 'back to the future' or transfix the poignancy of spiritual encounters in the faces of youth and age" (p. 10). Achenbaum saw media as affecting our notions of time, along with medicine and megadeath.

BOX 10.1. Going Out in Style
By James A. Thorson

A *Wall Street Journal* article recently leaked the secret to marketers that the baby boom generation spends lots of money. This no doubt came as a shock to those bent on selling chewing gum and cigarettes to teenagers. Consider, however, that the sale of just one yacht exceeds the expense of many lifetimes of chewing gum.

The fact is that old folks have dough, and the people who are *about* to be old are used to spending it.

It's a fact that cruise companies target AARP members. Steamship owners find that honeymooners and retirees (or, as they say, the newly wed and the nearly dead) pay the bills. Who, after all, is most likely to have money available after the house has been paid for and the kids have completed college? People with empty nests can at last spend their money on themselves. And the next generation of old people will know just how to spend it.

Baby boomers make up that demographically swollen group born between 1946 and 1964. One can trace this great lump of humanity as it crawls along the lifespan—gerontologists sometimes call it the "pig in the python," the large number of future elders. Beginning in 2010, the leading edge of the postwar baby boomers will start to become postwar senior citizens.

They will continue to be free spenders as this Golden Age market emerges. Current stereotypes of older people often characterize them as tight-fisted, or at as least frugal or thrifty. People who are now old were born or raised during the Great Depression. They learned to waste not and to want not, to clean up their plates, to save for a rainy day, and to not replace things until they are worn out.

BOX 10.1. *(Continued)*

All bets will be off when the throwaway generation gets old. These are people used to spending money on themselves. There's no reason to think that this will change as they become elders. They will continue to spend money hand over fist as they approach aging—and death.

Consider, in addition to everything else this generation represents, the fact that they are mortal. Actually, however, that does not mean that they'll stop spending.

It is a sad fact that even baby boomers will die. This despite all of the health food, the Botox treatments that make people's faces look like drum heads, the eyelid lifts, bosom enhancements, $200 jogging shoes, spa treatments, and truckloads of vitamin E.

What we will see as the baby boomers become old is a huge number of people confronting death, denying death, postponing death, looking to medicine to make them immortal, running headlong from reality. And, ultimately, accepting death. When your brothers and sisters start dying off, it is time to quit kidding yourself.

So, an unfortunate reality of the future is that the baby boom generation will represent a solid waste disposal problem.

The other day, I was watching the construction of a new mausoleum in a cemetery in our city that is overlooked by new high-rise condos. The irony occurred to me that the residents of the condos will, in a matter of not-too-many years, be moving from one filing cabinet to another, because the mausoleum compartment is the burial place of the future. If the land starts to run out, do not build out, build up. Cemeteries all over the country see their future expansion plans as piling sets of drawers one upon the other, and offering columbarium niches for those who have been cremated and thus reduced in size to fill a shoebox.

There is a buck to be made here.

I once asked an undertaker about people who do pre-need planning (buying their funeral ahead of time). I suspected that they were the ones anxious to have bare-bones ceremonies, simple affairs to save their relatives the expense of elaborate and expensive funerals. He said that, quite to the contrary, people who arrange their funerals ahead of time want control; they want to pick out the coffin, the music, and the headstone. They do not trust their tight-fisted heirs to do it right. They are afraid that the kids will try to get off on the cheap.

The baby boom generation represents as many as 77 million people. None of them is going to die for free. Figure that right now it is easy to spend $10 thousand on a funeral and burial. Simple math says that getting rid of the baby boomers could easily be more than a $700 *billion* proposition.

BOX 10.1. *(Continued)*

This could, as they say, represent some real money. And figure that inflation will make the average funeral much more costly. True, there is a trend for more and more people to look to cremation as a less expensive alternative. But not everyone is a cheapskate like me. Further, it is the creative undertaker who can turn a cremation into a profitable proposition. I know one who has three rent-a-caskets for viewing and ceremonies. They can charge for urns, tombstones, and vehicle rental for processions to the columbarium—it all mounts up.

So, there is no need to look at the disposal of the baby boom generation in negative terms. Let us think of it as a marketing opportunity.

Dr. Thorson is Jacob Isaacson Distinguished Professor and Chair of the Department of Gerontology, University of Nebraska at Omaha.

BOOMERS' LATER WORKING YEARS

Aging baby boomers, particularly those working in the youth-oriented media fields, continue to face problems with age discrimination. At age 57, for example, WBZ television reporter Paula Lyons was told by her news director that, despite 25 years of experience, the station was going in a "different direction" (Matchan, 2003, p. D1). Lyons told *The Boston Globe* that the decision was based on her age. "I thought age discrimination was supposed to be illegal," she said. "I'm amazed that the law hasn't properly responded to this. It's certainly not had the desired effect" (p. D1). In a more prominent case, National Public Radio found itself criticized in 2004 for reassigning long-time anchor Bob Edwards.

BOX 10.2. NPR Dumps Bob Edwards

Bob Edwards, host of National Public Radio's "Morning Edition" since the launch of the program in 1979, was ousted from the anchor seat in 2004. Edwards, 56 at the time, was named a senior correspondent.

Edwards told national media: "You have to figure it's going to happen someday and you get out before they do it, but I failed." The network said it was looking for "new ideas and perspectives." *The Washington Post* concluded that Edwards "has been told, more or less, that he is a dinosaur."

BOX 10.2. *(Continued)*

Source: National Public Radio (2004).

"My feeling is, you have people in the field and you have people here. . . . The childless and single would go out and cover wars, and the rest of us would be here at the microphone," Edwards told the *Post*. "But I guess that's not what they want anymore."

Linda Ellerbee, the wry and onetime network television news anchor, commented in the *Los Angeles Times* that the aging of the baby boomers should seen as different than previous generations. "Although nobody came right out and said so, it's clear that the new honchos at NPR believe the man whose voice has soothed millions of us into day after day of too much reality is, at 56, too old for the task." Ellerbee disagreed with the idea that networks must have younger news anchors in order to attract the advertiser-coveted younger audience.

Sources: CBS News (2004, March 23). NPR boots "Morning Edition" host. Retrieved from http://www.cbsnews.com/stories/2004/03/23/entertainment/main608265.shtml; Frey, J. (2004, April 29). Bob Edwards & the remains of the day. *The Washington Post*, p. C01; Ellerbee, L. (2004, March 26). All things weren't considered. *Los Angeles Times*, p. B, pt. 15.

TRENDS AND PREDICTIONS

Aging is a global issue. By 2000, there were 600 million people age 60 and over, and experts predict that this number will swell to 1.2 billion by 2025 and 2.0 billion by 2050 (World Health Organization, 2004). Among concerns are those related to communication disorders (hearing, language, speech, and voice deficits) related to the aging process (Van Vliet, 1995). Additionally, the older population faces communication issues related to changes in status, such as when one leaves the workforce and is perceived as losing power in relationships (Kastenbaum, 1995).

Nevertheless, mass media portrayal of baby boomer issues appears more optimistic and playful. Media around the country have identified a number of "trends" unique to baby boomers as they grow older:

- An interest in purchasing expensive mausoleums instead of typical grave sites
- A need for high-tech health care monitoring equipment to assist everyday living of older people
- A possibility that boomers will pay for medical advice in e-mails from their doctors
- An increasing level of concern about retirement and finances
- A desire by boomers for retirement homes may fuel the real estate market
- A tension between aging boomers and ongoing interest by media executives in younger viewers
- A desire for easier to see and use technology, such as video recorders, with larger buttons
- A use of the online interactive exercises designed to ward off memory loss

Another trend is a desire by older people to join the dating scene. Coupland (2000) studied dating advertisements for boomers over age 50. The study utilized dating advertisements to examine "age-identity negotiations" (p. 9):

> Older people's dating ads tend to express restrained, modest, and nonsexual relational goals. Their references to age often are mitigated. Appearance is given less emphasis and is represented less evaluatively than in texts written by younger advertisers. However, several instances stretch the boundaries of the dating ad genre. They find ways to comment on, and sometimes undermine, the ageist assumptions that restrict older people's relational and lifestyle ambitions. (p. 9)

Even before baby boomers reach retirement, some studies of senior citizens suggest that the conventional view of older people has given way to a world in which most elderly are engaged. In one Minnesota study, researcher Jan Hively found that three fourths of her subjects said they were healthy and active into their 80s: "I never expected that rate of good health. I expected that there would be many more who were receiving assistance from their kids than who were giving. Also, there was a high percentage, 39 percent, caring for sick and disabled. So this is a remarkably productive population" (National Public Radio, 2004, p. 1). Older people have begun to be redefined as an important resource rather than a liability. As people age, they are not just concerned about issues affecting the elderly. Instead, they have been found to have a wide range of social interests (Independent Television Commission, 2002).

Thompson's (1990) 5-point strategy to reach older consumers acknowledged the changing landscape by suggesting segmented messages toward a flexible age group of "joiners" (p. 29). At the same time, Schewe's (1991) 7-point approach to communicating with older people gave preference to print media and memory aids. As the boomers enter a new phase of life, they are likely to redefine issues, activities, and perceptions related to an aging population.

BOX 10.3. Aging Rockers Stress Hearing Loss Issue

The Hearing Education and Awareness for Rockers (H.E.A.R.) nonprofit organization was founded in 1988. The goal of the group is to raise awareness about the dangers of repeated exposure to high noise levels at, for example, rock concerts.

BOX 10.1. *(Continued)*

Rocker Pat Benatar in 2004 offered tips for baby boomers and others on how to detect, prevent, and treat hearing damage.

1. Look for warning signs of hearing loss:
   - Ringing in your ears
   - Sensitivity to loud noises
   - Difficulty distinguishing words and sounds, such as "flow" from "show"
   - Difficulty hearing others when there is background noise
   - People sound like they are mumbling or talking too quickly
   - You find yourself turning the TV volume louder than others
   - You hear the telephone better with one ear than the other
2. Take a proactive approach to managing your hearing health:
   - Wear earplugs to prevent hearing damage at rock concerts or clubs
   - Use noise-canceling headphones while mowing the lawn and using power tools around the house
   - Set volume limits with your family on car stereos, personal headphones, and home theater systems

Benatar, focusing on the rock 'n roll generation of boomers, said: "Our music defines us, but all those years of rockin' are beginning to take a toll." She has partnered with battery giant Energizer to tap the over-50 baby boomer market, which is likely to need hearing aids.

Sources: http://www.energizer.com; http://www.hearingloss.org; http://www.stltoday.com/business.

OTHER ISSUES

The 2000 U.S. Census found that 12.3% of American males and 15.2% of American females were age 50 or older. The Census Bureau projected those figures to rise to 16.6% of all American males and 19.5% of all American females by 2025. Increasing numbers, however, do not tell the entire story.

Older Americans, as well as aging baby boomers, are a diverse group. Studying those who are elderly (or will be some day) offers a unique focus, but it may produce overgeneralizations. It remains true that demographic variables (e.g., income, education, and social status) are important and cut across all generations and nations. Nevertheless, the aging baby boomers come to their later years at a unique time that offers new social and technological progress.

Aging baby boomers, even as they shift gears in later life, will continue to help redefine social and cultural assumptions about diversity on issues of gender, sexual orientation, race, and ethnicity, as well as advancements in health and medicine. Also, changes in sexual behavior and practices, use of pharmaceutical products, and use of innovative technologies should lead to an increasingly complex social landscape. This will present challenges for mass media, which report on society and typically go for simple themes and explanations. The decisions that media gatekeepers make about coverage of older people and their issues will influence public opinion.

SYNTHESIS OF THEORY AND RESEARCH

The ongoing impact of computer-mediated communication technologies, as well as other technologies that improve health care and make life easier, are bound to change media and interpersonal perceptions about what it means to be old. To the extent that baby boomers leave the workforce as experienced users of technology, they have the opportunity to harness it and make life better. As Mundorf and Brownell (1995) indicated, "Although familiarity, acceptance, and adoption of new communication technologies may not be as high among older as in younger adults, they will increase as older adults have a chance to learn more about the potential for these technologies to improve the quality of their lives" (p. 204). The importance of new technologies, such as robotics that assist older people, suggests there will be increased scholarly and industrial interest in why some people resist change and are categorized as "laggards" or "late adopters" of innovation:

> Laggards are the most localite of all adopter categories in their outlook. Many are near isolates in the social networks of their system. The point of reference for the laggard is the past. Decisions are often made in terms of what has been done previously, and these individuals interact primarily with others who also have relatively traditional values. . . . The laggard's precarious economic position forces the individual to be extremely cautious in adopting innovations. (Rogers, 2003, pp. 284–285)

Interestingly, age is not a consistent predictor of willingness to change. Rather, it appears that there may be a linkage between the degree of social disengagement of individuals and their suspicion about the value of new technologies. If baby boomers extend their time in the workforce and remain socially active, because of their increased levels of education and personal wealth, then they may be more likely to be enthusiastic about how technology, including media technology, can better their later years. The Internet is the best example of how baby boomers have increasingly shifted to interactive and engaging media, while demanding more from traditional media (radio, television, newspapers, and magazines). Older Americans, particularly those in the boomer group, increasingly rely on the Internet for news, health, and special interest information, and e-mail with family and friends (Pew Internet and American Life Project, 2001). Interactive media skills have sparked interest in new technologies, such as TiVo digital recorders and DVDs. These media technologies allow the boomer generation to actively select what they want, when they want it. At the same time, the oldest Americans, those who came before the baby boomers, are said to "remain entrenched in the offline world" (p. 6).

CHAPTER SUMMARY

There are 77 million American baby boomers born between 1946 and 1964, and this group will influence media coverage and social policy. The improvements in health care will extend life expectancies, and new technologies will create new opportunities and challenges. Baby boomers are predicted to seek a more active retirement lifestyle. At the same time, the number of elderly boomers will likely stress the social and economic systems, and media coverage of issues is likely to increase. Media portrayals of older people and their issues, however, often are too simplistic. Aging baby boomers, like previous generations, will ultimately face serious health issues and death, but they may tend to delay dealing with reality. In part, media coverage of baby boomers may reinforce boomers illusions about old age. Traditional negative stereotypes about the frail and powerless elderly may be replaced by positive stereotypes about active and influential baby boomers. In both cases, complex social reality is replaced by oversimplified media portrayals.

Mass media are likely to be addressing new definitions of work and retirement. Some boomers may want to retire early, whereas others may want to work well beyond traditional retirement ages. The government may need to extend further retirement age for purposes of Social Security and Medicare disbursements. Likewise, the relative lack of working age people and the need for health care workers may lead to social pressures on the elderly to remain in the workforce. It will be interesting to see if these changes affect traditional age discrimination problems, including those experienced by media professionals.

The issues related to aging baby boomers in the United States are similar to those in many other industrialized nations. The predicted worldwide population of 1.2 billion people over age 60 by 2025 and 2 billion by 2050 will produce significant challenges and opportunities for policymakers and media covering them. People around the globe will face similar questions and potential answers about how to redefine aging. Mass media will continue to play an influential role in reporting and interpreting events and issues, and assisting people in adapting to social change.

REVIEW QUESTIONS

1. What potential crises do gerontologists predict may impact aging baby boomers when they retire? Why will media coverage be important?
2. Why have critics accused media of offering simplistic stories about older people and their issues?
3. How might the audience perception of media coverage on aging baby boomers reinforce stereotypes about growing old?
4. What social conflicts might emerge as baby boomers reach retirement age?
5. How will new media technologies be a factor in combating social disengagement among aging baby boomers? Why are mass media important in encouraging adoption of innovative technologies and ideas?

References

AARP. (1998). *Boomers approaching midlife: How secure a future?* Public Policy Institute report. Washington, DC: AARP. Retrieved from http://research.aarp.org/econ/boomer_seg_toc.html

AARP. (2004a). *AARP/Modern Maturity sexuality survey*. Washington, DC: AARP. Retrieved from http://research.aarp.org/health/mmsexsurvey.html

AARP. (2004b). *Finding good health information online*. Washington, DC: AARP. Retrieved from http://www.aarp.org/health/Articles/a2003-03-17-wwwhealth.html

AARP. (2004c). *Health and wellness*. Retrieved from http://www.aarp.org/health

Achenbaum, W. A. (2001). The flow of spiritual time amid the tides of life. In S. H. McFadden & R. C. Atchley (Eds.), *Aging and the meaning of time* (pp. 3–19). New York: Springer.

Adams, W. C. (1978). Local public affairs content of TV news. *Journalism Quarterly, 55*(4), 690–695.

Adler, M. (2003, February 23). Women over the age of 65 still underrepresented on the Net. *Weekend Edition*, National Public Radio.

Adler, R. (1996, November 11). Stereotypes won't work with seniors anymore. *Advertising Age, 67*(46), 32–33.

Alan, J. (2003, November 12). What's the future of evening network news? *Shoptalk*. Retrieved from http://www.tvspy.com.

Alch, M. L. (2000). Get ready for the Net generation. *Training & Development, 54*(2), 32–34.

Alliance for Aging Research. (2003). *Ageism: How healthcare fails the elderly*. Washington, DC: Alliance for Aging Research. Retrieved from http://www.agingresearch.org/brochures/ageism/index.cfm

Alwin, D. F. (1998). The political impact of the baby boom: Are there persistent generational differences in political beliefs and behavior? *Generations, 22*(1), 46–53.

Anderson, D. R., & Burns, J. (1991). Paying attention to television. In J. Bryant & D. Zillmann (Eds.), *Responding to the screen* (pp. 3–25). Hillsdale, NJ: Lawrence Erlbaum Associates.

Aronoff, C. (1974). Old age in prime time. *Journal of Communication, 24*(4), 86–87.

Associated Press. (2001, September 10). Once urged, senior citizens surf the Web with gusto.

Associated Press. (2003, July 1). Granny celebrates 80th birthday by skydiving.

Associated Press. (2004, March 21). Cloudy future for retirees.

Atchley, R. C. (1991). *Social forces and aging*. Belmont, CA: Wadsworth.

Atkin, C. K. (1976). Mass media and the aging. In H. J. Oyer & E. J. Oyer (Eds.), *Aging and communication* (pp. 99–119). Baltimore, MD: University Park Press.

Atkin, C. K. (2001). Theory and principles of media health campaigns. In R. E. Rice & C. K. Atkin (Eds.), *Public communication campaigns* (3rd ed., pp. 49–68). Thousand Oaks, CA: Sage.

Atkins, T. V., Jenkins, M. C., & Perkins, M. H. (1990–1991). Portrayal of persons in television commercials age 50 and older. *Psychology: A Journal of Human Behavior, 27–28*(1), 30–37.

Auerback, D., & Levenson, R., Jr. (1977). Second impressions: Attitude changes in college students toward the elderly. *The Gerontologist, 17*(4), 362–366.

Babbie, E. R. (1992). *The practice of social research* (6th ed.). Belmont, CA: Wadsworth.

Bagshaw, M., & Adams, M. (1985–1986). Nursing home nurses' attitudes, empathy, and ideologic orientation. *International Journal of Aging and Human Development, 22*(3), 235–246.

Baker, J. A., & Goggin, N. L. (1994). Portrayals of older adults in *Modern Maturity* advertisements. *Educational Gerontology, 20*(2), 139–145.

Barak, G. (Ed.). (1994). *Media, process, and the social construction of crime*. New York: Garland.

Barnes, S. B. (2001). *Online connections: Internet interpersonal relationships*. Cresskill, NJ: Hampton Press.

Barnes, S. B. (2003). *Computer-mediated communication: Human-to-human communication across the Internet*. Boston: Allyn & Bacon.

Barrow, G. M. (1996). *Aging, the individual, and society* (6th ed.). St. Paul, MN: West.

Barton, R. L. (1977). Soap operas provide meaningful communication for the elderly. *Feedback, 19*, 5–8.

Barton, R. L. (1977). Soap operas provide meaningful communication for the elderly. *Feedback, 19*, 5–8.

Barton, R. L., & Schreiber, E. S. (1978). Media and aging: A critical review of an expanding field of communication research. *Central States Speech Journal, 29*(3), 173–186.

Bell, D. (2001). *An introduction to cybercultures*. London: Routledge.

Bell, J. (1992). In search of a discourse on aging: The elderly on television. *The Gerontologist, 32*(3), 305–311.

Benedetto, R. (2000). Bush, Gore target seniors, focus on taxes, Social Security. *USA Today*, p. 1A.

Berger, P. L., & Luckmann, T. (1967). *The social construction of reality, A treatise in the sociology of knowledge*. Garden City, NY: Anchor Books.

Berkowitz, D., & Adams, D. (1990). Information subsidy and agenda-building in local television news. *Journalism Quarterly, 67*(4), 723–731.

Bishop, J. M., & Krause, D. R. (1984). Depictions of aging and old age on Saturday morning television. *The Gerontologist, 24*(1), 91–94.

Bliese, N. W. (1986). Media in the rocking chair: Media uses and functions among the elderly. In G. Gumpert & R. Cathcart (Eds.), *Inter/media, interpersonal communication in a media world* (3rd ed., pp. 573–582). New York: Oxford University Press.

Bogart, L. (1980). Television news as entertainment. In P. H. Tannenbaum (Ed.), *The entertainment functions of television* (pp. 209–249). Hillsdale, NJ: Lawrence Erlbaum Associates.

Bone, P. F. (1991). Identifying mature segments. *Journal of Services Marketing, 5*(1), 47–49.

Botwinick, J. (1984). *Aging and behavior*. New York: Springer.

Bower, R. T. (1973). *Television and the public*. New York: Holt, Rinehart & Winston.

Bower, R. T. (1985). *The changing television audience in America*. New York: Columbia University Press.

Bramlett-Soloman, S., & Wilson, V. (1989). Images of the elderly in *Life* and *Ebony*, 1978–87. *Journalism Quarterly, 66*(1), 185–188.

Broadcasting. (1987, March 30). pp. 163-164.

Broadcasting & Cable Market Place. (1997). New Providence, NJ: Bowker.

Brock, F. (2003, November, 9). Assisted living to Viagra: A dictionary nod to aging. *The New York Times*, p. 9.

Brogden, M. (2001). *Geronticide: Killing the elderly*. London: Jessica Kingsley.

Brown, A. S. (1996). *The social processes of aging and old age* (2nd ed.). Upper Saddle River, NJ: Prentice-Hall.

Browne, H. (2000, April 19). Accessibility and usability of information technology by the elderly. Retrieved from http://www.otal.umd.edu/UUGuide/hbrowne/

Burgoon, J. K., Burgoon, M., & Buller, D. B. (1986). Newspaper image: Dimensions and relation to demographics, satisfaction. *Journalism Quarterly, 63*(4), 771–781.

Burnett, J. J. (1991). Examining the media habits of the affluent elderly. *Journal of Advertising Research, 31*(5), 33–41.

Burnett, R., & Marshall, P. D. (2003). *Web theory: An introduction*. London: Routledge.

Burns, G. (1996). Popular music, television, and generational identity. *Journal of Popular Culture, 30*(3), 129–142.

Butler, R. (1969). Ageism: Another form of bigotry. *The Gerontologist, 9*(4), 243–246.

Butler, R. (1995). Ageism. In G. Maddox (Ed.), *The encyclopedia of aging* (2nd ed., pp. 35–36). New York: Springer.

Butler, R. N. (2003, May 19). *Ageism in the health care system: Short shrifting seniors?* U.S. Senate Special Committee on Aging. Retrieved from http://aging.senate.gov/index.cfm

Cable News Network. (1993, November 12). *Love, sex and romance after 50—part 1*.

Campbell, R. (2000). *Media and culture: An introduction to mass communication* (2nd ed.). Boston: Bedford/St. Martin's.

Campbell, R. J., & Wabb, J. (2003). The elderly and the Internet: A case study. *Internet Journal of Health, 3*(1), 2–18.

Cardona, M. M. (2000, September 11). SunAmerica banks on boomer crowd. *Advertising Age, 71*, 69.

Carey, J. W. (1992). *Communication as culture: Essays on media and society*. New York: Routledge.

Carmichael, C. W. (1976). Communication and gerontology: Interfacing disciplines. *Journal of the Western Speech Communication Association, 40*(2), 121–129.

Carmichael, C. W., Botan, C. H., & Hawkins, R. (1988). *Human communication and the aging process*. Prospect Heights, IL: Waveland Press.

Carrigan, M., & Szmigin, I. (2000, January). Advertising and older consumers: Image and ageism. *Business Ethics: A European Review, 9*, 42–50.

Cassata, M. B. (1985). *Television looks at aging*. New York: Television Information Office.

Cassata, M. B., Anderson, P. A., & Skill, T. D. (1980). The older adult in daytime serial drama. *Journal of Communication, 30*(1), 48–49.

Cassata, M. B., Anderson, P. A., & Skill, T. D. (1983). Images of old age on daytime. In M. B. Cassata & T. D. Skill (Eds.), *Life on daytime television: Tuning-in American serial drama* (pp. 37–44). Norwood, NJ: Ablex.

Cassata, M. B., & Irwin, B. (1989). Going for the gold: Prime time's sexy seniors. *Media & Values, 45*(1), 12–14.

Chaffee, S. H., & Wilson, D. G. (1975, August). *Adult life cycle changes in mass media use*. Paper presented to the Association for Education in Journalism, Ottawa, Canada.

Chamie, J. (2003). *World population prospects: The 2002 Revision*. New York: United Nations. Retrieved from http://www.un.org/esa/population/publications/wpp2002/

Chandler, J., Rachel, J., & Kazelskis, R. (1986). Attitudes of long-term care nursing personnel toward the elderly. *The Gerontologist, 26*(5), 551–555.

Chen, Y., & Persson, A. (2002). Internet use among young and older adults: Relation to psychological well-being. *Educational Gerontology, 28*(9), 731–744.

Chura, H. (2002, February 11). Draft codger. *Advertising Age, 73,* 4–5.

Clements, M. (1993, December 12). What we say about aging. *Parade,* pp. 4–5.

Clydesdale, T. T. (1997). Family behaviors among early U.S. baby boomers: Exploring the effects of religion and income change, 1965–1982. *Social Forces, 76*(2), 605–635.

Cody, M. J., & Dunn, D. (1999). Silver surfers: Training and evaluating Internet use among older adult learners. *Communication Education, 48*(4), 269–289.

Cohen, A. A., Adoni, H., & Bantz, C. R. (1990). *Social conflict and television news.* Newbury Park, CA: Sage.

Cohen, H. L. (2002). Developing media literacy skills to challenge television's portrayal of older women. *Educational Gerontology, 28*(7), 599–620.

Cole, J. I. (2003). *The UCLA Internet report: Surveying the digital future, year three.* Los Angeles: UCLA Center for Communication Policy. Retrieved from http://www.ccpa.ucla.edu

Collins, S. (2003, May 22). Networks may face ratings reality, Generation gap surfaces between young, older viewers. *Hollywood Reporter.* Retrieved from http://www.hollywoodreporter.com

Comstock, G. A., Chaffee, S., Katzman, N., McCombs, M., & Roberts, D. (1978). *Television and human behavior.* New York: Columbia University Press.

Coulson, D. C., & Macdonald, S. (1992). Television journalists' perceptions of group ownership and their stations' local news coverage. In S. Lacy, A. B. Sohn, & R. H. Giles (Eds.), *Readings in media management* (pp. 21-33). Columbia, SC: Association for Education in Journalism and Mass Communication.

Coulson, I. (2000). Introduction: Technological challenges for gerontologists in the 21st century. *Educational Gerontology, 26*(4), 307–315.

Coupland, J. (2000). Past the "perfect kind of age"? Styling selves and relationships in over–50s dating advertisements. *Journal of Communication, 50*(3), 9–30.

Cumming, E., & Henry, W. E. (1961). *Growing old: The process of disengagement.* New York: Basic Books.

Dail, P. W. (1988). Prime-time television portrayals of older adults in the context of family life. *The Gerontologist, 28*(5), 700–706.

Danowski, J. (1975, November). *Informational aging: Interpersonal and mass communication patterns at a retirement community.* Paper presented to the Gerontological Society, Louisville, KY.

Davis, R. H. (1971). Television and the older adult. *Journal of Broadcasting, 15*(2), 153–159.

Davis, R. H., & Davis, J. A. (1985). *TV's image of the elderly.* Lexington, MA: Heath.

Davis, R. H., & Edwards, A. E. (1975). *Television: A therapeutic tool for the aged.* Los Angeles: University of Southern California.

Davis, R. H., Edwards, A. E., Bartel, D. J., & Martin, D. (1976). Assessing television viewing behavior of older adults. *Journal of Broadcasting, 20*(1), 69–88.

Davis, R. H., & Kubey, R. W. (1982). Growing old on television and with television. In D. Pearl, L. Bouthilet, & J. Lazar (Eds.), *Television and behavior: Ten years of scientific progress and implications for the eighties: Vol. 2. Technical reviews* (pp. 201–208). Rockville, MD: National Institute of Mental Health.

Davis, R. H., & Westbrook, G. J. (1985). Television in the lives of the elderly: Attitudes and opinions. *Journal of Broadcasting & Electronic Media, 29*(2), 209–214.

De Moraes, L. (2003, October 1). CBS leaves rivals in the dust in premiere week. *The Washington Post,* p. C7.

DeFleur, M. L., & Dennis, E. E. (1996). *Understanding mass communication.* Boston: Houghton Mifflin.

DeGraves, D. J., & Denesiuk, R. J. (2000). The seniors computer information program: A pioneer website for seniors. *Educational Gerontology, 26*(4), 345–355.

Dillman, D. A. (1979). *Mail and telephone surveys: The total design method.* New York: Wiley.

Dillon, J. (2003). The world wide web and life contentment issues among older Internet users. *Journal of American and Comparative Cultures, 25*(4), 290–297.

Dimmick, J. W., McCain, T. A., & Bolton, W. T. (1979). Media use and the life span. *American Behavioral Scientist, 23*(1), 7–31.

Dobrow, L. (2004, March 9). Young male viewers watching less TV, older men watching more. *Media Daily News.* Retrieved from http://www.mediapost.com

Dominick, J. R., Wurtzel, A., & Lometti, G. (1975). Television journalism vs. show business: A content analysis of eyewitness news. *Journalism Quarterly, 52*(2), 213–218.

Doolittle, J. C. (1979). News media use by older adults. *Journalism Quarterly, 56*(2), 311–317, 345.

Dorsey, T. (2003, December 15). Dwindling viewership threatens nightly news. *Louisville Courier-Journal.* Retrieved from http://www.courier-journal.com/

Downing, M. (1974). Heroine of the daytime serial. *Journal of Communication, 24*(2), 130–137.

Doyle, D. P. (1997). Aging and crime. In K. F. Ferraro (Ed.), *Gerontology, perspectives and issues* (2nd ed., pp. 341–359). New York: Springer.

du Gay, P., Evans, J., & Redman, P. (Eds.). (2000). *Identity: A reader.* London: Sage.

Durand, R. M., Klemmack, D. L., Roff, L. L., & Taylor, J. L. (1980). Communication with the elderly: Reach of television and magazines. *Psychological Reports, 46*(3), 1235–1242.

Dychtwald, K. (1999, November 8). In support of testimony given to the Senate Committee on Aging. Retrieved from http://aging.senate.gov/oas/hr42kd.htm

Dychtwald, K. (2003a, April 1). Niche experts: In his own words. *American Demographics.* Retrieved from http://www.AmericanDemographics.com

Dychtwald, K. (2003b, July). The Age Wave is coming. *P.M. Public Management, 85*(6), 6–12.

Dychtwald, K., & Flower, J. (1989). *Age wave: The challenges and opportunities of an aging America.* Los Angeles: Jeremy P. Tarcher.

Ebenkamp, B. (2002, October 7). When they're 64. *Brandweek, 43,* 22–25.

Elasmar, M., Hasegawa, K., & Brain, M. (1999). The portrayal of women in U.S. prime time television. *Journal of Broadcasting & Electronic Media, 43*(1), 20–34.

Elliott, J. (1984). The daytime television drama portrayal of older adults. *The Gerontologist, 24*(6), 628–633.

Endres, K. L. (2004). "Help-wanted female": *Editor & Publisher* frames a civil rights issue. *Journalism & Mass Communication Quarterly, 81*(1), 7–21.

Epstein, E. J. (1973). *News from nowhere.* New York: Random House.

Estes, C. L. (2001). *Social policy & aging: A critical perspective.* Thousand Oaks, CA: Sage.

Fang, I. (1985). *Television news, radio news* (4th ed.). St. Paul, MN: Rada Press.

Fattah, E. A., & Sacco, V. F. (1989). *Crime and victimization of the elderly.* New York: Springer-Verlag.

Ferguson, D. A., & Perse, E. M. (2000). The World Wide Web as a functional alternative to television. *Journal of Broadcasting & Electronic Media, 44*(2), 155–174.

Fisher, D. H. (1977). *Growing old in America.* New York: Oxford University Press.

Folkerts, J., & Lacy, S. (2001). *The media in your life: An introduction to mass communication* (2nd ed.). Needham Heights, MA: Allyn & Bacon.

Francher, J. S. (1973). "It's the Pepsi generation. . . ." Accelerated aging and the television commercial. *International Journal of Aging and Human Development, 4*(3), 245–255.

Freedman, D. H. (1995, November). Life in the virtual lane. *Inc., 17*(17), 136.

Frey, L. R., Adelman, M. B., Flint, L. J., & Query, J. L. (2000). Weaving meanings together in an AIDS residence: Communicative practices, perceived health outcomes, and the symbolic construction of community. *Journal of Health Communication, 5*(1), 53–72.

Friedan, B. (1993). *The fountain of age.* New York: Simon & Schuster.

Galbraith, J. (2004, March 23). Settle baby boomer Social Security crisis by taxing the wealthy. *Minnesota Public Radio.* Retrieved from http://mpr.org

Gamson, W. A., Croteau, D., Hoynes, W., & Sasson, T. (1992). Media images and the social construction of reality. *Annual Review of Sociology, 18,* 373–393.

Gans, H. J. (1968). *The uses of television and their educational implications.* New York: Center for Urban Education.

Gans, H. J. (1979). *Deciding what's news: A study of CBS Evening News, NBC Nightly News, Newsweek, and* Time. New York: Vintage.

Gantz, W., Gartenberg, H. M., & Rainbow, C. K. (1980). Approaching invisibility: The portrayal of the elderly in magazine advertisements. *Journal of Communication, 30*(1), 56–60.

Gardiner, S. (2001, February 26). New ad campaigns celebrate aging. *Marketing Magazine, 106*(8), 2.

George, R. A. (1997). Stuck in the shadows with you: Observations on post-Boomer culture. In R. D. Thau & J. S. Heflin (Eds.), *Generations apart, Xers vs boomers vs the elderly* (pp. 24–30). Amherst, NY: Prometheus.

Gerber, J., Wolff, J., Klores, W., & Brown, G. (1989). *Lifetrends: The future of baby boomers and other aging Americans.* New York: Stonesong Press.

Gerbner, G. (1969). Toward "cultural indicators": The analysis of mass mediated public message systems. In G. Gerbner (Ed.), *The analysis of communication content* (pp. 123–132). New York: Wiley.

Gerbner, G. (1990). Epilogue: Advancing on the path of righteousness (maybe). In N. Signorielli & M. Morgan (Eds.), *Cultivation analysis* (pp. 249–262). Newbury Park, CA: Sage.

Gerbner, G. (1993). *Women and minorities on television.* Research report. Philadelphia: University of Pennsylvania.

Gerbner, G., Gross, L., Signorielli, N., & Morgan, M. (1980). Aging with television: Images on television drama and conceptions of social reality. *Journal of Communication, 30*(1), 37–57.

Gill, B. (1998). *The portrayal of older adults in consumer magazines.* Unpublished thesis, University of Nebraska at Omaha.

Girion, L. (2000, November 12). Older writers press case. *Los Angeles Times.* Retrieved from http://www.writerscase.com/pdf/OlderTVWritersPressCase1112.doc

Gitlin, T. (1980). *The whole world is watching: Media in the making and unmaking of the new left.* Berkeley: University of California Press.

Glick, I. O., & Levy, S. J. (1962). *Living with television.* Chicago: Aldine.

Goedkoop, R. J. (1988). *Inside local television news.* Salem, WI: Sheffield.

Goodman, R. I. (1990). Television news viewing by older adults. *Journalism Quarterly, 67*(1), 137–141.

Graber, D. A. (1993, 1997). *Mass media and American politics* (4th, 5th eds.). Washington, DC: CQ Press.

Graber, D. A. (2001). *Processing politics: Learning from television in the Internet age.* Chicago: University of Chicago Press.

Grajczyk, A., & Zollner, O. (1998). How older people watch television. *Gerontology, 44,* 176–181.

Graney, M. J. (1975). Communication uses and the social activity constant. *Communication Research, 2*(4), 347–366.

Graney, M. J., & Graney, E. E. (1974). Communication activity substitutions in aging. *Journal of Communication, 24*(4), 88–96.

Greco, A. J. (1988). Representation of the elderly in advertising: Crisis or Inc. *Journal of Services Marketing, 2*(3), 27–35.

Greenberg, B. S., Korzenny, F., & Atkin, C. K. (1979). The portrayal of the aging. *Research on Aging, 1*(3), 319–334.

Gregg, A. R. (2003, August 11). Aging is as aging does. *Maclean's, 116*, 44–45.

Grey Advertising, Inc. (1988). The who and how-to of the nifty 50-plus market. *Grey matter alert*. New York: Grey Advertising.

Grossberg, L., Wartella, E., & Whitney, D. C. (1998). *Media making: Mass media in a popular culture*. Thousand Oaks, CA: Sage.

Grossman, M. B., & Kumar, M. J. (1981). *Portraying the president—the White House and the news media*. Baltimore, MD: Johns Hopkins University Press.

Hagevik, S. (1999, May). From Ozzie and Harriet to the Simpsons: Generations and workplace. *Journal of Environmental Health, 61*(9), 39.

Hall, C., & Tian, Q. (2001, April 18). Old for boomers isn't until the 70s. *USA Today*, p. 6D.

Hall, L. (1998, September 28). Panel mulls news' impact on kids. *Electronic Media*, p. 48.

Hansen, C. J., Stevens, L. C., & Coast, J. R. (2001). Duration and mood state: How much is enough to feel better? *Health Psychology, 20*, 267–275.

Harmon, M. D. (1989, August). *Featured persons in local television news*. Paper presented to the Association for Education in Journalism and Mass Communication, Washington, DC.

Hartman, J. K. (1987). *USA Today* and young-adult readers: Can a new-style newspaper win them back? *Newspaper Research Journal, 8*(2), 1–14.

Harwood, J. (2000). Communication media use in the grandparent–grandchild relationship. *Journal of Communication, 50*(4), 56–75.

Harwood, J., & Anderson, K. (2002). The presence and portrayal of social groups on prime-time television. *Communication Reports, 15*(2), 81–97.

Head, S. W., Sterling, C. H., & Schofield, L. B. (1994). *Broadcasting in America: A survey of electronic media* (7th ed.). Boston: Houghton Mifflin.

Hellbusch, J. S., Corbin, D. E., Thorson, J. A., & Stacy, R. D. (1994). Physicians' attitudes toward aging. *Gerontology & Geriatrics Education, 15*(2), 55–66.

Herzbrun, D. J. (1991, August 5). Broad market segmentation tricky when appealing to older consumer. *Advertising Age, 62*(32), 15–16.

Hess, B. B. (1974). Stereotypes of the aged. *Journal of Communication, 24*(4), 76–85.

Hiemstra, R., Goodman, M., Middlemiss, M. A., Vosco, R., & Ziegler, N. (1983). How older persons are portrayed in television advertising: Implications for educators. *Educational Gerontology, 9*(2–3), 111–122.

Hilt, M. L. (1992). Television news and elderly persons. *Psychological Reports, 71*(1), 123–126.

Hilt, M. L. (1997a). *Television news and the elderly*. New York: Garland.

Hilt, M. L. (1997b). The Kogan attitudes toward old people scale: Is it time for a revision? *Psychological Reports, 80*(3), 1372–1374.

Hilt, M. L. (2000). Descriptive analysis of news magazines' coverage of John Glenn's return to space. *Educational Gerontology, 26*(2), 161–168.

Hilt, M. L., & Lipschultz, J. H. (1996). Broadcast news and elderly people: Attitudes of local television managers. *Educational Gerontology, 22*(7), 669–682.

Hilt, M. L., & Lipschultz, J. H. (1999). Revising the Kogan scale: A test of local television news producers' attitudes toward older adults. *Educational Gerontology, 25*(2), 143–153.

Hindman, D. B. (2000). The rural–urban digital divide. *Journalism & Mass Communication Quarterly, 77*(3), 549–560.

Hine, C. (2000). *Virtual ethnography*. London: Sage.

Hodes, R. J. (2004, March 23). Alzheimer disease research. Testimony before the Committee on Senate Appropriations Subcommittee on Labor, HHS, Education. Washington, DC: Federal Document Clearing House.

Holladay, S. J. (2002). "Have fun while you can," "you're only as old as you feel," and "don't ever get old!": An examination of memorable messages about aging. *Journal of Communication, 52*(4), 681–697.

Holson, L. M. (2004, January 18). And the winner is . . . the older woman. *The New York Times,* Sec. 4, p. 12.

Horton, D., & Wohl, R. R. (1986). Mass communication and para-social interaction: Observation on intimacy at a distance. In G. Gumpert & R. Cathcart (Eds.), *Inter/media, interpersonal communication in a media world* (3rd ed., pp. 185–206). New York: Oxford University Press.

Howe, N., & Strauss, B. (2000). *Millennials rising: The next great generation.* New York: Vintage Books.

Howe, N., & Strauss, B. (2003, April 1). Demographic diamonds: In their own words. *American Demographics.* Retrieved from http://www.inside.com/product/product.asp

Hummert, M. L., Garstka, T. A., Bonnesen, J. L., & Strahm, S. (1993, November). *Attitude, age and typicality judgments of stereotypes of the elderly.* Paper presented to the 46th scientific meeting of the Gerontological Society, New Orleans, LA.

Humphreys, J. (2003, April 1). Demographic diamonds: In their own words. *American Demographics.* Retrieved from http://www.inside.com/product/product.asp

Ibelema, M., & Powell, L. (2001). Cable television news viewed as most credible. *Newspaper Research Journal, 22*(1), 41–51.

Independent Television Commission. (2002). *The numbers game: Older people and the media.* London: Help the Aged.

Ives, N. (2004, January 12). AARP aims to show marketers what they are missing in overlooking the consumer over 50. *The New York Times,* p. 8.

Iyengar, S., & Kinder, D. R. (1987). *News that matters.* Chicago: University of Chicago Press.

Jacobs, J. (1990). *Changing channels.* Mountain View, CA: Mayfield.

Jennings, M. K., & Zeitner, V. (2003). Internet use and civic engagement: A longitudinal analysis. *Public Opinion Quarterly, 67*(3), 311–334.

Jesdanun, A. (2001, September 9). Study says seniors enthusiastic online. *Associated Press.* Retrieved from http://wire.ap.org

Johnson, P. (2002, December 11). News channels losing battle for young viewers. *USA Today,* p. 3D.

Johnson, P. (2003, August 11). At "60 Minutes," clock ticking on change. *USA Today,* p. 3D.

Jones, S. G. (1997). *Virtual culture, identity and communication in cybersociety.* London: Sage.

Jordan, R. (2003). Age 50+ demographic not a homogenous group; income figures drop dramatically after age 55. Houston, TX: International Demographics. Retrieved from http://www.theMediaAudit.com

Kahai, S. S., & Cooper, R. B. (2003). Exploring the core concepts of media richness theory: The impact of cue multiplicity and feedback immediacy on decision quality. *Journal of Management Information Systems, 20*(1), 263–299.

Kaniss, P. (1991). *Making local news.* Chicago: University of Chicago Press.

Karsch, U., & Karsch, C. (1999). Migration and urbanization in Brazil: Implications for work and elder care. In V. M. Lechner & M. B. Neal (Eds.), *Work and caring for the elderly: International perspectives* (pp. 143–159). Ann Arbor, MI: Taylor & Francis.

Kastenbaum, R. (1995). Communication: Processes and issues. In G. Maddox (Ed.), *The encyclopedia of aging* (2nd ed., pp. 200–203). New York: Springer.

Katz, F. (2001, September 10). Grandma gets wired to e-mail children; family drives seniors' use of Net. *The Atlanta Constitution,* p. 3D.

Kelley, P. (2002, December 3). Ageism's stereotypes getting old. *The Charlotte Observer*. Retrieved from http://www.media-diversity.org/

Kellner, D. M., & Durham, M. G. (2001). Adventures in media and cultural studies: Introducing the keyworks. In M. G. Durham & D. M. Kellner (Eds.), *Media and cultural studies, Keyworks* (pp. 1–38). Malden, MA: Blackwell.

Kelly, C. (2000, July 10). Active lifestyle central to targeting. *Advertising Age, 71*, 8.

Kent, K. E., & Rush, R. R. (1976). How communication behavior of older persons affects their public affairs knowledge. *Journalism Quarterly, 53*(1), 40–56.

Kent, K. E. M., & Shaw, P. (1980). Age in *Time*: A study of stereotyping. *The Gerontologist, 20*(5), 598–601.

Klein, R. D. (2003). Audience reactions to local TV news. *American Behavioral Scientist, 46*(12), 1661–1672.

Kleyman, P. (2004). *Media ageism: The link between newsrooms and advertising suites.* San Francisco, CA: American Society on Aging. Retrieved from http://www.asaging.org/at/at–218/Media.html

Kogan, N. (1961). Attitudes toward old people: The development of a scale and examination of correlates. *Journal of Abnormal and Social Psychology, 62*(1), 44–54.

Kogan, R. (1992, August 14). Networks not following focus on older Americans. *Omaha World-Herald*, p. 45.

Kohut, A. (1997, April 18). Trust and citizen engagement in metropolitan Philadelphia: A case study. *Pew Research Center for the People and the Press*. Retrieved from http://people-press.org/reports/

Kong, D. (2002, February 10). AARP has seen the future, and it is Hispanic. *St. Louis Post-Dispatch*, p. A12.

Kornreich, M. (1991, July 22). Spotlight, the 50 plus market: A generation of caregivers. *Adweek's Marketing Week, 32*(30), 18.

Korzenny, F., & Neuendorf, K. (1980). Television viewing and self-concept of the elderly. *Journal of Communication, 30*(1), 71–80.

Kotarba, J. A. (2002). Rock 'n' roll music as a timepiece. *Symbolic Interaction, 25*(3), 397–504.

Kotlikoff, L. J., & Burns, S. (2004, March 19). The perfect demographic storm: Entitlements imperil America's future. *Chronicle of Higher Education, 50*(28), B6.

Kranish, M., & Johnson, G. (2000, November 8). Late-night drama battle in key states makes Gore–Bush race too close to call. *Boston Globe*, p. A1.

Kremer, J. F. (1988). Effects of negative information about aging on attitudes. *Educational Gerontology, 14*(1), 69–80.

Krout, J. A., & Coward, R. T. (1998). Aging in rural environments. In R. T. Coward & J. A. Krout (Eds.), *Aging in rural settings: Life circumstances & distinctive features* (pp. 3–14). New York: Springer.

Kubeck, J. E., Miller-Albrecht, S. A., & Murphy, M. D. (1999). Finding information on the world wide web: Exploring older adults' exploration. *Educational Gerontology, 25*(2), 167–183.

Kubey, R. W. (1981). Television and aging: Past, present, and future. *The Gerontologist, 20*(1), 16–35.

Lang, A. (Ed.). (1994). *Measuring psychological responses to media messages*. Hillsdale, NJ: Lawrence Erlbaum Associates.

Lang, G. E., & Lang, K. (1984). *Politics and television re-viewed*. Beverly Hills, CA: Sage.

Langreth, R. (2000, October 16). Hard sell. *Forbes, 166*, 56.

Levine, G. F. (1986). Learned helplessness in local TV news. *Journalism Quarterly, 63*(1), 12–18, 23.

Levinson, R. (1973). From Olive Oyl to Sweet Polly Purebred: Sex role stereotypes and televised cartoon. *Journal of Popular Culture, 9*(3), 561-572.

Levy, B. R., Slade, M. D., Kunkel, S. R., & Kasl, S. V. (2002). Longevity increased by positive self-perceptions of aging. *Journal of Personality and Social Psychology, 83*(2), 261–270.

Lewis, H. G. (1996, March). Another look at the senior market. *Direct Marketing, 58*(11), 20–25.

Lieberman, S., & McCray, J. (1994, April). Coming of age in the newsroom. *Quill, 82*(3), 33–34.

Lin, C. A. (1993). Adolescent viewing and gratifications in a new media environment. *Mass Comm Review, 20*(1–2), 39–50.

Lindlof, T. R. (1995). *Qualitative communication research methods.* Thousand Oaks, CA: Sage.

Lipschultz, J. H. (1994, March). *Craft v. Metromedia, Inc.* and its social-legal progeny. *Communications and the Law, 16*(1), 45–74.

Lipschultz, J. H., & Hilt, M. L. (1993). First amendment vs. business orientations of broadcast general managers and news directors. *Journalism Quarterly, 70*(3), 518–527.

Lipschultz, J. H., & Hilt, M. L. (2002). *Crime and local television news: Dramatic, breaking, and live from the scene.* Mahwah, NJ: Lawrence Erlbaum Associates.

Lopez, D. (2003, June 28). She'll take the flying leap. *The Californian.* Retrieved from http://www.californianonline.com/news/

Louis Harris and Associates, Inc. (1975). *The myth and reality of aging in America.* Washington, DC: National Council on Aging.

Louis Harris and Associates, Inc. (1981). *Aging in the eighties: America in transition.* Washington, DC: National Council on Aging.

Lowenthal, M. F., & Boler, D. (1965). Voluntary vs. involuntary social withdrawal. *Journal of Gerontology, 20*(3), 363–371.

Lull, J., & Hinerman, S. (Eds.). (1997). *Media scandals: Morality and desire in the popular culture marketplace.* New York: Columbia University Press.

Lumpkin, J. R., & Festervand, T. R. (1988). Purchase of information sources of the elderly. *Journal of Advertising Research, 27*(8), 31–51.

Lunsford, D. A., & Burnett, M. S. (1992). Marketing product innovations to the elderly: Understanding barriers to adoption. *Journal of Consumer Marketing, 9*(4), 53.

Mares, M. L., & Cantor, J. (1992). Elderly viewers' responses to televised portrayals of old age. *Communication Research, 19*(4), 459–578.

Markson, E., Pratt, F., & Taylor, S. (1989). Teaching gerontology to the business community: Project older consumer. *Educational Gerontology, 15*(3), 285–295.

Marshall, C., & Rossman, G. B. (1995). *Designing qualitative research* (2nd ed.). Thousand Oaks, CA: Sage.

Mason, A. (2002, November 29). Advertisers targeting baby boomers this holiday season. *CBS Evening News.* Lexis-Nexis.

Matchan, L. (2003, December 31). The problem of their age older workers are fighting back against employers who favor youth. *The Boston Globe,* p. D1.

Maynard, N. (2001, January 24). Current trends in evening news. *The Newshour With Jim Lehrer.* Retrieved from http://www.pbs.org/newshour/

McManus, J. H. (1994). *Market-driven journalism.* Thousand Oaks, CA: Sage.

McQuail, D. (1985). Gratifications research and media theory: Many models or one? In K. E. Rosengren, L. A. Wenner, & P. Palmgreen (Eds.), *Media gratifications research* (pp. 149–167). Beverly Hills, CA: Sage.

Media Audit. (2002). New research shows some local TV gain web audience; newspapers still dominate. International Demographics, Inc.

Media Literacy. (2003). Center for Media Literacy. Retrieved from http://www.medialit.org/reading_room/article37.html

Miller, C. (1991, December 9). Misconception, fear stall advance into mature market. *Marketing News, 25*(25), 11–14.

Miller, D., & Slater, D. (2000). *The Internet: An ethnographic approach.* Oxford, England: Berg.

Miller, D. A. (2001). Measuring the effectiveness of your Intranet. *Public Relations Strategists, 8*(3), 35–39.

Miller, L. (2003, December 14). The lost boy. *The New York Times Book Review,* p. 35.

Mills, D. Q. (1987). *Not like our parents: How the baby boom generation is changing America.* New York: William Morrow.

Morgan, M., & Signorielli, N. (1990). Cultivation analysis: Conceptualization and methodology. In N. Signorielli & M. Morgan (Eds.), *Cultivation analysis* (pp. 13–34). Newbury Park, CA: Sage.

Morrell, R. (2000). A survey of World Wide Web use in middle-aged and older adults. *Human Factors, 42*(2), 175–183.

Moss, M. S., & Lawton, M. P. (1982). Time budgets of older people: A window on lifestyles. *Journal of Gerontology, 37*(1), 115–123.

Mundorf, N., & Brownell, W. (1995). Communication technologies and older adults. In G. Maddox (Ed.), *The encyclopedia of aging* (2nd ed., pp. 203–204). New York: Springer.

Murphy-Russell, S., Die, A. H., & Walker, J. L., Jr. (1986). Changing attitudes toward the elderly: The impact of three methods of attitude change. *Educational Gerontology, 12*(3), 241–251.

Namazi, K. H., & McClintic, M. (2003). Computer use among elderly persons in long-term care facilities. *Educational Geronotology, 29*(6), 535–550.

National Council on the Aging. (1998). Half of older Americans report they are sexually active; 4 in 10 want more sex, says new survey. Retrieved from http://www.ncoa.org/content.cfm

National Public Radio. (2004, March 25). Trend of people continuing to work past traditional retirement age.

Newcott, W. R., & The Editors. (2004). *Movies for grownups 2003.* Retrieved from http://www.aarpmagazine.org/entertainment/movies/

Newspaper Association of America. (2003, 2004). http://www.naa.org

Nielsen estimates: National audience demographics report from November 1974. *Nielsen '75.* Chicago: A.C. Nielsen.

Nohlgren, S. (2001, February 8). For mature audiences only? Hardly. *St. Petersburg Times,* p. 1D.

Northcott, H. (1975). Too young, too old—age in the world of television. *The Gerontologist, 15*(2), 184–186.

Norton, J. M. (2001, July 30). Highway one touts SeniorsSurfers. *Adweek, 51*(31), 6.

Nuessel, F., & Van Stewart, A. (2000). "Prime time": The integration of the content of a weekly newspaper column on aging into the gerontology curriculum. *Educational Gerontology, 26*(7), 639–650.

Nussbaum, J. F., & Coupland, J. (1995). *Handbook of communication and aging research.* Hillsdale, NJ: Lawrence Erlbaum Associates.

Nussbaum, J. F., Pecchioni, L. L., Robinson, J. D., & Thompson, T. L. (2000). Mass media use and aging. In *Communication and aging* (2nd ed., pp. 64–84). Mahwah, NJ: Lawrence Erlbaum Associates.

Nussbaum, J. F., Thompson, T., & Robinson, J. D. (1989). *Communication and aging.* New York: Harper & Row.

O'Briant, D. (2001, February 6). AARP talking about My Generation. *Atlanta Journal and Constitution,* p. 3C.

O'Connell, V. (1998, August 5). Alcohol maker's new target: Drinkers over 50. *Wall Street Journal,* p. B1.

Ogles, R. M., & Sparks, G. G. (1989). Television violence and viewers' perceptions of criminal victimization. *Mass Comm Review, 16*(3), 2–11.

Omaha World-Herald. (2003, October 2). CBS still rates No. 1 with older crowd, p. 8-E.

Omaha World-Herald. (2003, October 4). Good, bad news for Americans: You're living longer but also larger, p. 1-A.

Osgood, N. J. (1995). Leisure. In G. Maddox (Ed.), *The encyclopedia of aging* (2nd ed., pp. 544–546). New York: Springer.

Owen, A. S. (2002). Memory, war and American identity: *Saving Private Ryan* as cinematic jeremiad. *Critical Studies in Media Communication, 19*(3), 249–282.

Paddon, A. R. (1995). Papers target older readers with special features. *Newspaper Research Journal, 16*(3), 52–63.

Palmgreen, P., Wenner, L. A., & Rayburn, J. D., II. (1980). Relations between gratifications sought and obtained: A study of television news. *Communication Research, 7*(2), 161–192.

Palmgreen, P., Wenner, L. A., & Rosengren, K. E. (1985). Uses and gratifications research: The past ten years. In K. E. Rosengren, L. A. Wenner, & P. Palmgreen (Eds.), *Media gratifications research: Current perspectives* (pp. 11–37). Beverly Hills: Sage.

Palmore, E. B. (1999). *Ageism, negative and positive* (2nd ed.). New York: Springer.

Papacharissi, Z., & Rubin, A. M. (2000). Predictors of Internet use. *Journal of Broadcasting & Electronic Media, 44*(2), 175–196.

Parks, M. R., & Floyd, K. (1996). Making friends in cyberspace. *Journal of Communication, 46*(1), 81–96.

Passel, J. (2003, April 1). Demographic diamonds: In their own words. *American Demographics.* Retrieved from http://www.inside.com/product/product.asp

Passuth, P. M., & Bengston, V. L. (1988). Sociological theories of aging: Current perspectives and future directions. In J. E. Birren & V. L. Bengston (Eds.), *Emergent theories of aging* (pp. 333–355). New York: Springer.

Paul, P. (2003, March). Targeting boomers: The demographics of media consumption. *American Demographics, 25*(2), 24–26.

Paul, P. (2003, September 15). Sell it to the psyche. *Time,* p. 78.

Pavlik, J. V. (1996). *New media technology: Cultural and commercial perspectives.* Boston: Allyn & Bacon.

Peale, B., & Harmon, M. (1991, August). *Television news consultants: Exploration of their effect on content.* Paper presented to the Association for Education in Journalism and Mass Communication, Boston, MA.

Pepper, J. (2002). Wired and retired: Assisted living residents go online. *Nursing Homes Long Term Care Management, 51*(10), 60–64.

Perloff, R. M., & Krevans, J. (2001). Tracking the psychosocial predictors of older individuals' television use. *Journal of Psychology, 121*(4), 365–372.

Perry, M. G. (1999). Animated gerontophobia: Ageism, sexism, and the Disney villainess. In S. M. Deats & L. T. Lenker (Eds.), *Aging and identity: A humanities perspective* (pp. 201–212). Westport, CT: Praeger.

Perse, E. M. (1990). Cultivation and involvement with local television news. In N. Signorielli & M. Morgan (Eds.), *Cultivation analysis* (pp. 51–69). Newbury Park, CA: Sage.

Petersen, M. (1973). The visibility and image of old people on television. *Journalism Quarterly, 50*(3), 569–573.

Peterson, R. T. (1995). The portrayal of senior citizens by banks in newspaper advertisements: A content analysis. *Journal of Professional Services Marketing, 12*(2), 95–101.

Petrecca, L. (2002, July 8). Savvy, aging boomers buy into pharma mantra. *Advertising Age, 73,* 8–9.

Pew Internet and American Life Project. (2001, September 9). *Wired seniors: A fervent few, inspired by family ties. Washington, DC: Pew Internet and American Life Project.* Retrieved from http://www.pewinternet.org

Pew Internet and American Life Project. (2003, November 23). Tech-savvy Americans are increasingly attached to their computers, the Internet, and cell phones. Retrieved from http://www.pewinternet.org

Pew Internet and American Life Project. (2004, March 25). *Older Americans and the Internet.* Washington, DC: Pew Internet and American Life Project. Retrieved from http://www.pewinternet.org

Pollack, R. F. (1989). Granny bashing: New myth recasts elders as villains. *Media & Values, 45*(1), 2–4.

Postman, N. (1986). *Amusing ourselves to death: Public discourse in the age of show business.* New York: Penguin.

Powell, L. A., & Williamson, J. B. (1985). The mass media and the aged. *Social Policy, 21*(1), 38–49.

Powers, M. H. (1992). *Saturday morning children's television and depictions of old age.* Unpublished master's thesis, University of Nebraska at Omaha.

Price, L. (1989). The mature market: 10 ways to reach seniors by mail. *Bank Marketing, 21*(8), 40–51.

Putnam, R. D. (2000). *Bowling alone: The collapse and revival of American community.* New York: Simon & Schuster.

Putnam, R. D. (2004). *Declining social capital: Trends over the last 25 years.* Retrieved from http://www.bowlingalone.com/index.php3

Quarderer, J. M., & Stone, V. A. (1989a, April). NDs and GMs define news "profitability." *Communicator, 43*(4), 10–12.

Quarderer, J. M., & Stone, V. A. (1989b, May). NDs and GMs describe their managerial "marriages." *Communicator, 43*(5), 32–34.

Rahtz, D. R., Sirgy, M. J., & Meadow, H. L. (1989). The elderly audience: Correlates of television orientation. *Journal of Advertising, 18*(3), 9–20.

Ramsdell, M. (1973). The trauma of TV's troubled soap families. *Family Coordinator, 22,* 299–304.

Rau, A. B. (2004, April 12). Valley cities brace for the boom when boomers retire. *The Arizona Republic.* Retrieved from http://www.azcentral.com

Reilly, P. (1999, May 28). Cell phones, wine coolers 'n' rock 'n' roll. *Wall Street Journal,* p. W1.

RIAA. (2003, May 15). RIAA releases 2002 consumer profile. Recording Industry of America. Retrieved from http://www.riaa.com/news

Riggs, K. E. (1998). *Mature audiences: Television in the lives of elders.* New Brunswick, NJ: Rutgers University Press.

Riggs, K. E. (2004). *Granny @ work.* New York: Routledge.

Roberts, D. (2002, September 9). *The image of aging in media and marketing.* U.S. Senate Special Committee on Aging. Retrieved from http://aging.senate.gov/events/090402.html

The Robert Wood Johnson Foundation. (2001, May). Increasing physical activity among adults age 50 and older. *Journal of Aging and Physical Activity, 9*(Suppl.)

Robinson, J. D., & Skill, T. (1995). Media usage patterns and portrayals of the elderly. In J. F. Nussbaum & J. Coupland (Eds.), *Handbook of communication and aging research* (pp. 359–371). Hillsdale, NJ: Lawrence Erlbaum Associates.

Rogers, E. M. (1995). *Diffusion of innovations* (4th ed.). New York: The Free Press.

Rogers, E. M. (2003). *Diffusion of innovations* (5th ed.). New York: The Free Press.

Romano, A. (2003, August 25). Wish you were younger? So do many cable nets. *Broadcasting & Cable, 133*(34), 12.

Romer, D., Jamieson, K. H., & Aday, S. (2003). Television news and the cultivation of fear of crime. *Journal of Communication, 53*(1), 88–104.

Roper Organization, Inc. (1989). *Public attitudes toward television and other media in a time of change, No. 14.* New York: Television Information Office.

Rosenfeld, F. H. (1981). Criminal victimization of the elderly. In D. Lester (Ed.), *The elderly victim of crime* (pp. 3–13). Springfield, IL: Thomas.

Rosengren, K. (1985). Growth of a research tradition: Some concluding remarks. In K. E. Rosengren, L. A. Wenner, & P. Palmgreen (Eds.), *Media gratifications research: Current perspectives* (pp. 275–284). Beverly Hills: Sage.

Rowe, J. W., & Kahn, R. L. (1999). *Successful aging.* New York: Dell.

Roy, A., & Harwood, J. (1997). Underrepresented, positively portrayed: Older adults in television commercials. *Journal of Applied Communication Research, 25*(1), 39–56.

Rubin, A. M. (1982). Directions in television and aging research. *Journal of Broadcasting, 26*(2), 537-551.

Rubin, A. M. (1988). Mass media and aging. In C. W. Carmichael, C. H. Botan, & R. Hawkins (Eds.), *Human communication and the aging process* (pp. 155–165). Prospect Heights, IL: Waveland Press.

Rubin, A. M., & Rubin, R. B. (1981). Age, context and television use. *Journal of Broadcasting, 25*(1), 1–13.

Rubin, A. M., & Rubin, R. B. (1982a). Contextual age and television use. *Human Communication Research, 8*(3), 228–244.

Rubin, A. M., & Rubin, R. B. (1982b). Older persons' TV viewing patterns and motivations. *Communication Research, 9*(2), 287–313.

Rubin, A. M., Perse, E. M., & Powell, R. A. (1985). Loneliness, parasocial interaction, and local television news viewing. *Human Communication Research, 12*(2), 155–180.

Rubin, A. M., & Step, M. M. (2000). Impact of motivation, attraction, and parasocial interaction on talk radio listening. *Journal of Broadcasting & Electronic Media, 44*(4), 635–654.

Russell, C. (1993). *The master trend: How the baby boom generation is remaking America.* New York: Plenum.

Ryff, C. D., Marshall, V. W., & Clarke, P. J. (1999). Linking the self and society in social gerontology: Crossing new territory via old questions. In C. D. Ryff & V. W. Marshall (Eds.), *The self and society in aging processes* (pp. 3–41). New York: Springer.

Sallot, L. M., Steinfatt, T. M., & Salwen, M. B. (1998). Journalists' and public relations practitioners' news values: Perceptions and cross-perceptions. *Journalism & Mass Communication Quarterly, 75*(2), 366–377.

Saltzman, J. (1979). How to manage TV news. *Human Behavior, 8,* 65–73.

Sanchez, P. (1999, August/September). How to craft successful employee communication in the information age. *Communication World, 16*(7), 9–15.

Sanders, M. (2002, November). *Older women and the media.* Paper presented to the United Nations Division for the Advancement of Women, Beirut, Lebanon.

Scales, A. M. (1996). Examining what older adults read and watch on TV. *Educational Gerontology, 22*(3), 215–227.

Schewe, C. D. (1991, August). How to communicate with older adults. *American Demographics, 13*(8), 53.

Schlossberg, H. (1992, September 28). Expert on aging warns against "stupid marketing." *Marketing News, 26*(20), 2–5.

Schonfeld, E., & Furth, J. (1995, December 25). Betting on the boomers. *Fortune, 132*(13), 78–83.

Schonfeld, R. (1983, September–October). Pop news, TV's growth industry. *Channels, 3,* 34–38.

Schramm, W. (1969). Aging and mass communication. In M. W. Riley, J. W. Riley, & M. E. Johnson (Eds.), *Aging and society: Vol. 2. Aging and the professions* (pp. 352–375). New York: Russell Sage Foundation.

Schreiber, E. S., & Boyd, D. A. (1980). How the elderly perceive television commercials. *Journal of Communication, 30*(1), 61–70.

Schudson, M. (1998). The public journalism movement and its problems. In D. Graber, D. McQuail, & P. Norris (Eds.), *The politics of news, the news of politics* (pp. 132–149). Washington, DC: CQ Press.

Segan, S. (2002, March 19). Old minds, new media, senior citizens feel at home on the Net. *ABC News.* Retrieved from http://www.abcnews.com

Sergent, J. (2002, September 23). Boomers not quite ready to leave jobs. *Evansville Courier & Press.* Retrieved from http://www.myinky.com

Severin, W. J., & Tankard, J. W., Jr. (2001). *Communication theories: Origins, methods, and uses in the mass media* (5th ed.). New York: Longman.

Shapiro, J. (2003, November 20). AARP's decision to endorse the GOP's prescription drug bill and their move to become more politically active. *National Public Radio.* Retrieved from http://www.npr.org

Shaw, M. E., & Wright, J. M. (1967). *Scales for the measurement of attitudes.* New York: McGraw-Hill.

Shea, J. (2003, November 8). Dividing geezers into groups; age category too broad, so breakdown is needed. *Hartford Courant,* p. D1.

Sherkat, D. E. (1998). Counterculture or continuity? Competing influences on baby boomers' religious orientations and participation. *Social Forces, 76*(3), 1087–1115.

Shicor, D., & Kobrin, S. (1978). Criminal behavior among the elderly. *The Gerontologist, 18*(2), 213–218.

Signorielli, N., & Gerbner, G. (1978). The image of the elderly in prime-time television drama. *Generations, 3*(1), 10–11.

Smart, T., & Pethokoukis, J. M. (2001, June 4). Not acting their age. *U.S. News & World Report, 130,* 54–59.

Smith, C. (1988). News critics, newsworkers and local television news. *Journalism Quarterly, 65*(2), 341–346.

Smith, S. J. (2003). How will Julia and other over–35-year-old stars cope with aging? *Netscape Celebrity.* Retrieved from http://channels.netscape.com/ns/celebrity/

Somerville, R. (2001). Demographic research on newspaper readership. *Generations, 25*(3), 24–30.

Spring, J. (1993). Seven days of play. *American Demographics, 15*(3), 50–55.

Starr, B. (1997, March). *It ain't just paint: Aging and the media.* A paper presented at the 1997 meeting of the American Society on Aging. Retrieved from http://www.media-diversity.org/

Statistical Abstract of the United States. (1994). Table 16: Resident population projections by age and sex: 1993 to 2050. Lanham, MD: Bernan Press.

Steel, K. (2002). Changes associated with aging. In C. E. Koop, C. E. Pearson, & M. R. Schwarz (Eds.), *Critical issues in global health* (pp. 346–355). San Francisco, CA: Jossey-Bass.

Steinberg, J. (2003, November 30). At 72, a dogged Rather is not yet ready to yield. *The New York Times.* Retrieved from http://nytimes.com

Steiner, G. A. (1963). *The people look at television.* New York: Knopf.

Stempel, G. H., III. (1988). Topic and story choice of five network newscasts. *Journalism Quarterly, 65*(3), 750–752.

Stempel, G. H., III, Hargrove, T., & Bernt, J. P. (2000). Relation of growth of use of the Internet to changes in media use from 1995 to 1999. *Journalism & Mass Communication Quarterly, 77*(1), 71–79.

Stephens, N. (1991). Cognitive age: A useful concept for advertising? *Journal of Advertising, 20*(4), 37–47.

Stevenson, N. (1995). *Understanding media cultures.* London: Sage.

Stone, G. (1987). *Examining newspapers: What research reveals about America's newspapers.* Newbury Park, CA: Sage.

Stone, V. A. (1988, September). News directors move for professional advancement. *Communicator, 42*(9), 16–18.

Surratt, C. G. (2001). *The Internet and social change.* Jefferson, NC: McFarland & Co.

Sutel, S. (2003, December 17). Aging boomers pose dilemma for radio industry. *Associated Press.* Retrieved from http://newsobserver.com/

Swayne, E., & Greco, A. (1987). The portrayal of older Americans in television commercials. *Journal of Advertising, 16*(1), 47–54.

Szmigin, I., & Carrigan, M. (2001, June). Learning to love the older consumer. *Journal of Consumer Behavior,* 22–34.

Tebbel, J. (1975). *Aging in America: Implications for the mass media.* Washington, DC: National Council on Aging.

The Economist. (2002, August 10). Over 60 and overlooked. *The Economist, 364,* 51–52.

ThirdAge. (2004). *ThirdAge.* Retrieved from http://www.thirdage.com/

Thomas, V., & Sullivan, M. P. (1989). The mature market: A golden opportunity. *Bank Marketing, 21*(8), 32–34.

Thompson, F. G. (1990). Workshop: Reaching America's aging market place. *Public Relations Journal, 46*(2), 28–30.

Thornton, J. E. (2002). Myths of aging or ageist stereotypes. *Educational Gerontology, 28*(4), 301–312.

Thorson, J. A. (1995). *Aging in a changing society.* Belmont, CA: Wadsworth.

Trigoboff, D. (2002, June 3). Programming, station break. *Broadcasting & Cable,* p. 30.

Tuchman, G. (1978). *Making news: A study in the construction of reality.* New York: The Free Press.

Tulloch, J. (2000). *Watching television audiences: Cultural theories & methods.* London: Arnold.

UCLA World Internet Project. (2004, January 14). Significant "digital gender gap" in many countries. Los Angeles, CA: UCLA World Internet Project. Retrieved from http://www.ccp.ucla.edu

Underwood, E. (1990, December 3). 50-plus marketing: Three strategies for reaching older consumers in the 1990's. *Adweek's Marketing Week, 31*(49), 30.

U.S. Census Bureau. (2000–2002). *Historical income tables; money income in the United States: 2001; and projected resident population—2002.* Retrieved from http://www.census.gov

U.S. Department of Health and Human Services. (2000). *Healthy people 2010: Leading health indicator.* Retrieved from http://www.cdc.gov/nchs

U.S. Newswire. (2003, November 21). Hastert rallies with seniors for support of the bipartisan Medicare bill. Lexis-Nexis, Newswires.

U.S. Senate Special Committee on Aging. (1987). *Aging America: Trends and projections.* Washington, DC: U.S. Government Printing Office.

USA Today Magazine. (2001, March). Move over kids—adults like video games, too. p. 6.

Usdansky, M. L. (1992, November 10). "Nation of youth" growing long in the tooth. *USA Today,* p. 10A.

Van Vliet, L. (1995). Communication disorders. In G. Maddox (Ed.), *The encyclopedia of aging* (2nd ed., pp. 198–200). New York: Springer.

Vann, K. (2003, October 28). Seniors embrace Internet shopping. *Hartford Courant,* p. D4.

Vasil, L., & Wass, H. (1993). Portrayal of the elderly in the media: A literature review and implications for educational gerontologists. *Educational Gerontology, 19*(1), 71–85.

Vivian, J. (2001). *The media of mass communication.* Needham Heights, MA: Allyn & Bacon.

Waldrop, J. (1992, April). Old money. *American Demographics, 14*(4), 24–29.

Wallace, H. (1998). *Victimology: Legal, psychological, and social perspectives.* Needham Heights, MA: Allyn & Bacon.

Wallack, L., & Dorfman, L. (2001). Putting policy into health communication. In R. E. Rice & C. K. Atkin (Eds.), *Public communication campaigns* (3rd ed., pp. 389–401). Thousand Oaks, CA: Sage.

Wass, H., Almerico, G. M., Campbell, P. V., & Tatum, J. L. (1984). Presentation of the elderly in the Sunday news. *Educational Gerontology, 10*(4-5), 335–348.

Weaver, J. (2003, July 17). More people search for health online. *MSNBC.* Retrieved from http://www.msnbc.com

Weissman, R. X. (1999, August). Money to burn. *American Demographics, 21*(8), 36–37.

Wenner, L. A. (1976). Functional analysis of TV viewing for older adults. *Journal of Broadcasting, 20*(1), 77–88.

Wenner, L. A. (1984). Gratifications sought and obtained in program dependency: A study of network evening news programs and 60 Minutes. *Communication Research, 11*(3), 537–562.

White, E. (2001, October 19). One out of two viewers is still over the age of 55. *Media Life.* Retrieved from http://www.medialifemagazine.com/news2001/

White, H. (2002). A randomized controlled trial of the psychological impact of providing Internet training and access to older adults. *Aging and Mental Health, 6*(3), 213–222.

White, J., & Weatherall, A. (2000). A grounded theory analysis of older adults and information technology. *Educational Gerontology, 26*(4), 371–386.

Whitman, D. (2000, November). Unhappy and up for grabs. *U.S. News & World Report, 129*(18), 22.

Whitmore, R. V. (1995). *The portrayal of older adults in the* New York Times *and the* Omaha World-Herald, *1982 and 1992.* Unpublished master's thesis, University of Nebraska at Omaha.

Wicks, R. H. (1989). Segmenting broadcast news audiences in the new media environment. *Journalism Quarterly, 66*(2), 383–390.

Will boomers never die? (2003, November 11). *Time,* p. 78.

Williams, A., & Nussbaum, J. F. (2001). *Intergenerational communication across the life span.* Mahwah, NJ: Lawrence Erlbaum Associates.

Williams, A., & Ylanne-McEwen, V. (2000). Elderly lifestyles in the 21st century: "Doris and Sid's excellent adventure." *Journal of Communication, 50*(3), 4–8.

Williamson, J. B. (1998). Political activism and the aging of the baby boom. *Generations, 22*(1), 55–60.

Wimmer, R. D., & Dominick, J. R. (1997). *Mass media research* (5th ed.). Belmont, CA: Wadsworth.

Wolfe, D. (1987). The ageless market. *American Demographics, 9*(7), 27–29, 55–56.

Wolfe, D. B. (1992). Segmenting your market: The key to marketing to older consumers. *Journal of Business Strategy, 13*(6), 14–18.

World Health Organization. (2004). Global movement for active ageing. Retrieved from http://www.who.int/hpr/globalmovement/background.htm

Wright, C. R. (1986). *Mass communication: A sociological perspective* (3rd ed.). New York: Random House.

Wright, K. (2000). Computer-mediated social support, older adults, and coping. *Journal of Communication, 50*(3), 100–118.

Wurtzel, A. (1992, March). *The changing landscape of network television.* Paper presented to the ABC television affiliate stations.

Yin, P. (1985). *Victimization and the aged.* Springfield, IL: Thomas.

Young, T. J. (1979). Use of the media by older adults. *American Behavioral Scientist, 23*(1), 119–136.

Author Index

Subject Index